To

Mr. Wm Zielman

friend & neighbor

Poultney Bigelow

July

1930

HOW EUROPE MADE PEACE WITHOUT AMERICA

BOOKS BY FRANK H. SIMONDS

History of the World War, 5 Vols.
They Shall Not Pass—Verdun

HOW EUROPE MADE PEACE WITHOUT AMERICA

By

FRANK H. SIMONDS, D. LITT.

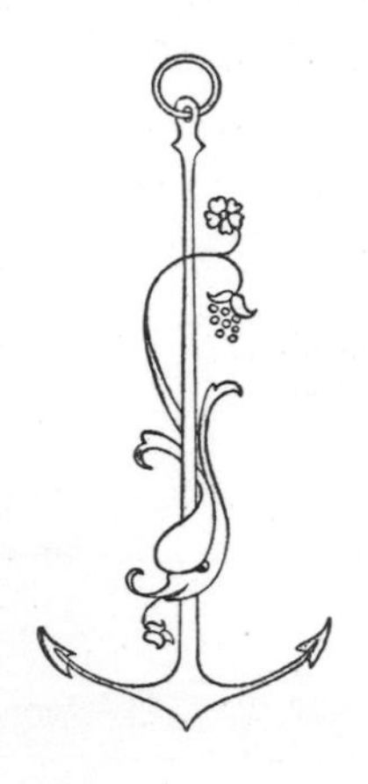

GARDEN CITY NEW YORK
DOUBLEDAY, PAGE & COMPANY
1927

PRINTED IN THE UNITED STATES AT THE COUNTRY LIFE PRESS, GARDEN CITY, N. Y.

FIRST EDITION

THIS BOOK IS RESPECTFULLY
DEDICATED TO

KATHARINE SIMONDS

CONTENTS

Part I. Democratic Control of Foreign Policy

Part II. The Failure of the Treaty of Versailles

Part III. National Consequences of the Failure

Part IV. The Anglo-French Duel

PART ONE

DEMOCRATIC CONTROL OF FOREIGN POLICY

HOW EUROPE MADE PEACE WITHOUT AMERICA

CHAPTER ONE

HOW EUROPE MADE PEACE IN 1814

AMONG all the political changes which crowded the century separating the fall of Napoleon Bonaparte from the flight of William II none was more far reaching than that which transferred the control of foreign policy to parliamentary and democratic hands. Nor did any change that was in fact a revolution ever come more imperceptibly.

Two generations after the Congress of Vienna, that of Berlin seemed, in all outward circumstances at least, to preserve the traditions of the famous assembly which liquidated the wars of the French Revolution and of the Empire. But four decades later, the Paris Conference which made the Versailles Treaty, differed from the Vienna and Berlin congresses in every essential circumstance.

In the larger sense, the study of the period between Versailles and Locarno is in reality the examination of the consequences of this transfer of control of foreign policy. It is in these consequences that there is to be found the explanation of all the international anarchy which extends from the moment of the signing of the Treaty of Versailles in the Hall of Mirrors in the palace of Louis XIV to the welcome of the German delegation in the Hall of the Reformation in the city of John Calvin.

To establish the extent and the character of the change, too, there is, perhaps, no more satisfactory method than to contrast the personalities and compare the circumstances and conditions of the two great settlements, those of 1814 and 1919.

In examining the problem which was set for the sovereigns and diplomats who met in Paris immediately after the military defeat of the great Emperor, and even in advance of the First Abdication, the fact which claims instant attention is that the situation of Europe itself was not in the main largely different from that which existed immediately after the World War.

In both cases, a long, bloody, and enormously expensive conflict had exhausted the whole Continent. In both instances, a great nation had been beaten by a coalition and with defeat had changed its régime. When the Allied sovereigns made peace with France in 1814, Napoleon was about to set out for Elba. When the Conference to Make Peace assembled in Paris in 1919, William II was in Holland. In the earlier time, the Bourbon Monarchy had been restored in France; in the later, Germany had become a republic.

Again, if the Allied peoples had loudly proclaimed that they were fighting to make the world safe for democracy, the Allied sovereigns had never mistaken the fact that they were fighting to make the world safe for monarchy. Thus the victors of our own time had precisely the same reasons for desiring the survival of the German Republic as those of the previous century for wishing the Bourbon Monarchy to endure.

The problem of peace in 1814 was not largely unlike that of 1919. Nor were the surrounding circumstances different. If the Allied peoples of our own time were still moved by passionate anger at German deeds, the Allied sovereigns of the earlier time were face to face with the people who, by killing their own king, had struck a blow at the very root of the monarchical principle and shattered the system of privilege by the wholesale and savage murder of their aristocrats.

If, between 1914 and 1918, German armies had ranged destructively over Belgium, France, and Poland, and accumulated ruins still bore testimony to their recent presence, the armies of Revolutionary and of Napoleonic France had for twenty years travelled all the roads from Madrid to Moscow, quartered themselves in the palaces of kings, levied enormous tribute upon all the conquered peoples, taken provinces and cities, created new states and destroyed old. On balance, the claims of the victors of 1918 were not impressively greater than those of the conquerors of 1814.

Again, if the problems of peace in the two centuries

were not in any larger aspect different, it is also true that at bottom the problem of peace differs little from war to war and from century to century. By victory nothing is changed except the fact that one nation or coalition of nations, which was seeking to enforce or establish its will by arms, is forced by defeat or by exhaustion to abandon its purpose. It has to submit and it does submit.

By contrast, the victorious nation or coalition, which has sought to establish an opposing will, is now in a position to do it. Power is completely in its hands. It can proceed to translate its purposes into action. Upon the defeated it can impose such conditions as it may choose. It can take provinces, demand indemnities, impose military occupation of the territories of the defeated country.

Yet always there are very definite limitations imposed upon the victor which lie outside of his eventual control and beyond the circumstances of the immediate present. The nation which is beaten will endure and continue. The weakness incident to defeat will not last. Thus the France which was broken in 1870 reappears in 1919 as one of a victorious coalition.

There are, therefore, limits beyond which it is not profitable or even safe to impose terms based upon transitory military decision, since the will and power of every people to exist are permanent. History is full of illustrations of this fact.

When, in the War of the Spanish Succession, still

another coalition had triumphed and the victors were face to face with Louis XIV, beaten to his knees, seemingly without further resource to resist, as France appeared without capacity to make war, when the Grand Monarch, himself, recognizing defeat, proposed to surrender all the provinces which represented a life-time of successful wars, his conquerors asked one thing more. They demanded that the old king make war upon his grandson, whom he had seated on the throne of Spain.

But this demand went beyond the limit. It struck not the king but the grandfather, and Louis repulsed it. As a consequence, the war was resumed. France rallied to its sovereign, and when peace did come at last, France retained all that would have been surrendered had her foes restricted their demands to territorial cessions.

There is in peoples, too, even when their power to make war nationally has been broken, a capacity for resistance which can hardly be measured. Napoleon found this out in Spain and Germany. The facts and circumstances of modern life have, too, tended rather to fortify than to weaken this last resource of the vanquished.

In the last analysis, the terms of any peace based upon military decision in war are rigidly limited to that maximum, which the man in the street calls "all the traffic will bear." No matter how complete and far-shining his military success, no matter, also, how great and undeniable his wrongs, if the victor exceed the load limit, the bridge, which is the proposed settlement, will crash.

Immediately or eventually, the unbroken will of the conquered, the will to exist, will reassert itself and the violence of the reaction may compromise everything, the circumstances which were tolerable together with those which were unbearable. Thus the victor will lose what he might have kept because he demanded what was beyond the endurance of the defeated.

The truth of all this was perfectly well known to the kings and diplomats who had to make peace with France after the fall of Napoleon. They knew that if, by the peace which they were going to make, they wounded the spirit of France or put unbearable fetters upon the French people, that settlement would not endure beyond the time during which France recovered her power to act.

And they also knew that, if the Bourbon Monarchy, which they had brought back to Paris in their baggage, were associated with national humiliation or intolerable diminution of the Fatherland, it could not last; that France, the French people, having recovered their freedom, would cast it out and revert to the Napoleonic-Revolutionary régime, which for the victors of 1814 was as terrifying as was the Hohenzollern system for the conquerors of the German Empire.

Therefore, in the first Treaty of Paris, made in April, 1814, the victorious allies left to France every foot of territory which had been hers at the beginning of the great cycle of the wars of the Revolution and the Empire. What France had taken by the sword, they took back, although, even in defeat, they left her Savoy, which had not been hers in 1792. In addition, they levied no tribute and they imposed no occupation of French soil.

Were they enlightened and generous, after all, these servants and masters of the ancient régime? If anyone thinks that, let him study what they did to the Polish, the Belgian, the Italian, the Saxon peoples, to all helpless peoples, at Vienna a few months later. They were harsh, cynical, greedy men, and the Fourteen Points in the halls of Vienna in the winter of 1814–15 would have been greeted as an echo escaping from Bedlam. They made peace with the strong, but only to do violence to the weak.

They were also, however, men who had learned their trade. They had been at school steadily in all the years from Valmy to Fontainebleau. They knew their Europe, their France, and they also knew their job, which was to restore peace without delay and on the terms which would be most profitable to themselves within the limit of possible profit. They remembered that, even after Leipzig, they had offered Napoleon the left bank of the Rhine from Switzerland to the sea, and he had refused. Now, in less than two years, he was on his way to Elba and they were in Paris.

The work of the treaty-makers of 1814 was presently subjected to two rigid tests. Within the year, Napoleon came back from Elba and all their settlement was put in jeopardy. Had the Treaty done violence to the spirit of France, had it reduced France beyond the limits of French endurance, 1815 was bound to be 1792, and the French people would have gone to the frontiers again. As it was, the veterans of the Grande Armée rallied to their great commander, and he took them to Waterloo. But France stood still.

The second test was that of time. Peace between France and Great Britain has endured to the present hour. It lasted between France and Prussia to 1870 and between France and Austria to 1859. By contrast, the settlement made at Versailles in 1919 had to be revised within less than five years and, so far from producing peace, was the immediate prelude to a new period of anarchy and chaos.

What explains this different outcome? Why did the Allied sovereigns and diplomats of the early Nineteenth Century successfully solve their problem while the prime ministers and President of the Twentieth failed completely in the face of conditions which were not essentially different?

The answer must be found in the change which had come with the passage of a little more than a century. The settlement of 1814 was made by men who were the fine and finished product of a system which had long endured and, with the passing of centuries, had acquired a competence and technique in dealing with precisely the questions which constituted the task of Paris after the Napoleonic debacle.

In all the centuries following the period when kings on horseback led their subjects to war, foreign affairs had remained the chief and exclusive business of sovereigns. They no longer fought wars, but they made and directed them. They retained in their hands the management of the machinery by which wars were conducted and terminated. And with the passing of time they had learned to associate with themselves those of their subjects whose brains, knowledge, and character permitted them to become great foreign ministers or successful military captains. The favours of royalty were thus bestowed upon the ministers who did the will and the soldiers who directed the armies of the monarchs.

The business of the people was to pay taxes and to furnish conscripts for their kings. There was nothing approaching contemporary public opinion in any of the Continental countries which had fought France. Nor was there anything even remotely suggesting representative parliaments through which public opinion could make itself felt.

The situation was materially different in England, but the difference was more apparent than real. The Crown had surrendered much to Parliament. There were a press and a public opinion. But Parliament was not representative in the contemporary sense, the press was still in its infancy and public opinion was left consistently in the dark.

Castlereagh, who represented Britain at Paris and Vienna, had acquired an enormous prestige at home as well as abroad. When he was backed by the Duke of Wellington, as was almost invariably the case, his will was supreme, and for public opinion in our modern sense both had a contempt which was equal and without limit. As a consequence, Castlereagh did not even deign to keep Parliament informed of his negotiations.

Thus there existed at the close of the Napoleonic Period and at the moment when Europe made peace with France, a number of highly trained statesmen and diplomats, responsible to royal masters who themselves knew Europe, or were, at least, beyond the control of any popular or democratic force. By reason of their relation to the events of the past two decades, too, these men not only knew Europe intimately, but they knew equally well the statesmen of the several countries with whom they had to deal. In fact, the sovereigns had themselves made the last campaign together.

It is not only possible but obviously tempting to exaggerate the extent to which this combination of knowledge and experience did function smoothly. In point of fact, it never functioned at all smoothly and was always on the point of an open break. Yet the break never came, and in the end, decisions were always reached by unanimity.

Thus, it is exact to say that the men who made the settlement of Paris in 1814, as they also made the decisions of the Congress of Vienna and the later peace after Waterloo, were men for whom the business in hand had been a life work, and that their knowledge, experience, and ability, subject to royal pleasure, which did often hamper and harass them, had full scope. And never under any circumstance had they to consider the question of public opinion as we know it, or submit to the immediate restrictions of parliamentary supervision.

CHAPTER TWO

THE SITUATION IN 1919

WHEN one turns to the consideration of the situation which existed a century after the Paris Peace of 1814, on the eve of still another Paris conference, the contrast with the circumstances of the earlier day is impressive.

The kings had gone. Parliaments, beginning with the British, had become representative. The men who were to act for the great European states, and in reality they were Clemenceau and Lloyd George, were not diplomats. Neither had any claim to expert knowledge of foreign affairs. Neither had ever manifested any particular interest in this field. And this was also true of Woodrow Wilson, who acted with them to make the decisions of the "Big Three" and thus to make the settlement of Versailles.

Both the European premiers were lifelong parliamentarians. Both had come to power in the dark days of the war because of their unique power to give impulsion to legislative bodies and stimulus to democratic peoples facing the tremendous strain incident to the great struggle.

Clemenceau had once been president of the Council and thus measurably conversant with foreign affairs for a brief moment before the war, but both he and Lloyd George had been distinguished throughout their long careers almost exclusively because of their mastery of that peculiar technique which permits contemporary politicians to control majorities, sway public opinion, make or break ministries.

They were, themselves, moreover, in the last analysis, entirely at the command of their respective parliaments which could dismiss them within the hour. For them, as for all premiers, the conditions of continued power were found always in the necessity to maintain control of parliament by that highly difficult device of retaining popular approval, for parliaments are jealous bodies and are ever ready to lay hold upon public opinion as a stick with which to assail the Minister of the moment.

In the field of domestic affairs, moreover, the people have with the passing decades acquired undeniable capacity. Although they may be frequently misled, sometimes deceived, often frankly mistaken, within the limits of their own national existence and experience the people have acquired a grasp of the fundamentals. They know here what they want and why. They are acquiring and they continue to acquire the discipline and self-restraint which are necessary. They have learned to compromise, and rarely, except in transitory bursts of passion, demand the absolute.

But in the nature of things they can, as yet, bring nothing like the same knowledge or the same experience to foreign affairs. The complex problems of international relations and the baffling mysteries of other national existences lived under different conditions of geography, dominated by other traditions and illuminated by other histories are to them unintelligible. They must measure the policies and purposes of every other people by the yardstick of their own experience.

Thus, they will bring to foreign questions the same standards, express the same will, insist upon the same tests which they employ in domestic affairs. They will never question their own knowledge or competence. And, in the last analysis, the choice of any Prime Minister must often be between openly flouting national will, and throwing this national will into violent collision with the similar will of another people.

Thus the absolute break between the conditions of 1814 and 1919 is established. The men who made the older settlement knew the material with which they had to work. They knew it because it was their trade to know it, and their presence at Paris and Vienna was the ultimate proof of their mastery of that trade. Finally, together with knowledge, they had power.

On the contrary, the men who held power in 1919 had come to office by reason of their capacity to deal with an utterly dissimilar set of problems from those presented at the Paris Conference. They had learned a totally different art from that of negotiating abroad, they were masters of the art of dealing with a modern parliamentary democracy. They knew all about this business that a lifelong training could teach them, and they were at Paris precisely because, in the terrible hours of the World War, they had displayed the supreme mastery of this art of leading the peoples.

There is a further circumstance to be noted in presenting the contrast between 1814 and 1919. In its long struggle with monarchy and autocracy, democracy had not only wrested control of domestic affairs from the enemy and thus automatically succeeded to the direction of foreign affairs, it had in the progress of the battle also acquired an instinctive and dominating distrust for methods of the older order, for what it described as "old-fashioned diplomacy" and the men who plied that trade.

As a consequence, although diplomacy had on sufferance continued to play a part, its influence in foreign affairs had steadily diminished in all the years from the Congress of Berlin to the World War. Moreover, after 1914, democracy tended to arrive at the conclusion that this world-wide catastrophe was itself in some mysterious fashion to be charged to diplomacy.

Accordingly, when Clemenceau, Lloyd George, and Woodrow Wilson undertook to make peace at Paris, none of them even thought of employing importantly the machinery of the Foreign Office, the Quai d'Orsay, or the State Department. Diplomatic opinion was rarely asked, diplomatic experience and knowledge were seldom appealed to. On the contrary, all three manifested the same impatience and contempt for the representatives of the profession to which Talleyrand and Metternich had belonged a century before.

Between the situation of Lloyd George and Clemenceau on the one hand, and that of Woodrow Wilson on the other, in their relation to their respective legislatures, there were points of close resemblance and of tremendous contrast.

From the beginning of its history the United States had adopted a system which in reality forbade all foreign relations save the most rudimentary. The Atlantic Ocean and, later, the Monroe Doctrine were the bases of American foreign policy, which was comprehended in the double purpose to keep out of Europe and to keep Europe out of the Americas.

All power, save that of mere formal negotiation, was from the outset vested with Congress and in practice with the Senate. The President had power, subject to the consent of the Senate, to appoint ambassadors, who represented the country abroad. But, in practice, ambassadors had seldom been more than messenger boys in evening dress and diplomatic posts either inexpensive rewards for party service or a form of inverted Purgatory between the lost Paradise of public office and the impending Hades of enforced private life.

The President had also the power to negotiate treaties, but all treaties, when negotiated, were without validity until they had been ratified by the Senate. For four years the President was beyond the reach of political accident, save in the remote contingency of impeachment, but in all this time, while he had absolute freedom of action, he was without power to bind or to loose.

Under the American system, there was always the possibility of a collision between the Executive and the Legislature, but in practice, at least since the War of 1812, no President had ever seriously attempted to act in foreign affairs save in close relation with Congress, drawing negotiators either from that body or from the ranks of the two parties therein represented.

The fundamental difference between the American and the European system lay in the fact that, in Europe, the executive was a member of the legislative branch. He was daily and hourly subject to its will and pleasure. He could disappear overnight. But, while he remained, as the agent of the Parliament he had all power. In negotiating with other countries, he was compelled always to retain the majority of his own Parliament and, therefore, to keep it informed and consenting.

On the other hand, when the Prime Minister had made a treaty under these conditions, ratification of the document by the Parliament was generally automatic. By contrast, when President Wilson had made a treaty, he had then to begin at the beginning. He had first to inform and then to persuade Congress.

These details in the American system, which had decisive importance later and were never understood or appreciated in Europe, have a value at this point, only as they serve to make clear the fact that in the United States, as in France, Britain, and all Allied states represented in the Peace Conference, democratic control of foreign policy through parliaments or Congress had become absolute—and, of course, in the case of the United States there never had been any other tradition.

Such, then, was the revolution which had taken place in the control of foreign policy in the European world. But the Conference of Paris in 1919 was precisely the first occasion when and where the consequences of the revolution were to be disclosed. If the Congress of Vienna had been the culminating point of the old order, Paris was just as clearly the first authentic revelation of the arrival of a new system and another age.

But if the Paris Conference was the first disclosure of this great transformation, what occurred there was steadily repeated in all the succeeding years. All prime ministers and foreign ministers in Europe, from Versailles to Locarno, were equally helpless in the face of their own public opinions. Each was compelled to adopt policies and resort to measures in which he did not believe, either to avoid disaster at home or save a foreign associate, equally handicapped by a similar national state of mind.

Peace after the first fall of Napoleon, and again after Waterloo, was restored in a few weeks because those who had power were aware of the realities of the international situation. Peace after 1918 was postponed for seven years, because the peoples which had all power at home were uninformed as to the limits of their own power abroad and unaware of the necessity for compromises without which settlement was impossible.

What the monarchs and diplomats had learned before the settlement of 1814, the sovereign peoples learned only after the making of the Treaty of Versailles in 1919.

CHAPTER THREE

AMERICA AND THE PARIS CONFERENCE

IF THE elements of the problems of 1814 and 1919 were in the main similar, if not identical, there was, however, one factor in the later situation without parallel in the earlier, and that was the American.

After the Armistice, two million American soldiers still remained upon European soil. They had supplied the added weight which had made the military decision possible. Their presence testified eloquently to the meaning of the American intervention and to the fact that the forthcoming Peace Conference had not merely to make peace with the German enemy, but to establish the bases of any future relation between the American people and those Allied nations with whom they had been associated in the common victory.

The importance of the American factor could not be overlooked then, it cannot be neglected now. From the very outset of the Peace Conference, it was apparent that the character of the settlement to be made with Germany would not alone be enormously shaped by the views of the American representative as to proper terms, but by the extent to which the American representative could and would bind the American people to share in the task of compelling execution of the Treaty when made.

In reality, it lay within the power of the United States, if not in its purpose or thought, to play the part at Paris in 1919 that Britain had played in 1814, and the role of Castlereagh was open to President Wilson. The European hope and need to obtain the continuing aid of the United States gave to the American President incalculable power, which was not lessened by the fact that his country was asking for no share in the war booty itself.

In estimating the importance of the American factor, it is also necessary to go beyond the material circumstances and appreciate the moral effect upon Europe of the sudden and decisive intervention in a Continental struggle of a people, which, throughout all its previous history, had followed a policy of complete and defiant isolation and had existed rather as a dream than a reality for the European masses, the dream of an El Dorado where everyone was rich and happy and the streets were literally paved with gold.

This effect was, in truth, little short of revolutionary. Accustomed through long centuries not merely to conduct their own struggles within European limits, but to intervene powerfully and profitably in the affairs of other continents, the European peoples beheld with wonder and amazement the arrival upon their shores of a power superior to all in every material circumstance. Physically exhausted, they were struck by the still unwearied strength of American youth; financially stricken, they were made aware of the seemingly inexhaustible American wealth which the American soldier and civilian spread about with lavish disdain. Mortally sick with the agony and horror of the long war, they listened captivated to the words in which the American President proclaimed the arrival of a new age of peace, prosperity, and safety.

For the moment, the American phenomenon filled all eyes, captured all imagination, defied all rational appraisal. Knowing nothing about America, the Allied peoples believed everything which their own misfortune and the patently incalculable good luck of the American people could suggest.

Yet, aside and apart from all this delirium, there were facts which could not safely be forgotten. There was above all the central fact, disclosed in the situation of Europe at the moment the United States entered the war, that situation which might approximately be restored if the United States withdrew.

Before the United States became a belligerent, the World War had been, after all, little different from other struggles which had shaken and devastated Europe in all the centuries following the rise of modern states. Whatever the origin of the conflict itself, once it had been entered upon, it unmistakably took the form of the old familiar battle for the balance of power.

The British, French, and Russian peoples, together with the smaller nations allied with them, were conducting precisely the same form of combat which similar coalitions had waged against France in the era of Louis

XIV and again in the period of Napoleon Bonaparte. The issue of the conflict would determine whether Germany would be able to acquire over Europe that hegemony which in the end had escaped both the Sun King and the great Emperor.

Against such a trial, too, Europe had been visibly preparing in all the years from Tangier to Serajevo. This preparation alone explained the Anglo-French Entente, the Franco-Russian Alliance, and the final merging of the two combinations into that Triple Entente which confronted Germany at the moment of the outbreak of the World War.

By the close of the year 1916, that is, well in advance of the American entrance into the war, that inevitable state of balance which marks European history had been reëstablished. The Germans had lost their chance of a military decision at the Marne, which must hereafter rank with Leipzig as one of the decisive battles of all time. Their later defeats at Verdun and the Somme in 1916 had further reinforced the decision of the campaign of 1914.

On the other hand, the Allies were not within striking distance of any actual military decision, and the collapse of Russia, which was impending, was bound to abolish that hope of a military success, which was, otherwise, not unreasonable.

Europe was, in fact, actually in a state of deadlock and headed for that "peace without victory" of President Wilson's unpleasantly accurate phrase. Behind the firing lines, the two coalitions were becoming similarly, if not equally, exhausted. For, on balance, the Central Powers, with fewer natural resources and shut off by the ever-tightening blockade, were suffering more severely. This fact, too, was a counterweight to the imposing, but actually less significant, advantages disclosed by the war maps and the occupation of Allied territory.

At this moment, Germany made the colossal blunder of forcing the United States into the war. It was a mistake as monumental as Napoleon's march to Moscow, and it had as fatal results. But it had its origin in the realization by the German soldiers that a decisive military victory was no longer possible and that peace by negotiation was inescapable unless they risked this last gambler's throw.

American intervention instantly destroyed the state of balance between the forces engaged. Thereafter, the single question which was posed was whether Germany could get a military decision by one final and desperate offensive before the weight of American military strength could make itself felt decisively. Thus in 1918 the campaign became a gigantic Waterloo, with our European associates playing the part of Wellington, while the rôle of Blücher's Prussians fell to the Americans. Like the Prussians, the Americans arrived in time, although in both cases the wait was agonizing. Thereafter, the inevitable Armistice finally left Germany helpless before her conquerors.

The defeats of Napoleon in 1814 and in 1815 had,

however, changed nothing in the actual balance of power in Europe. No new force had been added, no old force had been subtracted. France remained after Waterloo, after all diminution which could conceivably be imposed upon her, the strongest single state on the Continent.

The situation was utterly different in 1919. The future value of sixty millions of Germans in the European equation would depend, not upon the populations of the Allied states, but upon the relation to Europe which would be henceforth assumed by one hundred and twenty millions of Americans.

If the United States were going to remain in Europe, peace could be made on that basis. It could be an imposed peace, and its terms need have little regard for the wishes and less for the feelings of the German people. It would, in reality, be a compact with the United States rather than with Germany.

On the other hand, if the United States were determined to resume its former isolation, if its intervention had been no more than an accident, fortunate but fugitive, then the situation and condition of 1916 would return, not completely, thanks to the military decision achieved with American aid, but measurably. Then peace must be made with the German people on the basis of their position in Europe, in a Europe without the United States.

But, at the precise moment when the Conference of Paris was assembling, Woodrow Wilson arrived on the

Continent bringing with him his proposal for a League of Nations. His presence and his proposal together convinced the people of all Allied countries that the stay of the United States as a force in Europe was to be permanent. That this force would, too, continue in the future as in the immediate past to be exerted against the German they could not doubt, for to all the German remained the enemy.

The League of Nations, to the minds of all Europeans, statesmen and peoples, could be nothing more or less than the perpetuation of the alliance which had won the victory, the eternal guarantor of that cause of right and justice which to their minds was their own. The victory had been won with American aid, peace would be made with the same support, and this peace, with the fruits of victory, would be guaranteed for all time by American presence insured by the League.

For every Allied public, indeed, for the American public as well, the German was outside the pale. He was a Hun and a Boche. The war was a crime for which he was uniquely responsible. Not only was the German the enemy of all democratic peoples, but he would remain so for a future still undetermined. Hence the basis of common action and association was patent.

Mr. Wilson and those of his fellow countrymen who shared his views conceived that the proposal for a League of Nations was the promise of a new system of world peace. The European peoples saw it as a future guarantee of their own security against a German menace which had only been temporarily stayed and could not permanently be restrained save by the constant union of irresistible forces.

Mr. Wilson imagined that he was hailed in Europe as a deliverer come to free the older continent from the evils inherent in an existing system of national policies and international rivalries. Allied Europe saw in him the head of that state which, by its intervention in the war, had delivered it from the crushing weight of the German attack and would henceforth, by reason of its enormous strength and incalculable resources, insure it against the perils of a new war and in the enjoyment of the profits of the recent victory.

But if this view of the peoples was natural, perhaps inevitable in the circumstances, and if it was shared by the British, French, Italian, and Belgian peoples equally, there remained to be considered the views of the American people. And precisely here diplomacy and statesmanship of the older period would have paused to consider the realities of the problem.

All Allied peoples, on the contrary, accepted the existing circumstances as they saw them, interpreted the fact that America had entered the war and that Mr. Wilson had come to Paris as final proof that the people of the United States would unhesitatingly consent to bear all the burdens, run all the risks, accept all the difficulties incident to perpetual intermixture in European affairs.

None paused to ask the simple question of what material and practical return the American people could derive from a policy which imposed such manifest burdens and dangers. None inquired on what basis of legitimate self-interest the American peoples would consent to stand guard on the Rhine, or the Vistula, or the Dniester.

In the minds of all European peoples in January, 1919, and throughout the succeeding months, the price which Europe was to pay the United States was comprehended in the acceptance of Mr. Wilson's League of Nations, and that not unconditionally. If Paris had once been worth a mass, America was worth just this and nothing more.

At the moment when the Treaty of Versailles was being made, all the European Allied peoples were demanding passionately, incessantly, unreservedly the realization of all their material claims. Yet all took it as a foregone conclusion that the people of the United States, who had resigned all title and interest in the fruits of the common victory, would be satisfied to accept a contract by which Europe subscribed, with reservations, to the vaguest sort of moral principles, while the United States undertook the most specific and far-reaching material responsibilities.

Diplomacy of the old order, of any order—for it must be perceived at once that the troubles incident to the making of the Treaty of Versailles were not due to the presence of old-fashioned diplomacy but to the absence of diplomacy of any fashion—would not have been thus deceived by its own desires.

At the moment, and for the purposes of this study, however, it is essential to establish the circumstances surrounding the making of the Treaty and the view the Allied peoples took of the future relation of the United States to their own problems. What was put into the Treaty of Versailles is not otherwise explicable, save as it is understood in advance what was expected of the United States.

Nor is it otherwise possible to appreciate why Europe, after the American rejection of the Treaty, charged the people of the United States with the responsibility for the anarchy and chaos which followed. For it was upon their interpretation of the future relation of the United States to Europe and to its associates of the war that the Allied statesmen did construct their settlement with Germany. And when the United States withdrew, the foundations of the structure were removed.

PART TWO

THE FAILURE OF VERSAILLES

CHAPTER FOUR

THE TREATY OF VERSAILLES

IN ALL the centuries during which nations have made war with arms and terminated them by treaties of peace, no settlement has ever been more generally condemned than that of Versailles and none less frequently examined.

It has been denounced unreservedly as a treaty of violence in its territorial clauses, yet few of the critics have ever undertaken with historical and ethnographic atlases at hand to study the problems of the Polish frontier, which are the crux of the whole matter.

The military clauses have been assailed with equal vehemence, yet these, like the territorial, were unmodified in the later and voluntary agreement of Locarno. Under these, Germany has been disarmed and the later tasks by mutual consent transferred to the League of Nations. The evacuation of the first Rhineland zone took place, if not on the date fixed by the Treaty, within the year, the negotiations to shorten the stay of Allied troops in the remaining zones are going forward hopefully. Moreover, neither the Germans nor the Allies dream that in any event the occupation will endure beyond the Treaty date.

Even the reparations clauses, which were absurdly and fantastically contrary to reality, were never applied. On the contrary, under the Dawes Plan, Germany is to-day paying annually and without protest more than was ever demanded in any one year under the Treaty.

The failure of the Treaty of Versailles was complete and abysmal. But the primary cause lay outside the territorial, military, and reparations clauses. It was not the text but the spirit of the Treaty which made the settlement intolerable for all Germans. Interpreted in the spirit of Versailles, applied in the temper in which it was drafted, it seemed in all German eyes a vast and coherent programme designed to plunder and to destroy a great people on the pretext of moral guilt.

The spirit and the design, which alike seemed to have inspired the material clauses, explained all German resistance. Between the conditions which the Germans later fulfilled and those they were compelled to accept in 1919, the verbal changes were few. Whatever modifications were subsequently established in practice, the textual revisions were inconsiderable. Actually what Germany rejected, when it was applied in the spirit of Versailles, it accepted and at least measurably fulfilled in the spirit of Locarno.

While the German people did resist, however, the Treaty of Versailles could not be executed. Territories could be taken, provinces occupied, military forces used as a means of coercion, but all the financial clauses and all the disarmament provisions, which in the last analysis depended for vitality upon the German will to fulfil, could not be made to work.

As to the territorial clauses themselves, they were severe. Germany was deprived of territories amounting to one seventh of her metropolitan area and containing one tenth of her total population. Nevertheless, considerable as were these cessions, save for the Eupen-Malmedy cantons and the Memel strip, relatively insignificant in the aggregate, all that was taken had been acquired by Prussia or by the German state by acts of aggression against other nations.

Alsace-Lorraine, Schleswig, the Polish frontier lands, even Silesia, had come by the sword or by the abominable partitions of the Eighteenth Century. Whether, in point of contemporary expediency, the creation of the Polish Corridor was wise may fairly be debated, although that it was historically just, cannot be denied. But the Treaty of Versailles, while invariably condemned for sinning against morality, has rarely been charged with offending against expediency.

It is true that all the German colonies were swept away at one stroke, but at the least this was only in accordance with a time-honoured practice recently observed by the United States in dealing with the foreign possessions of Spain.

In addition to the cessions demanded outright, the victors imposed a number of plebiscites in frontier districts. Of these several popular tests, only two had even passing importance and only one was the cause of bitterness which still endures.

Thus, in the case of the East Prussian and Schleswig applications of the principle of self-determination, all the later elections proceeded without disorder and with complete fairness. In every case, save that of the northern Schleswig district, the Germans were decisively victorious, and here the size of the Danish majority silenced all German protest.

In the matter of the Saar and of Upper Silesia, the situation was totally different. In both cases, too, sentimental circumstances were reinforced by material conditions, for both contained great coalfields and each was the seat of a great industrial establishment which was a vital unit in German economic and industrial prosperity.

With respect to the Saar, which long remained the basis for German protest and distrust, it is sufficient to say that the French demand for a plebiscite, like the original demand for annexation outright, was based upon the fact that, before the French Revolution, much, if not quite all, of the territory had been French. Even in the settlement of 1814, the portion on the left bank of the river, including Saarlouis, the birthplace of Marshal Ney, remained French. Only after Waterloo was all taken. Yet, in 1919, the Saar was as German as the Ruhr. And only the later perception and acceptance of this fact by the French people removed the whole question from among the controversial issues of the peace settlement.

As for Upper Silesia, the plebiscite, when taken disclosed a very formidable Polish vote. The size of this vote warranted the taking of the count; the later application of the results of the election belongs to another phase of the present study.

Prohibition of Austrian union with the German Reich aroused later protest, but the same denial was made to the Belgian peoples in 1814 and again in 1830, when they desired union with France. Yet Belgium has, in the course of nearly a century, achieved national unity. Moreover, the opposition to *Anschluss*, both in Austria and in Germany, is far from negligible.

The military terms were not in themselves more excessive or more open to just and reasonable criticism. Germany was to be disarmed, her huge conscript army reduced to the narrow limits of a volunteer system modelled upon the British and American. Her western frontier was to be demilitarized and for a period of fifteen years occupied by Allied armies, which were to retire in three echelons, beginning in 1925.

As to the military occupation, it could be justified by the precedents of 1815 and 1871, in both of which years Prussian troops had been left in France to insure the fulfilment of the terms of the treaties of Paris and Frankfort respectively. Recalling the triumphant evasions of Prussia after Jena and the decisive intervention of Prussian troops upon the battlefields of Leipzig and Waterloo, these precautions could hardly be termed unreasonable, the more as Germany contained, after the Armistice, five million trained veterans. With such a field for recruitment what could Napoleon not have done on his return from Elba?

The reparations clauses, on the other hand, were conceived in folly and born to futility. Germany was asked to pay sums totally beyond her capacity. She was, in fact, held liable to pay more than $33,000,000,000, while, by comparison, the British government was later able to persuade a not too indulgent creditor on this side of the Atlantic that the American war debt claim of $5,000,000,000 was beyond British capacity.

In principle, then, but never in practice, Germany was required to pay what was beyond her ability—and inevitably the requirement abolished all incentive to pay at all. Since German soil was occupied by Allied armies which might remain until fulfilment was assured, since they might even advance and take more territory in the face of failure, the Treaty of Versailles became potentially an engine of incredible oppression.

Yet it is essential to preserve a sense of measure, to recognize that no super-Machiavellian brain planned this impossible combination of clauses, and to perceive that accident and not design was responsible for what was worst and seemed most wicked. The preposterous reparations totals were the consequence of the fact that the problems of transfer of wealth from one country to another were not only incomprehensible to the popular mind, but hardly less insoluble to the minds of the political economists themselves.

Men talked easily in billions and measured Germany's capacity to pay by the extent of the ruin German arms had wrought. The question was conceived to be moral, not material. After 1870, France had paid a billion, and payment had been without great difficulty. Since 1870 the world had expanded incredibly in wealth. The very magnitude of German industrial development in the previous decades seemed to warrant unlimited demands which could never in any event equal the losses incident to German devastations in the war.

Finally, it was not the reparations clauses which wrecked the Versailles Settlement. They had to be revised, but revision was not impossible, and execution to unreasonable and impossible limits was never demanded. When the revision came, with the Dawes Plan, when, in fact, Germany consented to fulfil, the reparations problem disappeared and the military clauses became without menace to German rights. The reparations clauses were, in a sense, like the mainspring of a watch; if that will not function, the watch will not tick or tell time, but if the mainspring is repaired, the watch will go.

Actually, the Paris Conference failed because in dealing with Germany it was dominated at all times by the spirit and the conception which were disclosed in the famous "guilt clause" of the Treaty itself. This clause read:

> The Allied and Associated Governments affirm and Germany accepts the responsibility of Germany for causing all the loss and damage to which the Allied and Associated Governments and their nationals have been subjected as a consequence of the war imposed upon them by the aggression of Germany and her Allies.

This did not relate merely or primarily to the legal liability for damage which had been accepted by Germany in the Armistice. It was designed to establish the fact that the war had been caused by Germany, and it was required of German representatives to sign this document as a confession of crime. It was the disclosure of the purpose of the Allied peoples to deal with the Germans as a guilty people.

Allied action, moreover, supplied the best evidence of Allied spirit. The Germans were not permitted to discuss the terms of peace. Summoned to receive the document, they were confined behind wooden fences in the Trianon gardens at Versailles through which Sunday crowds peered at them as at caged beasts. Called at last to appear before the treaty-makers, as criminals coming up for sentence, they were brought into the Hall of Mirrors, where, less than half a century before, the German Empire had been proclaimed. There the "Big Three," Clemenceau, Lloyd George, and Woodrow Wilson, with their minor associates, sat as the human embodiment of Divine Justice, Divine Wisdom, and Divine Mercy, and

Woodrow Wilson, who in this interesting trinity might be assumed to be the member representing Divine Mercy, openly showed his displeasure when Brockdorff-Rantzau for the Germans protested against this guilt clause.

If the whole performance was modelled upon the processes of the criminal court, too, in one respect Versailles went far beyond its model. For the criminal convicted by a jury and presented to his judges for sentence is still suffered to enjoy the ultimate solace of professing his innocence. Even this was denied the Germans, who were not only tried in their absence, condemned without defence, but under immediate duress in the shape of Allied military power operating within their country, required to sign a confession of their own guilt which they did not, and in the nature of things could not, believe.

Peoples may believe that they have been deceived, misled, mistaken. They may, as a consequence, cast off their rulers or suffer them to depart, as the French had done with Napoleon, and more recently the Germans themselves had done in the case of William. They may abandon policies, change régimes, dismiss political leaders. All these things constitute in themselves admissions of error. But no people can believe in the moral turpitude of their race.

The question of whether the Germans were uniquely responsible for the war could not be affected by any confession thus extorted. Such a confession could, in fact, only testify to the extent of German weakness and the completeness of Allied power. It was accompanied, as it was bound to be, by the disclosure that what the German delegates signed, they repudiated, and their fellow countrymen repudiated also and equally.

The victors, however, did not rest on the confession. After, as before the signature, they continued to treat the Germans as a guilty people. In proof of this, Germany was denied admission to the League of Nations for a time undetermined. Thus, in principle and by practice, was established the view that the German people were and remained a pariah people, that they were, as Allied press and publics continued to call them, Huns and Boches.

Laying aside every consideration save that of common sense, how could peace be made with a great people on this basis? If the Germans were in fact a guilty and therefore a criminal people, the single alternative was between destruction and permanent restraint. Since sixty millions of people, however guilty, could not be destroyed, there was left only the resource of restraint.

In practice, how could or can peace be made with any great people on the basis of restraint, inequality, inferiority? Who can measure the chaos and anarchy, leading to ultimate strife, which the effort to enforce any such judgment must involve? Nor is the situation made more tolerable by reason of the fact that those on whom falls the duty to enforce the moral law have selfish and material reasons for desiring the enforcement.

Could the German people believe that they were innocent? The fact is they did, they do, and they will. No man or woman can have travelled even casually in Germany and not been struck by the phenomenon of German reaction to the war-guilt charge. What is, perhaps, even more incredible to Allied minds, the German people not only believe themselves innocent, but dare to think that other people were guilty.

Edmund Burke had once admitted that he was unable to discover a method by which to draw an indictment against a whole people. The victors of 1918 succeeded where he failed. In fact, they not only drew the indictment, but they compelled the accused to sign it. Further, they emphasized their decision by denying to the German people admission to the League of Nations to which entrance was not refused the Asiatic and African races.

Against this indictment, against the spirit which it disclosed, against the policy which expressed it, the German people were bound to revolt. Disarmed, exhausted, reduced to a condition of domestic chaos by the collapse of the old régime and by the weakness of the new, they could not resort to arms. Only passive resistance remained, but this endured precisely as long as the Allied peoples arrogated to themselves the right to treat the German people internationally as guilty, as moral inferiors, on any basis save that of complete political equality.

In the eyes of every German, resistance to the Treaty

of Versailles was resistance to a verdict which not merely condemned his race on the ground of moral turpitude, but thereby supplied the pretext for the physical destruction of his country as well. The moral verdict he rejected. To prevent the physical destruction, he struggled desperately, if at times hopelessly. Moreover, since he repulsed the moral condemnation, the policy which expressed it seemed to him sheer violence based upon patent hypocrisy.

Allied pretence to moral elevation was measured by Allied performance in German premises. In that performance the German saw the purpose to plunder thinly veiled by the profession of lofty principles. The sentence passed upon himself, as a criminal, he felt unjust. The use made of the sentence was for him the proof that the judgment had been rendered solely for the purpose of licensing a policy of unlimited persecution and of unrestrained plunder. Angered by the extent of the exactions, his indignation at what were for him utterly hypocritical explanations was intense. Helpless at the moment of the Armistice, on the morrow of the publication of the Treaty of Versailles, he felt himself armed by the acts of transparent injustice of his conquerors.

With impartial exactitude, therefore, the authors of the Treaty of Versailles had aroused the resentment and insured the resistance of every inhabitant of the Reich, not because he was a Junker or a Communist, a Monarchist or a Republican, but precisely because he was a German. Human ingenuity could go no further.

The Treaty of Versailles did not fail because of the material clauses, although some are severe and some impossible. It failed because the victors attempted to translate a military victory into terms of moral superiority and to make this alleged superiority a basis for their later treatment of a great people. In doing this they overpassed the limit. As a consequence, they failed to make peace with the German people.

Undoubtedly, the German people would have resisted the material clauses of the Treaty of Versailles, even had the moral implications been absent. Certainly the creation of the Polish Corridor, the cession of Danzig, the loss of Upper Silesia would have aroused nationwide resistance. But it was the sense of moral injustice which actually made the German revolt formidable, and this feeling was shared by all factions of the population. It was this consciousness of injustice which armed the spirit of the German for a conflict which was always unequal and inevitably disastrous.

Locarno did not amend the material clauses, it abolished the moral assumptions. It did not revise the fact of Versailles, but it exorcised the spirit. In so far, the victors of 1918 surrendered to the vanquished. To this extent the German resistance was successful. When, however, during the resistance, the campaign was extended to envisage possible escape from the material consequences of defeat, failure followed inexorably.

Even to the present hour, however, in Allied countries the German revolt against the Treaty of Versailles continues to appear no more than the extension of the war. It is interpreted as an effort to escape physical consequences of defeat. Those who sympathize with the German explain it as resistance to unjust and impossible terms. Those who continue to see the German in wartime light regard it as an effort to evade reasonable terms by dishonourable methods. Both interpretations, however, miss the sense of moral injustice, which was never absent, which alone made the resistance formidable.

In the Treaty of Versailles, itself, was included the Covenant of the League of Nations, which was the objective of all Mr. Wilson's Paris endeavours. To the settlement were also appended the two treaties, one binding Britain, the other the United States, to the defence of French security against any fresh and unprovoked German aggression.

This double guarantee was the corner stone of the whole settlement from the point of view of both European countries. For France it insured Anglo-Saxon aid in case of new German attack, and by the very fact of such overwhelming strength thus arrayed, abolished the danger that Germany would even consider such an aggression. In the French eyes, the American guarantee had moral value rather than military, but the British had both.

For the British people the American signature both to the Treaty of Versailles and the Treaty of Guarantee had almost as broad a meaning. It insured that in all the future conferences and meetings which must inevitably take place and direct the practical task of reordering Europe, American presence would promise Anglo-Saxon coöperation. Since both countries were pledged to support and defend France, too, both countries would be able to exercise a powerful influence upon the French to persuade them to accept Anglo-Saxon views as to the course necessary to bring Europe and the world back to economic peace and industrial prosperity.

For France, the settlement was a guarantee against Germany, for Britain it was an insurance against France, while for both equally it was the foundation of the whole peace structure.

CHAPTER FIVE

WHY THE TREATY FAILED

WHEN the fact of the failure of the Treaty of Versailles began to be unmistakable, there arose in the world a debate over the responsibility for the breakdown which has continued with little-decreasing violence to the present hour. Indeed, this debate over the responsibility for the failure of the Treaty of Versailles has divided the field with that over war guilt itself.

At the outset, the Democrats in the United States blamed the Republicans and the Republicans blamed Woodrow Wilson. After the national election of 1920, the people of the United States reproached Europe, which responded by condemning the United States.

As the failure began to have serious consequences in Europe, the French criticized the British and the British censured the French, while the Germans, with far greater consistency, indicted all their enemies with varying degrees of bitterness, as the circumstances dictated.

Presently the argument took a new form and entered into the field of domestic politics in Europe as it had done at once in the United States. In this discussion, the parties and groups which had been out of power in 1919, and therefore without responsibility, in the main the Liberal, Radical, and Pacifist elements, condemned the parties and leaders holding office at the moment the Treaty was made.

Since the groups which were in power in 1919 were those which had supported the war, and the leaders, the men who had led their democracies to victory, were alike Nationalists and had insisted upon victory before peace, their opponents denounced them as Militarists, Imperialists, and Super-nationalists.

Then, as the debate tended to become academic after the arrival of the Dawes Plan and the Locarno pacts, all peoples of all countries, having taken little part in the debate hitherto, settled down to the comforting conclusion that in 1919 they had unanimously demanded a peace of justice and conciliation, and that their desire had been thwarted by narrow, unenlightened, and vindictive statesmen.

Each European country, while conceding the mental limitations of its own representative, found satisfaction in condemning the moral limitations of his associates representing other nations, which did not quite share the noble aspirations now professed by all, *ex post facto*. As for the people of the United States, while repudiating the part played by the President, they derived solid satisfaction from the belief that the ultimate collapse was due to errors and evils which were peculiarly European.

Europe, by contrast, clung and clings to a similarly

fundamental conviction that all would have been well, if only the United States had been what Europe imagined it to be in January, 1919, and it condemns the American people for continuing to follow American traditions, in the face of the opportunity and the duty to tread pathways marked out for them by European expectations and interests.

Viewed in retrospect, too, each European people is conscious of the fact that, in January, 1919, its consuming and dominating desire was for peace. How could it be otherwise? Tortured and afflicted by four years of continuous and incredible agonies, exhausted by efforts which have been unequalled in any other age, the longing of all European peoples for peace at the moment of the Armistice cannot be denied.

But what kind of peace did the several peoples desire? To what extent did any desire peace at any price? What were the demands made by the peoples upon their Ministers at the moment when the military decision had placed it within their power to write the terms of a settlement? Here and perhaps only here it may be possible to discover the origin of the causes of the later failures.

The case of the British people is perhaps most illuminating, and it relates to the reparations clauses, which were the cause of so much disaster. In December, 1918, before the Paris Conference had assembled, Lloyd George went before the people of Britain in the notorious "Khaki election." Rightly he judged that this was the moment most propitious for the man who had "won the war" to win another mandate.

Trustworthy contemporary report records the fact that at the outset of this campaign Lloyd George was in a moderate and reasonable mood. But no sooner had his foot touched the platform than with that incredible flair for popular opinion which has made him the greatest politician of modern times, he sensed the temper of the British electorate.

Under the lash of press propaganda, under the stimulus of popular emotion still reacting to the war, responding to continuous heckling of press and audiences alike, Lloyd George promised the British people that, if they would give him a majority, he would go to Paris and "hang the Kaiser" and make the Germans "pay the last farthing," that he would squeeze the Germans "until the pips squeaked." And on this understanding the British public gave him an enormous majority.

In this episode it would be difficult to discover anything of that secrecy later alleged against the treaty-makers. No open covenant was ever more openly arrived at than this between Prime Minister and people. No detail in proposed foreign policy was ever more frankly and freely submitted to that solemn referendum which is that of the ballot box. Patently the reparations clauses were not inspired in the dark corridors of Paris, but in the great open spaces of the British electoral arena.

It might, perhaps, be conjectured, however, that, since this popular decision was unmistakably based upon transitory war passion and the British public was at the moment incapable of knowing its own mind, it would later and relatively promptly adopt more generous and reasonable conceptions. But, in point of fact, it was the other way—it was Lloyd George who saw the truth first.

In contact with the American financial commission, which could and did view the question objectively, since the United States was not making a reparations claim, Lloyd George was convinced that excessive reparations could not be collected, that the "last farthing" was not available. In conference with the younger economists of his own delegation, he was brought to see that, for a trading and commercial people, reparations even to the extent of the possible might be of doubtful advantage.

But, although he began to see the truth, Lloyd George was daily faced by the contract, and with each edition the London press spread the disquieting rumour that "L. G. Sells Pass" that the Prime Minister, "Wants to Let the Hun Off." The members of Parliament who were chosen with Lloyd George in the recent election became disturbed by the unrest at home, and their protests crowded the wires to Paris.

The British people had sent Lloyd George to Paris to impose a hard peace on the German people; were they going to permit him to impose a soft peace upon themselves? Hardly; if anyone believes that they were prepared for this, let him study the British press of March and April, 1919.

In the end, then, Lloyd George, although he knew better and told the American financial delegates that he knew better, sent General Smuts to President Wilson and obtained the President's consent to include pensions and war allowances in the bill against the German. By this method only could the British share in reparations be more than trifling, because all the devastation was on Continental soil. But by this device the sum total was trebled. There was the origin of the reparations folly, but the choice of the British Prime Minister was between the course he took and an adverse vote in the House of Commons.

The French case is equally illuminating although a trifle less obvious. Clemenceau and all the French people knew what they needed, as Lloyd George and the British people did not perceive in their own case at the outset. Security was for France the primary objective in the peace-making.

But the French people saw security only in terms of traditional and military solutions. Permanent occupation of the left bank of the Rhine by Allied armies, definite separation of the populations of the left bank from Germany, these were the French demands, and Clemenceau presented them to the Peace Conference.

Instantly, these demands encountered British and American opposition. They were contrary to all Mr. Wilson's conceptions based upon the Fourteen Points; they were utterly inconsistent with all British foreign policy for centuries. Neither the British nor the American people were willing to keep armies perpetually on the Rhine or permanently to support what was in reality an eternal state of war with the German people.

Unable to establish these demands, which were the demands of the French people at the moment, furiously pressed by the Paris newspapers, Clemenceau accepted, instead, an Anglo-American promise to guarantee French security against any new German aggression.

This was not only the maximum to be obtained, but it was the true line of French policy, for it was the single possible line which promised any security. Clemenceau's course was amply vindicated later when the Locarno pacts did give France the British guarantee which was the objective of all his Paris effort.

In the face of all popular opposition, Clemenceau forced the ratification of the Treaty when made. He bullied a hostile Chamber of Deputies which was at the moment more fearful of a "Tiger" in front of it than a people somewhat in the background. To achieve the ratification, Clemenceau had to treat Poincaré, the President of the Republic, like an impertinent butler, and Foch, the marshal of victory, like an insubordinate corporal.

But although the Chamber ratified the Treaty, the French people refused to accept it. They rallied against Clemenceau, now come to private life, and under their stimulus Parliament denied him the Presidency of the Republic which had fallen vacant. The "Father of Victory" became for his people the man who had lost the peace.

Lloyd George bowed to the mistaken will of the people, and he lasted for nearly four years after the Paris Conference. Clemenceau imposed the wise policy upon the French people, and they punished him and continue to reproach him, even when they have accepted what he sought to obtain for them.

This present volume is limited to the discussion of the events which directly concern Germany and her British, French, and American opponents, but there is, perhaps, warrant for appealing to an Italian example, since it is illuminating and apposite. When the question of Fiume arose at the Peace Conference, it precipitated a dispute which threatened to wreck the whole negotiation. It produced a deadlock at a moment when Europe was patently disintegrating.

In this situation, President Wilson, who steadily adhered to the belief that the poeple, as contrasted with their leaders, were always generous and enlightened, put his doctrine to the test. He had been in Italy during his grand tour before the Conference met. Nowhere had he been welcomed so warmly, cheered so enthusiastically, acclaimed so deliriously. Perhaps there came back to him the memory of the night when he leaned from a Roman balcony and threw kisses to the mad throngs below.

At all events, he suddenly issued an appeal to the Italian people over the head of Orlando, their representative at Paris, who was holding out for Fiume. This appeal was based upon an eloquent and moving statement of the perils to the world of continued delay. It was a request of the Italian people to disown the unregenerate and selfish nationalism of their Paris representative and by an act of national self-abnegation remove the stumbling block to the restoration of peace in the world.

What happened? From the Alps to Sicily there burst forth a unanimous, passionate, violent denunciation of Woodrow Wilson. After years, the embers of this nationwide conflagration are discoverable in Italy, and they are not yet cold. Obedient to this will thus expressed, D'Annunzio later went to Fiume, following the example of Garibaldi and his Thousand, and took the city by force against the will of Europe.

When one turns to the question of the guilt clause, the reef on which the whole settlement ultimately wrecked, the fact is beyond discussion that this indictment of sixty millions of Germans proceeded directly from the peoples of the Allied democracies.

No people, no considerable minority within any nation, no popular voice audible to the sentient ear of any politician ever raised a protest against an indictment which was impossible in fact and unwise in policy. For all peoples equally and for all elements within national frontiers, the German people were the people who had invaded Belgium, sunk the *Lusitania*, devastated northern France. They were by virtue of these facts, which were incontrovertible, a criminal people.

That the physical terms of the Treaty must be sufficiently reasonable to permit the Germans to live, at least to exist, was generally perceived. But that the moral condemnation should be other than definite, drastic, unequivocal, no one even dreamed. President Wilson went to Paris to insure that no new Alsace-Lorraine should be created, but Brockdorff-Rantzau's protest against the guilt clause not only left him cold but aroused his resentment as something irrelevant and immaterial.

The guilt clause expressed what the Allied peoples, with utter unanimity, believed of the German people when the treaty was made and for years thereafter. It expressed what many still believe. The Germans must be guilty because all Allied peoples unanimously believed and knew them to be guilty. In no democracy was there opposition; in all the verdict was unanimous. The very failure of the German people to acknowledge the truth thus established became a new proof of the accuracy of the indictment.

No portion of the whole tremendous and ponderous volume, which is the Treaty of Versailles, came so directly and unmistakably from the people, and no representative of any country, not Lloyd George, not Clemenceau, not even Woodrow Wilson, would have dared to face his own people having opposed this judgment at Paris. And, of course, none ever thought of doing that.

And, in fact, this same phenomenon, less definite, less remarked, may be discovered in the case of the American Civil War, which was, after all, the first struggle between two modern democracies. When the North had triumphed and the passions of war were accentuated by the assassination of Lincoln, for which the South had not the remotest responsibility, it unhesitatingly undertook to adopt toward the beaten Confederates policies and methods which it frankly based upon moral grounds.

The result was, too, the same after 1865 as after 1918. All the shame and scandal of the Reconstruction Era were the consequence of this attempt. Reconciliation was postponed for a generation, not because the South thought of resuming the conflict, but because the North was still acting on the basis of moral superiority. Those who wore the gray were in no doubt as to the decision of the battlefield. Time would even bring the later survivors in many cases to rejoice in that. But what force could compel the men and women of the Confederacy to confess that they had been morally guilty, merely because the war began with rebel shots fired at Fort Sumter?

At Paris, the British people wanted peace with reparations, the French people peace with security, the Italian people peace with Fiume. All peoples demanded and asserted the right to pronounce a moral sentence upon the recent enemy. Excessive reparations meant ruin for the British people; security, as the French people sought it, insured dangers incalculable, Fiume for the Italian people created a peril of war which has never lessened to this hour. The guilt clause as a basis of policy made German resistance inevitable.

But how can the responsibility for these things be placed upon the shoulders of Clemenceau, Lloyd George, Orlando, or Woodrow Wilson? Clemenceau and Orlando were repudiated because they failed to get what their people demanded, Lloyd George was rewarded because he obtained what was and in its consequences continues to be a curse to his country.

There remains the case of the American people, and it is on the surface, but only on the surface, quite different. In fact, the American people asked nothing of President Wilson affirmatively. Yet their negative demand was not less definite because it was not disclosed until the Treaty was made.

When Mr. Wilson returned from Paris, bringing the Treaty of Versailles, which he told his fellow countrymen was a peace of justice, it was never examined on that basis. It might have been rejected with reason for the thing which it was, but examination to disclose this reality was never undertaken.

Instantly and to the bitter end the American debate turned upon the single question as to whether the American President, in signing the Versailles document, had compromised those American rights which were comprehended in the American tradition and instinct for isolation, for freedom from all commitments which would involve participation in European struggles.

The American people were prepared to accept the reparations schedules, the territorial annexations, the guilt clause, which they endorsed as unanimously as their European associates, but they were not ready to waive the smallest fraction of that interest which for them was controlling. Mr. Wilson could tell the Senate of the United States that the reservations to his Covenant cut the heart out of the system for world peace and reconciliation, the Senate did not deny the system of world peace, but it insisted upon the reservations because, without them, the Treaty compromised American interests which at most were national and parochial.

Thus, in reality, the American relation to the Treaty of Versailles was not different from that of the European associates. All peoples wanted what they wanted, and all peoples repudiated the leaders who failed to further or safeguard interests which were exclusively national.

CHAPTER SIX

WOODROW WILSON AT PARIS

NO STUDY of the decisions of the Paris Conference can be complete, however, without reference to the part played by Woodrow Wilson. No other circumstance, moreover, supplies as satisfying a measuring rod for the forces actually in play at that moment.

At the outset, however, one is faced by the double question: What did Europe, the peoples of the Allied countries, conceive Mr. Wilson's coming to mean? what did the President of the United States regard his mission to be? And unmistakably there are between the answers to these two questions a divergence almost incalculable and explanatory of most if not all of separation in sympathy which afterward took place.

For the European peoples, the intervention of the United States in the war itself had meant salvation and victory. For them the presence of Mr. Wilson and the programme which he brought to Europe with him meant peace on their own terms and protection from the enemy who remained the enemy. Mr. Wilson was the symbol of that American guarantee against a European menace. All else was beyond the power of men and women in the circumstances of the Europe of that hour to grasp.

In Mr. Wilson's view the conditions were quite

different. He was a scholar and a student, and even the incredible uproar of the World War had not disturbed the academic calm in which he approached the post-war problem. Moreover, to preserve that calm, he resisted every effort to influence his emotions and to cloud his judgment. The best example of this was his refusal to visit the devastated regions of France, a refusal which cost him French understanding from the start.

As a writer upon American history, Mr. Wilson's attention had been concentrated upon national development, and he had little or no expert knowledge of European questions. By contrast, he had naturally thought of European problems before the war, and the struggle itself forced him to consider more or less of the details of geography and history which make up the Continental puzzle.

Wrestling with these problems, too, he inevitably discovered that at the bottom of all lay the conflicting interests of race and nation. At the beginning of the war, however, Mr. Wilson was not a partisan of any belligerent, least of all of the German, as was later alleged. His whole nature forbade partisanship. As a scholar, he examined the problem calmly, objectively, whereas many of his fellow countrymen approached it on the basis of violent sympathy and dominating partisanship. This very calmness, this aloofness, this dispassionate objectivity angered many and puzzled more.

In all the whirling storm of clashing propaganda and mutual recrimination the President detected naturally andex pressed frankly the striking fact that each coalition professed something like the same high moral purposes, announced substantially the same war aims and charged with equal assurance that the war itself was the result of evil men, statesmen and rulers animated by wicked designs. He saw, for example, that the German people laid the catastrophe to the policy of "encirclement" of Edward VII, while the Allied peoples charged it to the mad ambition of William II.

Like many of his fellow countrymen, Mr. Wilson did not believe one but both of these accusations. He believed both because each equally well fitted in with his fundamental conception that all peoples are peace-loving, generous, just, and that wars come only because these people are led into nationalistic, imperialistic, and militaristic policies by representatives of an old and non-democratic era.

Being what he was, Mr. Wilson was bound to go beyond analysis and seek remedies. But his remedies would naturally go along with his diagnosis. Believing that the peoples were essentially right and their leaders fundamentally wrong, his solution would infallibly take the form of some system which would restrain the leaders and give free expression to the popular will.

Thinking deeply upon this subject, Mr. Wilson presently adopted the not unknown thesis of a League of Nations. In his conception, this league would be some international seat of reason and justice, from which could issue appeals, and even commands, to the peoples of all countries, whenever they were tempted by ambitious leaders to follow pathways which led to war. Such an international machine would always have access to the ear of the people, its voice would undeniably be that of justice and reason, and the people would inevitably respond. They would dismiss their faithless leaders and accept the advice of the League.

But in the situation which existed in the world at the moment, the President reasoned that, unless something were done at once, the politicians, the agents of the old system, would be able to make a treaty of peace which would perpetuate all the evils out of which they fashioned their policies. They would be able to create feuds, embitter races, perpetuate secular quarrels. Therefore he conceived that the first step must be to put all the politicians on record as accepting certain general principles on which the peace was to be based. Thereafter he could hold the politicians to this declaration.

Here is alike the origin of the Fourteen Points and the basis of all of Mr. Wilson's Paris mission. In the President's conception, proposing these Fourteen Points had been supreme strategy. When he had succeeded in getting the Allied statesmen to accept, he was satisfied that he had them. For him, Paris was no more than the problem of holding the European premiers to their word which was already recorded.

To accomplish this he relied upon the support of the peoples of all countries, whom he believed equally alive to the significance of the Fourteen Points and without exception determined upon a peace of justice. In case of resistance on the part of Lloyd George, Orlando, Clemenceau, any public man, Mr. Wilson could, in the last analysis, appeal to the people of Britain, Italy, or France, and they would respond. Moreover, this power to appeal constituted a sword which he held over the heads of all European diplomats and politicians. Mr. Wilson believed this implicitly, and so did most of his immediate associates who accompanied him to Paris.

But success or failure in the whole adventure would depend in the final circumstance upon the accuracy or unsoundness of this major premise. It assumed popular support, it rejected the notion that the people of any country could be exclusively nationalistic. It based all upon that fierce passion for justice which Mr. Wilson regarded as the dominating fact in any democracy.

Thus Mr. Wilson went to Paris expecting to meet the contemporary heirs to the policy and methods of Metternich, Talleyrand, Bismarck, but against them he was armed to the teeth with the Fourteen Points. And behind him was not merely the force of the American people, but of all people. There, succinctly, is the Wilsonian conception of the Paris Conference in advance of assembling.

In the accepted sense, too, the President never thought of himself as going to Paris to make a peace treaty. For him and for his followers alike, the Paris journey was nothing less than another apostolic adventure. As St.

Paul went forth to preach a new gospel to the decadent Roman Empire, President Wilson embarked to proclaim a new faith to a sinking Continent.

When, too, the peoples of all Allied countries greeted him with an enthusiasm which passed all known precedents, when he was welcomed in London, Paris, Rome, in all cities and towns and villages, with an emotion and a delirium which only those who witnessed the progress could even imagine, Mr. Wilson's last doubt vanished. This was for him ultimate proof of the soundness of the principle which he had adopted, and also conclusive evidence of the popular acceptance of the Fourteen Points and of his programme for a peace of justice and reconciliation.

As a consequence, when at the outset of the sessions of the Peace Conference itself, President Wilson encountered the squat, square, solid figure of Georges Clemenceau in his pathway, when M. Clemenceau insisted upon the discussion, not of the Covenant of the League of Nations, but of the security of France, Mr. Wilson and his followers were first impatient, then irritated, finally frankly denunciatory. What concern had Woodrow Wilson with a narrow, parochial question of French security, since under the Covenant of the League the security of all countries was assured?

Clemenceau's voice was the voice of the old order. Clemenceau was the enemy Mr. Wilson and all his friends had expected to encounter. Security in the sense the French Premier meant it and under the conditions by which he sought to attain it was exactly the thing Mr. Wilson had come to fight.

Out of this irritation, presently rising fairly to the point of moral indignation, proceeded the familiar but fantastic picture of the President, already broken in health, physically weak but morally invincible, single-handed in the dark council chamber, fighting the battle of the nobler to-morrow with the grim, sinister, gray-gloved Clemenceau, the incarnation of militarism, imperialism, chauvinism, in fact, of the unregenerate yesterday.

By coincidence, however, a Frenchman with equal fidelity to the fact as he saw it, at the same moment, produced a portrait of Clemenceau, now almost eighty, physically spent by the tremendous and superhuman exertions which had saved his country, carrying in his body the bullet of a recently attempted assassination, wearily seeking to protect, not merely the rights but the safety of France against the attacks of another Don Quixote, mounted not upon Rosinante, but upon the Fourteen Points.

There is a third picture, which might perhaps be drawn with even greater faithfulness to detail. It is the picture of the same Woodrow Wilson a few months later, still more stricken in health, no longer in Paris, but in Washington, face to face now, not with French nationalism but American, confronting not Clemenceau, Lloyd George, and Orlando, but Borah, Brandegee, and Hiram Johnson. The President's champions might, perhaps, claim that he was still fighting the same old devil in a fresh disguise, but they should at least concede that Borah did not speak French, nor Hiram Johnson "European."

There exists a second myth, slightly more ingenious then the first but infinitely less romantic. It borrows all that portion of the first which contains the conceptions of European wickedness, it adopts the legend which makes Paris the battle between American idealism and European militarism, but it varies to assert that Mr. Wilson was beaten, not victorious, because he was a dupe and not a hero. It asserts that he set out to hitch the European wagon to his star and ended by tying his star to the tailboard of the European wagon.

This second version has the double advantage that it enables Mr. Wilson's opponents, who father it, to escape from any concession of virtue to the President and it places the responsibility for American retirement from Europe squarely upon European shoulders. Thus is avoided any awkward allegation that the American withdrawal from Europe was based upon any selfish or national grounds.

The quaint and equal absurdity of these twin myths lies in the fact that neither bears the smallest relation to the realities of the case. At the Paris Conference, Mr. Wilson was not at grips with any peculiarly European and therefore particularly vicious form of nationalism. His experiences with Britain over reparations, France over security, Italy over Fiume, were identical. His final struggle in Washington was of the same order.

Mr. Wilson's trouble arose from the fact that his quarrel was with nationalism wherever found. This quarrel was inevitable because at the bottom of his whole conception lay the vital assumption that, whenever his programme for international adjustment clashed with the view of any people as to their own essential national interests, that people would waive its convictions.

This, no people would do. Not the French, not the British, not the Italian, least of all the American people. Mr. Wilson might arrive at a compromise with Clemenceau by offering France an American guarantee to replace the traditional French form of security. Clemenceau could accept it whole-heartedly, but only because he thought the material value greater.

In the same way, the President might have offered Italy New York City instead of Fiume. And because at the bottom of the Italian aspiration lay the desire to recover Italian populations, the million in New York might have seemed more desirable than the scant thousands in the Adriatic seaport.

In reality, in accepting the treaties guaranteeing for French security, the President was only accepting French reservations to his proposed Covenant, reservations which the French believed were necessary safeguards to their vital interests. When he refused to accept reservations offered by the United States Senate to safeguard American interests which it believed were similarly vital, Mr. Wilson was lost.

Because the President began abroad, not at home, because he encountered French nationalism in Paris long before he met American nationalism in Washington, because the American people know nothing about the history, tradition, or circumstances of France, and the French people were and remain, to say the least, equally ignorant of American, Mr. Wilson's supporters were able to create this legend of collective European wickedness and especial French political immorality, all because European peoples adopted the course which the people of the United States took later for the same reason and in the same premises.

No understanding of Mr. Wilson's experience in Paris, no grasp of the reality of that Conference itself, is possible until it is perceived that all the moral elements injected into the proceedings by the President's friends and foes alike are extraneous and unreal.

There was not one battle in Europe and another in the United States. There was not one nationalism more intransigent than another. The French and British in Paris, the Irreconcilables and the Mild Reservationists in Washington, supported by the traditions of their respective countries, were animated by the same spirit. The people of France would not sacrifice their security to Mr. Wilson's dream, the people of the United States would not surrender their isolation to his vision. The fact as contrasted with the fiction is all here.

There is, too, peculiar irony in the German circumstance. Mr. Wilson sincerely believed that at Paris he was seeking to protect what he conceived to be German rights against unjust attack. Yet, for the German people he is to-day the man who signed the guilt clause and created the eastern frontier. Seeking to prevent the French from establishing another Alsace-Lorraine on the Rhine, he erected a Polish Corridor on the Vistula.

Mr. Wilson's failure at Paris arose from the fact that all he did and strove to do was based upon a major premise which was not only inexact but completely untrue. He believed that he represented a world constituency, a world opinion which overran all frontiers and would override all parochial nationalisms. He believed that he was the champion of all peoples against their elected but unrepresentative leaders.

In fact, no such situation existed. Mr. Wilson put his theory to the test in the case of every nationality—even the German—and all, including the American, repudiated him. He believed that the people of each country would support him against its Paris representatives and, in the end, each people assailed its own representatives for sacrificing national rights to Mr. Wilson's insistence.

Lloyd George and not Woodrow Wilson was the true embodiment of the spirit of that hour. Like Mr. Wilson, he knew nothing about Europe. He could confuse Silesia with Cilicia, as Mr. Wilson "overlooked" the thousands of Germans in the Upper Adige. He could believe that the Emperor Charles was the grandson of the Kaiser Francis Joseph and eloquently harangue against the policy of "visiting the sins of the father upon the child." He was not abashed to inquire, "Where is Teschen?"

But Lloyd George did know one thing which Woodrow Wilson never dreamed of, and that was the art of managing a legislative body backed by the infinitely dangerous public opinion of that hour. He never tried to give the people what he decided that they should desire. His business was to give the people what they wanted, when they wanted it, and to the limit, without regard to any questions of reality or morality.

Mr. Wilson failed because he undertook to make American and European peoples live up to an abstract standard he had set up for them; Lloyd George succeeded and survived politically because he always lived down to the views the people had for themselves at the given moment. Mr. Wilson undertook to be an international compass; Lloyd George was always satisfied to be a domestic weather vane.

But there is in the Wilson episode one further circumstance which must be noted. The President and his later biographers have always asserted that the Paris conflict was a battle between the old order and the new. And this is true, but not in their sense.

Control of foreign policy had been wrested from the executive, from the king, in the Nineteenth Century; it had been vested by the people in the legislative branch which they controlled. Mr. Wilson's fight in Europe was against the prime ministers who represented their respective legislatures, and in the United States against the American Congress itself. His was the position of all kings and every dictator. Had he been successful, there would have been created in American political life the precedent that foreign affairs are the province of the Executive. This would have been to set the clock back indefinitely.

There, after all, is the infinite tragedy of Mr. Wilson's adventure and the grotesque absurdity of the interpretations supplied by his biographers and champions. Mr. Wilson did not abandon his principles or sacrifice his ideals to selfish and opportunist compromises; that is a mean and unworthy libel. His very devotion to his principles killed him. But he was fighting for the old order against the new. He believed that he was representing the will of the people, but in fact he was merely advocating the method of the kings'.

Surviving from the period of acute controversy is the charge made alike by unfriendly critics and disappointed and disillusioned followers, when they saw that Hell's brew which they conceived the Treaty of Versailles to be, that Mr. Wilson should have come home when he discovered the facts of the Paris situation.

The President might have done that. It was always in his power to do it, and he at least played with the idea when he summoned the *George Washington* on a memorable occasion. But if he had come home he would have brought his Covenant and his League with him, killed by that act.

For at that moment in Europe there was not the smallest substantial political or popular support for a League of Nations save as it was the consideration to be paid by Europe for American participation in European affairs on Allied terms. His retirement would have removed the value and the project would have disappeared beneath the turbulent waters of that flood of wrath American retirement would have loosed.

And in this last stage of the Paris experience Mr. Wilson, himself disillusioned and perhaps a little enlightened, fell back upon the ultimate basis of his faith in the people. He conceived that, however mistaken they might be at that moment, as he increasingly felt them to be, when war passions and war propaganda had subsided, their final decisions would vindicate his original conceptions. When that moment came the League would be available.

By staying, the President did save and insure the League of Nations. Whatever it may become in the future, the glory will be justly his. And at the moment the League does still live, and nothing in its recent record invites rash forecast.

PART THREE

NATIONAL CONSEQUENCES OF THE FAILURE

CHAPTER SEVEN

GERMAN WILL

THE situation of the German people in all the period following the failure at Paris constitutes one of the most amazing paradoxes in history. They were beaten, disarmed, helpless. Allied armies could go whither they pleased on German soil. Allied fleets could resume the "Hunger Blockade" at will. Property could be seized, citizens arrested, communications interrupted.

Affirmatively, the German people could do nothing. Never was a nation more completely without power. And yet, negatively, it held the fortunes of its conquerors in its own hands. As long as the German people chose to resist, British prosperity was compromised. While they declined to pay, French bankruptcy was daily made more inevitable.

Resistance was, to be sure, a form of national suicide. The end was inescapable ruin for the German people. But, provided they were resolved to hold out, if their will to resist remained firm, their conquerors, Europe as a whole, might be dragged down with them in the final collapse of European civilization.

It was possible, barely possible, that German resistance by precipitating a collision of British and French interests, might bring about an Anglo-French conflict.

If this happened, Germany, although it had lost the war, might win the peace. But the hope was slight, the risk incalculable. All depended, must depend, upon the German will to resist. And, since any German government must be powerless, action must come from the people.

To fathom this German will, to measure the political circumstances in Germany, is far more difficult than to make similar estimates of British and French national situations. In both of these countries, the storm of the war passed over the existing democratic structure and left it substantially intact. The illusion of victory covered the reality of disaster. The first post-war parliamentary elections had about them nothing which was novel or unfamiliar.

In Germany, on the contrary, all was changed. The strongest state in modern history, the most efficient governmental machine, the most effective bureaucracy, were suddenly swept out of existence. A dynasty, which from the remoter days of the Great Elector to the still recent period of Bismarckian splendour, had been associated with the rise and unification of the German people, had disappeared into exile. And certainly nothing became it less well than the manner of its leaving.

The greatest war in human history, in which German arms had won new battles and fresh laurels, had through four years stimulated national pride, only to end in complete and limitless disaster. Almost to the final hour, too, triumph had seemed assured. The offensive of July was to bring victory and peace. All the frightful collapse had come between August and November. It was September before the first suspicion of approaching defeat reached the German masses.

Then swiftly all fell, the armies, the dynasty, the state itself. Surrender abroad was accompanied by revolution at home. For some days, too, this revolution seemed destined to follow the precedents of the great French explosion or the even more terrifying example of the contemporary Russian upheaval.

On November 9, 1918, the German nation had felt itself on the edge of the Soviet abyss. From that madness it had reacted violently. The proletariat, itself, had not only rejected this solution of Lenin, but hungry, weary, exhausted, it had nevertheless rallied to the leadership of Ebert and permitted the bloody repressions of Noske.

The German Revolution was, moreover, real, though this fact was not perceived beyond German frontiers. The people, the working people, had seized power. The first elections for a National Assembly had placed control in the hands of the Socialists, supported as they were by the Catholic Centre and the liberal Democrats. The spirit which Bismarck had ruthlessly stifled in the far-off days following 1848 had once more asserted itself. Two generations of Prussian rule had not quite extinguished a tradition of liberalism.

What did the German people feel at this moment? For no question is it harder to find an adequate answer.

They felt so many things: Weariness and exhaustion following the sacrifices and sufferings of the war. Hunger and misery as a result of the blockade, which in defiance of all human considerations still continued and would continue until the signing of the Treaty.

Beyond these immediate sensations, there was the vast disillusionment which defeat always brings. Nearly two millions of Germans had died in battle. This sacrifice had been in vain. The German people had dared everything, suffered everything, the magnitude of their effort still remained in their eyes incredible, and all had been for nothing. Everything given in the period of struggle, lives, fortunes, all was now not only lost permanently but lost uselessly.

Looking abroad, the German people still failed utterly to comprehend the state of mind of the Allied peoples. Even in their dejection, they believed that the magnitude of their own effort against the world in arms would command the admiration of the conquerors. The passion with which they had entered the war, the violent, bitter, hateful accusations which they had flung at their enemies, the "hymns of hate" which they had sung, were now forgotten.

The words of President Wilson had inspired the belief in Germany that a similar change had taken place in the Allied countries. Having suffered their kings to depart, having adopted the forms of democracy, they easily accepted the idea of a peace of conciliation. The German journalists who accompanied their delegates to Versailles in April, 1919, to receive the peace terms, came prepared and expecting to attend the Paris Opera, to find the Paris which they had left less than five years before!

Guilty the German people did not feel themselves to be, then or ever thereafter. But they were at this moment intensely aware of the immense folly of their leaders, the stupid rashness of their Emperor, the blindness of the statesmen whom they had trusted so implicitly. Beyond all else, they had appreciated the complete and devastating weakness of their military commanders and of that Great General Staff, which before the war had been the apparent depository of all human wisdom and of all superhuman virtues. For them an immense bubble had been pricked. The revelations of the Marne, Verdun, and the frightful campaign of 1918 were not misinterpreted. The legends born of Waterloo, Sadowa, and Sedan had been dissipated.

In the moment of physical weakness, the German undertook the task of moral self-appraisal. His mood was the mood of the Frenchman after 1870. The men who had now come to power—and, in fact, it was the people—had no responsibility for what had happened. Nor had they any temptation to defend those mistakes which seemed to them folly and to their conquerors crime. The contemporary revelations, made from the official archives by Kautsky, were adequate proof of this fact.

If they hoped for a peace of reconciliation, the German

people were not blind to the fact that the price of defeat must be paid. They were ready to reconstruct the ruins of France and Belgium. They realized that Alsace was lost irrevocably, that the Schleswig strip would return to Denmark inevitably. The reference in the Fourteen Points to a renascent Poland insured the cession of most of Posen. There, too, every German knew Prussia had failed as Britain had failed in Ireland, and for precisely the same reasons.

As to the fact of military defeat, despite all Allied suspicions, the German people recognized it. They might receive their returning soldiers under arches of evergreens and with an acclaim which seemed inappropriate to defeat. But they were a military people; millions had served in the ranks. All knew that an army which in July was fighting on the Marne and in November was behind the Meuse was not victorious. If there had been no ultimate disaster like Waterloo, the surrender was as complete as that of France in 1814.

German democracy was in control in the opening months of 1919. It did desire peace. It did cling almost childishly to the glittering promise of President Wilson's programme. It had no conception, nor had the German people, as a whole, of the consequences of German acts upon Allied minds. It expected to make material sacrifices, but it was totally unconscious of moral judgments.

The real proof of the fundamental character of the German Revolution is to be found not alone in the

Constitution made at Weimar in the spring and summer of 1919, but in the men who made it and the ideas expressed at the moment. No objective examination of the circumstances of Weimar and the Constitution there made can fail to establish the conclusion that democracy in Germany at this moment was authentic.

But it was at Weimar, in the midst of this task of creating a Constitution for the German Republic, that German democracy was overtaken by the verdict of Versailles. Upon the new and struggling republic was thus visited the sins of the ancient régime. Democracy was called upon to pay all the costs of the offendings of monarchy.

For all Germans—Republicans, Royalists, Junkers, and Communists—the Versailles Settlement became instantly and remains still "the appalling treaty." By its territorial clauses it destroyed German unity in erecting the Polish Corridor. By the plebiscites which it imposed, it menaced the sources of German industrial prosperity in the Saar and in Upper Silesia. In Europe, it forbade the union of the German peoples by prohibiting the association of Austria with the Reich. In Africa and in Asia, it swept away all the colonial establishments which had been for the German people a source of pride and a symbol of world power.

On the financial side, the magnitude of Allied demands appeared at once to the practical and industrially experienced German mind preposterous. The unmistakable fact that these financial clauses were to be enforced by French bayonets made them instantly the disclosure of a purpose of oppression. Every German schoolboy had been taught the story of the French struggle for the Rhine frontier. Now French armies were put on the Rhine for years; that they would stay forever was the inevitable German conviction.

But terrible as were all the material circumstances of the Treaty, the moral content was even more devastating to the German mind. In the spirit of the conquerors revealed in the guilt clause, the continuing "hunger blockade," the refusal to negotiate, the denial to Germany of admission to the League of Nations, in every circumstance and detail, there was discoverable the double purpose to destroy Germany physically and morally. Germany was not only sentenced to die, but to die as a criminal nation, as a "guilty" people.

Thus, by the most cruel and fatal of all conceivable circumstances, the Allied peoples, who had fought to make the world safe for democracy, were now demanding that the German people sign a treaty which would make democracy impossible for all Germans. Having set out to hang the Kaiser, they were now undertaking to strangle the German Republic, not by design, but in fact.

To sign this treaty was for the members of the Weimar assembly to sign the death warrant of the German Republic. The fact was not mistaken, but, despite all hesitations, the signature could not be refused, for behind the Allied demand were the bayonets of the armies of Foch. The men who had come to power in Germany had to choose between new war which might bring a revival of that Soviet peril, only recently exorcised, and the less immediate but hardly more terrible consequences of acceptance of the Treaty.

In point of fact, too, the decision reached at Weimar was made under the shadow of an adjacent Communist threat. A local insurrection on the day of decision long left the delegates in doubt as to whether they would spend the night in debate or in prison. Noske, summoned to testify to his ability to maintain order if the Treaty were rejected and Allied armies advanced, responded in the negative. As a consequence, the National Assembly yielded.

But when the Treaty had been signed, the decline of the fortunes of the German Republic began. The old order, which had taken refuge in the remoter corners of Eastelbia, again raised its head. To preserve order in the first terrible days, Ebert and Noske had been compelled to turn to the army. They had surrendered power which could not now be recovered. Moreover, the decisions of Versailles confirmed all that Ludendorff and his associates had forecast.

In the last months of the war, the German people had permitted the fighting arm to be paralyzed, because, weary and exhausted, they had begun to doubt the words of their leaders and soldiers. Theirs was the mood of the French people after Moscow and Leipzig. Like the French people, they had no longer believed that the fortunes of their country were identical with those of the master of the military forces. Departing, the discredited Quarter Master General had warned them that they would pay dearly for their weakness, had admonished them that the enemy who uttered conciliatory words was actually seeking the destruction of the German people.

In the terms of the Treaty of Versailles, the German people saw full confirmation of the forecasts of Ludendorff. In 1914, they had believed that they were forced to fight in self-defence; now the faith which had sustained them through four years of incredible suffering and appalling losses returned. Trusting Woodrow Wilson, they felt that they had been deceived; having been deceived, they were now disarmed, disarmed in the presence of enemies who had proclaimed the purpose to make moral judgments the pretext for physical dismemberment and material exactions.

Resistance to the Treaty of Versailles, therefore, came from the very soul of the German people; it was instinctive, instant and unanimous. It could not be otherwise. Condemned as a pariah people; subjected to treatment which wounded every sensibility and aroused every surviving circumstance of national pride, of racial dignity; surrounded by a moral blockade after war, only less terrible than the hunger blockade itself, they were thrown back upon themselves and within themselves. They were placed outside the frontiers of civilization.

Having signed the Treaty under duress and ratified it

under the shadow of immediate invasion, the German democracy was henceforth caught between the upper millstone, which was the terms of the Treaty, and the nether, which was the will of the German people to resist, to evade, to escape, the determination never under any circumstances to accept that position of a politically inferior and morally guilty people, which had been assigned to it at Versailles.

In reality, therefore, the wretched ministers of the German Republic henceforth existed between the bayonets of the armies of Foch and the passions of their own people. To resist Allied demands was to invite Allied sanctions, new invasions, and fresh hardships; to comply with Allied demands was to insure the utter discrediting of the democratic régime and for Erzberger, Haase, and Rathenau it led to assassination.

A year after the ratification of the Treaty came the Kapp Putsch. As a political manœuvre, as an effort to restore the old order, it failed. But the Ebert régime which fled to Leipzig to escape the *coup d'état* came back without prestige. It had survived, but solely because the old order, perceiving the madness of inviting foreign invasion, had stayed its hand. For it, time was working and would continue to work.

Henceforth, however, the army was beyond civil control. Not only had the government no power to compel disarmament, it had no public sentiment behind it. In every such undertaking, it became in the eyes of its fellow countrymen the instrument of foreign oppression.

The policy of fulfilment was to every German the policy of national betrayal. And always it was the Republic which, under Allied coercion, must attempt to follow this policy.

Always, too, in each election from that for the Weimar Assembly onward, control slipped steadily through Republican hands. The Social Democrats lost it at once. The Weimar Bloc, composed of popular and Bourgeois parties, both Republican, held it precariously until the occupation of the Ruhr resulted in the destruction of any Republican majority.

As the democratic spirit declined, too, the voices of the old order were heard in the land. The Republic had become not merely a symbol of foreign humiliation, it was the sign of domestic misery. The people who, after defeat, were angry and bitter toward the imperial blunderers, began inevitably to contrast the pre-war days of prosperity with the post-war period of privation. Life, which was once easy, the circumstances of the little people, of the millions, had now become intolerable.

As hatred mounted, too, hope began to return, for the break-up of the Anglo-French Alliance went forward visibly, and American withdrawal was unmistakable. The will to resist was strengthened by the prospect that continued defiance might lead to ultimate deliverance. And as the hope grew, the resentment against all who advised fulfilment increased concomitantly. And the Republic was the symbol of fulfilment. So the fortunes of the Republic declined steadily until, at last, after the

Ruhr, as the first president had been an ex-saddler, the second was a former field marshal. The story is all told in this contrast.

Had there been anything of nobility, of dignity, anything to stir the pulse or arouse the loyalty of the German people in the person of the Kaiser or the promise of the Crown Prince, had there been in all German public life a man of Bismarckian stature, it is unbelievable that the Republic could have survived these national humiliations. From the final consequences of their mistaken policies, the Allied peoples were saved by the utter and contemptible weakness of that House of Hohenzollern, to overthrow which half the world had taken arms.

But, although the Republic survived and survives to-day, control in it has passed, at least temporarily, from the hands of those who created it. Under the shock of the Ruhr occupation, the Republic itself almost disappeared. And all the profit and all the advantage which flowed from Allied policy or impolicy flowed to the leaders and the political groups, who represented the principles and the purposes, which in Allied minds had made the war inescapable.

In all the period from Versailles to the Ruhr, however, it is this spirit of the German people which must be appreciated to understand the course of German action. The German people resisted the material clauses of the Treaty, and this resistance precipitated the political conflict, but it was against the moral judgments that the German people were in rebellion. The passive resistance which was, in itself, madness is not otherwise comprehensible. For what the German people suffered from the beginning of the resistance to the end of the inflation period is almost beyond comprehension.

From the physical consequences of military defeat, the German people could not escape. In so far as resistance undertook to reverse the decision of the battlefield it was a failure, and foredoomed to be a failure. But from the moral sentence of the conquerors, the German people could escape and did. Locarno and Thoiry were a final demonstration of the defeat of Allied policy based upon the guilt clause. Nor is there any more astonishing circumstance than the fact that, what the German people had lost under arms, they won back without them.

CHAPTER EIGHT

FRENCH RESOLUTION

BETWEEN the French and German situations in the post-war period, the contrast was most striking. Germany had no power and could prevent everything; France had power and could accomplish nothing. Moreover, each French attempt to use her power to attain her own ends, while disadvantageous to Germany, was disastrous to Great Britain.

French strength was both military and political. The demobilization of the British army and the withdrawal of the American gave France a military supremacy in Europe unequalled since the Napoleonic era. Britain was powerless, Italy negligible, Germany helpless, America was remote and uninterested, while Russia, after the debacle before Warsaw, ceased to be a European force.

In the face of German dangers, Belgium, Poland, and Czecho-Slovakia were inevitable allies of France. French support of the territorial and political system created by the Paris Settlements was equally valuable to Rumania and to Jugo-Slavia. For all five states, the French army was the single solid guarantee of survival.

Yet, possessing this power, the French people saw themselves helpless. The rejection of the Guarantee treaties by their allies compromised the future security of France. German resistance to the reparations clauses of the Treaty of Versailles hastened national bankruptcy. Although the return of Alsace-Lorraine had brought full possession of the richest iron deposits in Europe, German action rendered this possession without profit.

These three French interests were of unequal importance: That of security was paramount, that of reparations subordinate, the question of iron was relatively minor. But failure in all three directions combined to mould French opinion and dictate French action.

Twice invaded in less than half a century, France had, as a consequence of the first invasion, lost two flourishing provinces. As a result of the second, she had seen ten of her richest departments reduced to ruins. For the French people, on the morrow of the Armistice, therefore, the first condition of acceptable peace was that they should have permanent guarantees against a third attack. This was the primary condition of continued national existence.

Between the psychology of a people which had recently been invaded and that of the American, which had never known a serious foreign incursion, or of the British, which had enjoyed nine centuries of immunity, there were bound to be gulfs in experience as wide as the Channel and the Atlantic. And, in fact, France had not only been invaded recently, but periodically in all her long history.

For the American and British people, the war was

over at the Armistice. The objects for which they had fought were attained. Both could look forward tranquilly to peace and prosperity now apparently assured by victory and fortified by distance. But the people of France still gazed fearfully across the devastated area to that gap in their eastern frontiers, through which in all ages invasions had come, through which the latest had recently burst and narrowly missed achieving their complete ruin.

Even victory had not brought security, for in the years following the Franco-Prussian War, Germany had developed her industries and expanded her population. France, by contrast, had remained chiefly an agricultural country with a stationary population. Thus the balance of power between the secular enemies had been forever destroyed. Although at the Marne and at Verdun French courage and military genius had flamed forth as brilliantly as ever in the millenary history of the race, every Frenchman knew that, had France stood alone, Germany would have won the war.

This demand for security, too, was but the latest expression in the face of contemporary facts of an instinct as old as history. Cæsar had solved the same problem for Gaul two thousand years before, by setting the Roman Legions to maintain the watch on the Rhine. While the legions had remained, Gaul behind them had known peace and prosperity. When the legions were withdrawn, the barbarian floods had swept across the river, and all Latin civilization had been submerged.

More than a thousand years later, when a compact French monarchy had emerged, the struggle for security at the Rhine began again. Henry II took the first forward step when, in 1552, he seized Metz, Toul, and Verdun, and with them control of the crossings of the Meuse and the Moselle. Two centuries and a half later the dream was realized, when the soldiers of the French Revolution victoriously descended the Rhine valley and French garrisons were established in all the old Roman stations from Cologne to Basel.

And amidst all the confusing details, French history in these centuries was dominated by this effort to restore the "natural frontiers." It was the basis of all French policy from Henry of Navarre to Napoleon III. It was also the foundation of all military doctrine, from Julius Cæsar to Ferdinand Foch.

But what the French Republic gained, the Napoleonic Empire lost. The First Abdication swept away all the conquests of the Revolution and brought French frontiers back to the limits of 1790. Waterloo cost Landau and Saarlouis. Sedan deprived France of Alsace-Lorraine and, with Strasbourg, she lost her last foothold on the Rhine, while with Metz went the control of the crossings of the Moselle.

Before 1870, French aspiration to regain what had been lost in 1814 remained constant. It was a dream which exercised a fatal influence upon the mind of Napoleon III. After 1870, however, French hope was limited to the recovery of the lost provinces. And with years even this longing weakened. Yet, after victory in 1918, nothing was more certain than that the dream of all the centuries, the desire for security guaranteed by possession of the left bank of the Rhine would reappear.

Time, however, had brought changes which could not be abolished. Belgium and Holland had risen to national existence. French control from Switzerland to the sea and from the Rhine to the frontiers of 1870 was no longer possible. Moreover, while the independence and integrity of Belgium and Holland were beyond question, Mr. Wilson's principles and British policies, equally, forbade annexation of the territories of the Rhineland, with their millions of German inhabitants.

In this situation, Marshal Foch prepared that famous plan which undertook to reconcile the military teachings of Cæsar with the moral doctrines of Wilson. The Foch scheme envisaged the establishment of permanent allied garrisons on the Rhine. Autonomous states, wholly independent of the Reich, were to contain the German populations of the left bank. In sum, this programme undertook to restore the situation which had existed at the moment of the French Revolution.

Of the Foch Plan, which made a tremendous noise at the time and had continuing evil consequences, it is necessary now to say but one thing. It was a typical product of the military mind. It was the companion piece to that strategic conception of Field Marshal von Schlieffen, who prepared in advance the invasion of

Belgium in 1914. It was identical in spirit with the proposal of Admiral Sir John Fisher to "Copenhagen" the German fleet in a time of full peace. It ignored the imponderables; it did violence to the most elementary principles of right and justice; it was the perfect example of the military mind dealing in absolutes and concerned only with the technical questions of the soldier's trade.

The Foch Plan was, then, preposterous. Schlieffen had undertaken to repeat Hannibal's victory at Cannæ in a Twentieth Century Europe. Foch set out to found a new military system based upon the denial of the right of self-determination in a world in which national consciousness had reached its fullest expression. Designed to insure French safety, it would have compromised it permanently. Advocated as a measure of peace, it would have promised perpetual war. At the very least, the French instinct for security was not stronger than the German will for unity. And there were sixty million Germans and less than forty millions of French.

Yet this plan had the support of the French press. It satisfied French conceptions of French needs. It realized the age-long instinct of the people. It had all the authority which inevitably accompanied the word of the Marshal of Victory. It had the support of the President of the Republic. Whether it actually had the personal approval of Clemenceau, who laid it before the Paris Conference is, however, open to doubt.

At all events, Clemenceau's major conception at Paris was to preserve the alliance which had won the war. For him, the security of France was to be guaranteed only by the continuing support of the great Anglo-Saxon allies. When their opposition to the Foch proposal demonstrated that this programme could only be realized at the cost of the destruction of the association which was to Clemenceau vital, he abandoned it. But he only abandoned it in return for the treaties of Guarantee.

When, however, the United States Senate rejected the treaty of Guarantee, and the British insurance fell consequently, Clemenceau was disarmed in the presence of the soldiers, statesmen, press, and public opinion which he had flouted. What was infinitely worse, France was without all promise of security. To obtain these Anglo-American pledges, Clemenceau had, in the Treaty of Versailles, abandoned in advance every detail of the Foch programme. Now this surrender was beyond recall.

For every Frenchman, therefore, the Treaty of Versailles became at once a gigantic fraud. The rejection of the Guarantee treaties was similarly a colossal betrayal. Clemenceau had been duped and France deserted. What had been won by the victory had been lost by the peace treaty. What had been saved at the Marne and at Verdun had been sacrificed at Versailles. A million and a half of French soldiers had died in vain, and France was again in danger.

There is, too, in the French nature a terrible tenacity. It is the quality which made Verdun at once an immortal epic and a lasting expression of the soul of a peasant people. In her long history, France has rarely been as dangerous to Europe and to the world as when she has felt herself alone and in peril. She now felt herself isolated and in eventual danger, and German resistance to the Treaty instantly accentuated the peril and emphasized the betrayal of the Treaty.

In this situation, French troops were on the Rhine. Under the terms of the Treaty they could stay long. If Germany refused fulfilment, they might stay perpetually. But this was the Foch plan. What had been lost in the security treaties might be regained in the reparations clauses. Always, too, power, for all present time, irresistible force, remained in French hands. To believe that the French people would in the last analysis hesitate to use it was to forget the Committee of Public Safety, the popular rising of 1792, the despairing defence of 1870, after Sedan and Gravelotte.

Moreover, from the outset, the French people saw what the British people declined to believe. They recognized that German resistance was to the Treaty, not to any single provision or any particular category. If they did not understand the cause of the German revolt, they did appreciate the fact of it. And for them this fact had immediate and deadly danger. While the British argued on behalf of a Germany which could not pay, the French knew themselves in the presence of a Germany which would not disarm.

As for reparations, French necessities here were vital.

In the end it was the exhaustion of French resources and the expansion of French credit incident to reconstructing the devastated areas which produced the collapse. Here, and not in military expenses, foreign subventions or tax evasions, was the ruin of French finance. And German refusal to pay precipitated this ruin.

Throughout the war and the first days after the Armistice, the French people had been sustained by the hope that Germany would pay the enormous costs incident to restoring the villages and clearing the fields. In considering German capacity, the French people were peasant-minded. France was in reality an Eighteenth Century country, measuring the conditions of the modern age by the standards of a distant time.

Every French peasant recalled, too, that after 1870 France had paid. The milliards of the Treaty of Frankfort were a national memory. Not only had France paid, but in that unhappy time no voice had come from London or from Washington protesting on behalf of France. Yet from both countries now came protests on behalf of the German foe. And the voices were of the nations which had denied France security.

By the victory Britain had acquired colonies, ships, property. She purposed to retain all these. By the war America had been made rich, she held all her European associates to their debts, contracted in the common struggle. She intended that these should be paid. But all revision of reparations was uniquely at French expense, while the profit was to be divided between the Anglo-Saxon Allies who had deserted France and the enemy who still defied and menaced her.

Even if the British now demanded revision of reparations figures, the French people well remembered that while he had believed payments would be advantageous to England, Lloyd George had joined with Clemenceau in defeating Woodrow Wilson's efforts to hold them down. The British people had not, as they pretended, suffered a change of heart but only a change of head. Germany could still pay, but British interests were no longer served by such payments.

Finally, assuming that the German people could not pay, at least they could disarm. Yet every British military commission was forced to give testimony to the fact of German violations of the disarmament clauses, to acknowledge that behind evasion was a spirit of intransigeance, of hate, the will for revenge. Nevertheless, the British people, who asked the French to sacrifice money payments, desperately needed, refused France all guarantee against this German spirit. Could sacred egoism go further?

The French people always believed that Germany could pay. They accepted fantastic stories of the rapidity of German recovery. They contrasted their ruins and the frightful sufferings and privations of the peasant of Champagne, Picardy, and Flanders with the flourishing factories and the prosperous existence of the German. They not only believed that Germany could pay, but they explained German refusal as due uniquely to Anglo-American encouragement.

Looking toward that future in which they foresaw the inevitable resumption of the Franco-German duel, the French people saw themselves physically inferior, financially bankrupt, facing the superior numbers and the assured prosperity of a vengeful Germany. They recalled the rise of Prussia after Jena, insured by a policy of successful evasion.

Faced squarely with the necessity to choose between German recovery and German ruin, provided Germany refused to pay—even if she paid but refused to disarm morally and physically—the French people would undoubtedly have decided against German recovery. But the decision was always over the policy to be pursued with respect of a Germany which would neither disarm nor pay.

In this situation, the French people believed that they had justice on their side. They knew that in the Treaty they had the law. Little by little they realized that in their army they had the power. Always, to the moment of the Cannes Conference, the promise of a British guarantee might have restrained them from using this power. Afterward, although the guarantee was there proffered, it was too late. But in all this formative period of the French mind, the guarantee was the touchstone of all British sincerity.

If, however, the moment ever came when France, the whole French people, should feel themselves betrayed, abandoned, imperilled, then the ruin of Europe, the economic collapse of Great Britain, the paralysis of world prosperity would count for little in their eyes. And it was the growth of this conviction which moved France, not rapidly, but ineluctably, toward the Ruhr.

When one turns to the question of the relation of the issue of iron to French politics as contrasted with French public opinion, one enters instantly into the area of a familiar and invariably sordid circumstance of national life. There is always a material interest lurking in the background of a popular emotion and seeking to exploit it. And in the eyes of the political opposition at home and of the critics abroad, this material interest is always dominating. It controls public men, it dictates national action, it explains national policy.

The iron issue in the French situation in 1919 was in itself simple. The annexation of Alsace-Lorraine by Germany in 1871 had divided the great minette beds of Lorraine. Approximately half were on either side of the new Franco-German frontier, in the valleys of the Moselle and the Meurthe.

In the great industrial development of Germany after the war, Lorraine iron had been an important detail. The iron of Lorraine and the coal of the Ruhr had been combined. Even the French iron across the frontier had been largely dependent upon the German market. Partially treated at the minehead, the ore had in the main been carried to the Ruhr for final transformation. And on the basis of this coal and iron Germany had constructed that enormous industrial system which not alone gave her prosperity in peace but rendered her powerful in war.

One of the enduring German war aims, too, had been the annexation of the French iron deposits. Thus, in all German peace programmes until the last moments, "slight rectifications of the frontier" had concealed the intent to take the Briey district, which was the richest of the French iron regions.

The return of Alsace-Lorraine to France gave the French instant control of this vast and valuable iron supply. The value was not merely economic, it was also military. The inevitable ambition of French business and French statesmanship, alike, was to make this restored control the basis of economic supremacy in the heavy industry of Europe, and also of immediate military supremacy in case of new war. The two interests were indissoluble.

But, after the signing of the Treaty of Versailles, the Ruhr coal-owners turned to Sweden and Spain for their iron. It was far cheaper to bring iron to coal than coal to iron. France therefore found her new acquisitions without expected profit and the iron masters of Lorraine saw the prospect of industrial supremacy in Europe vanishing.

These French iron masters had wealth. They controlled newspapers. They influenced politicians. Their position was quite analogous to that exploited by German industrialists before and during the war. Between these two sets of industrialists a battle for control was at once joined. The ultimate reunion of the Ruhr coal and the Lorraine iron was almost inevitable. But, in such an amalgamation, which national faction would control? This was the stake of the battle.

In the battle, the value of the French army was patent. The importance of the threat or even of the fact of a military occupation of the Ruhr was obvious. Under such coercion, the German industrialists might be brought to terms. Failing this, French iron might lack a market and French industrial expansion be prevented.

The French iron masters had the ear of Poincaré—not because he was corrupt. On the contrary, he was and he remains singularly free from any suspicion of financial irregularity. He is an honest man, but he saw the question nationally. He saw it in the terms of the greater France never absent from his mind. He saw it in the light of the problem of French strength in the face of a new German attack, which he always expected.

The French iron masters did not make French public sentiment either with respect of security or reparations. The Allies and the Germans did that. But the French iron masters did exploit this sentiment. On the rising tide of popular emotion and passion they certainly launched their own ships. And their programme was, after all, material, selfish, and not lacking in sordid aspects.

In their struggle with the German industrialists, too, military occupation of the Ruhr was the last card of the

French. In the end, the playing of the card was as disastrous for them as it was expensive for their country. But unmistakably they favoured it. Conceivably they hastened it. That they caused it is less demonstrable, although widely charged. In reality, far greater forces and influences had been loosed.

The occupation of the Ruhr was, beyond all else, the final expression of the will of the French people at the moment. It was the ultimate consequence of the fears, sufferings, passions, which the war had created and the disappointments and disillusionments of the peace period had stimulated. It was the almost inescapable consequence of the German resistance. But beneath the cover of national, patriotic, human emotions, it is necessary to perceive these other forces working. They are rarely absent and seldom without some influence.

Finally, it is necessary to perceive that the conflict of material interests was not unilateral. Similar forces were working in the same fashion and for the same stakes on either side of the Rhine. If the German industrialists were now defending the Ruhr, they had set out in 1914 to annex the Briey district. Nor were they less obviously fighting to control that heavy industry in which they had enjoyed continental supremacy before the war. In the last analysis, too, the influence of each national group was equally considerable in politics, the press, and in moulding public opinion.

Moreover, like every other detail in Franco-German differences, there was nothing new in this battle. It was the German iron masters who had drawn the famous "green map" for Bismarck before the war of 1870. If they had left Briey to France, it was only because its ore beds were then unknown. And if the critics of France alleged that the occupation of the Ruhr was the consequence of the intervention of the French iron industry, in other eyes, the war itself was due to the desire of the German industry to complete the acquisition of the Lorraine iron mines.

CHAPTER NINE

THE BRITISH CASE

IN THE British situation in the period of international anarchy following the failure of Versailles, there was a paradox as complete as that in the French or German. Britain was the political ally of France. But, economically, all her interests were linked to those of Germany. German resistance to the Treaty inevitably provoked French sanctions, but no French reprisal could fail to do violence to British interests.

In all the post-war period, the British experience is alike the most challenging and the most illuminating. This is because Great Britain was and remains the most typical example of a modern industrial state, and precisely for this reason the economic consequences of the continuing European conflict were at once and continuously most disastrous for the British people.

No better example can be supplied of the meaning of war and of international anarchy in our contemporary age than that which is to be found in the British circumstances between 1914 and the present hour. And what was most costly for England was only less expensive for all European states, since all, in varying degrees, were subject to the same economic laws and lived under something of the same industrial conditions.

In the opening years of the present century, the British people were to all outward appearance the most powerful and prosperous on earth. Their empire was the most successful since that of Rome. In trade, commerce, finance, British supremacy had long been established. "The City" in London was the financial centre of the universe. Based on this economic foundation and backed by the supreme fleet, British political power had never been seriously challenged since the Napoleonic era.

Imposing as was the façade of the British imperial structure, it nevertheless had within it elements of grave weakness. More than forty millions of people were crowded into the narrow limits of one small island. They were really concentrated in the congested districts of a few great cities. Since, with the industrial revolution, domestic agriculture had been practically abandoned in the British Isles, all these millions were obliged to obtain abroad all their food save the supply for a few weeks in each year.

In addition, prosperous in appearance as was the United Kingdom, the vast majority of its inhabitants lived from hand to mouth. If capital continued to increase marvellously in the hands of the few, for the millions the problem of life remained excessively difficult. Labour was still largely exploited. Wages were low, standards of living depressed. Moreover, the annual income of the nation, had it been distributed equally, would not have permitted the people to enjoy a standard of living even remotely comparable with the American.

In reality, while the British people appeared to live prosperously, they actually lived perilously. In the last analysis, they relied for their existence upon the continuation of those conditions in the world which would permit them to sell abroad the products of their mines, their factories, and their hands and, in return, buy the food for their daily existence.

All foreign disturbances had therefore immediate and evil consequences for the British people. A riot in China or a revolution in Latin America might bring unemployment to factories in Manchester or Birmingham. Half a century before, the American Civil War had brought acute distress to all Lancashire.

Thus, for the British people, a general war which paralyzed trade, forbade commerce, reduced the purchasing power of peoples and abolished foreign markets had something of the menace that a famine had for their great East Indian Dominion. Nor did the British people possess greater power to insure the permanence of peace than the East Indians to control the weather upon which their crops depended.

Yet, in the face of a peril which was real, British population continued to increase rapidly and even recklessly. Each year multiplied the mouths to be fed, and the additional hands to be employed necessitated the finding of new markets. Aways the purchasing power of the world must increase, always the British share in foreign markets must remain proportionate to the growing domestic population.

Moreover, even in time of full peace, the British situation was becoming compromised to a degree. In competition with Germany and the United States, both rising commercially and industrially, British industry was lagging, British methods were falling behind. Again, with the development of hydro-electric power on land, and with the growing use of oil on the seas, the world market for coal was declining. And coal was the foundation of British economic prosperity.

Finally, at the moment when foreign competition was becoming most acute, British industry was facing an inevitable struggle between Capital and Labour at home. The working man was coming to political power and a Labour party was forming. The demands for shorter hours, improved social conditions, higher wages, and protection against old age and temporary disability were becoming insistent. But all this involved higher taxation and increased cost of production.

Politically, Britain remained the soundest country in the world. Socially, industrially, and economically, however, its domestic conditions were disturbing. And, beyond the parochial problems, there was always the great and growing peril incident to any world-wide conflagration.

There were, too, imperial problems hardly less serious than those of the United Kingdom itself. The Russo-Japanese War had produced a dangerous effervescence all over the Far East. India was stirring, and the old order, founded upon the prestige of the white race, was visibly passing. The future was at least obscure and disquieting. Anything which further lowered Asiatic esteem for the Western peoples might have in it the seeds of disaster.

As for the great white Dominions, if they still remained loyal and would soon prove this loyalty in the World War, they were now becoming nations. Their interests were increasingly limited by their own frontiers. The efforts of Joseph Chamberlain to find an economic unity for the far-flung political association, which was the British Empire, had failed and had been abandoned.

Between the Dominions and the United Kingdom there was a fundamental divergence of interests which might find dangerous emphasis if a European war compelled the former colonies to come to the aid of the mother country and spend billions in money and risk hundreds of thousands of lives in defending it. The imperial tie which had been an inexpensive symbol of power might assume a different appearance, if it bound the Dominions indefinitely to costly participation in European conflicts.

Last of all, there was the eternal Irish crisis, flaming up dangerously at the moment when the World War was impending. In the face of this latest Irish trouble, too, the British government had displayed disquieting indecision, while the British army had been on the edge of approximate revolt. And this was a phenomenon practically without parallel in British history.

Thus, from every conceivable angle, the World War was an immediate and well-nigh irreparable calamity. No triumph on the battlefield could balance the losses and injuries incident to the struggle. No fruits of victory could match the costs, not alone the cost in blood and in treasure, but those which resulted from the dislocation of that system of world peace by which the British millions lived, at best dangerously.

No people in the world could less afford to go to war than the British in 1914. No nation had more to lose and less to win. Even had Great Britain remained neutral, the immediate gains incident to supplying the belligerents could hardly have offset the ultimate losses due to the destruction of world purchasing power. War was little less than a suicide for the British people because, in destroying their foes and crushing enemy states, they were actually doing violence to prospective customers and essential markets.

Moreover, what was true to an almost unlimited extent in the British case was measurably the same for all peoples. Modern industrial and economic conditions had so inextricably intermingled the interests and fortunes of all great peoples, that military triumph could not counterbalance economic disasters, and military defeat only slightly increased the extent of the inevitable calamity.

To all the obvious misfortunes which war was bound

to bring to the British people, there was added one which could hardly have been foreseen. It was disclosed in the fact that, while the British people fought the war, the American neutral won it. More and more as the costs of the struggle mounted, the British were obliged to exchange their American investments for war materials. When at last the United States became a belligerent, the British were compelled to mortgage the future, and new war loans became the war debts of the post-war period.

When the war terminated, not only had the financial supremacy in the world passed from London to New York, but the political centre of gravity had also shifted. America, and not the British Empire, had supplied the decisive force in the campaign of victory. The United States, and not the United Kingdom, emerged from the conflict the greatest power among the nations. The position which had been British at the close of the Napoleonic conflict was American at the end of the World War.

At a relatively small cost, the United States had won everything. At incalculable expense, Britain had barely saved herself from military defeat. From the colossal struggle, America came forth at last a world power and a creditor nation. Britain, despite the specious symbols of military victory, had lost power and prestige, and the very foundations of her national existence had been sapped by the storm.

Since the war had been so complete a disaster, British

policy, following the termination of the fighting, was dictated by every interest, material and political. The restoration of pre-war conditions, the conditions of peace and tranquillity, was the prerequisite to British recovery, to British survival. Every moment of delay, every hour of postponement, must cost the British people dear.

Yet, at Versailles, Lloyd George, obedient to British public sentiment of the hour, signed a treaty of peace which, so far from making peace, prolonged the struggle. The settlement, too, while it was for Britain an economic absurdity, was for France a political reality. The terms which the German people would not accept were themselves inimical to British interests. But, by the treaty provisions, France had the right, and in her army the power, to enforce them.

Since all reparations payments made by Germany could only be in goods, and since all German goods were competitive with British, Britain could only receive payment at the cost of unemployment. Since payments to France, which could take them, must be of the same character, British sales to France would similarly diminish. To keep all reparations down to the lowest level was the first consideration of wise policy. Yet, at Paris Lloyd George had assisted in expanding them to astronomical figures.

Once the blunder of Versailles had been made, the need to repair it was instant and imperative. Lloyd

George had foreseen the demand, but he had calculated that, when the moment for revision came, the United States, having ratified the Treaty, would stand beside Britain. The two Anglo-Saxon peoples, which were the guarantors of French security under the treaties, could speak then with authority.

But the rejection of the treaties by the United States left the British to face France alone. The French people, too, were now not only indignant at the loss of the Treaties of Guarantee, but also aroused and fearful, as a consequence of German resistance.

There remained to Lloyd George a single basis of bargain. He could still offer the French nation a British guarantee for its security in return for French consent to a revision of the reparations terms. But in their postwar state of mind, facing the well-nigh irreparable consequences of a recent continental adventure, the British people were in no mood to undertake fresh engagements which might lead quickly to new struggles.

From the Dominions, too, came insistent protest against further intermixture in European affairs. Hundreds of thousand of soldiers from Canada, Australia, New Zealand, and South Africa had fought in Europe and on Asiatic and African battlegrounds. The debt which had been discharged to the mother country by these sacrifices had been paid loyally, but against new responsibilities Dominion sentiment was aroused.

For the British people, too, the French effort to couple

the questions of reparations and security seemed a monstrous fallacy. Like all peoples after the war, they had come to see their sacrifices as completely unselfish. They had fought to save France. French security had been established by a victory which had cost a million British lives. To ask new sacrifices was not only unfair, it was unreasonable.

As for the problem of reparations, itself, that was simple. Either the German people could pay, or they could not. The sums demanded were either reasonable or preposterous. Since, in fact, they were demonstrably impossible, to attempt to make the Germans pay beyond their capacity was stupid. To use force to attain this end was wicked.

If the French people really desired reparations, as they proclaimed, then patently they must permit the German people to recover economically. If, however, the French people were merely employing the reparations claims as a pretext, if while demanding money they were actually seeking to destroy Germany, such a policy was plain hypocrisy. To pursue it at British expense was ingratitude, to use it as a means to extort a British guarantee sheer blackmail.

There was, of course a gigantic inconsistency about the British popular view. While the British people had believed that they could get the money, they had insisted upon a treaty which gave them the last farthing. Now, when they saw that money was unavailable and reparations in kind undesirable, they assailed the French for seeking to collect not the last but an intermediate farthing.

In the mood of the Khaki election, they had demanded that the German be "squeezed until the pips squeaked." Now, when the French undertook to do a little "squeezing," they solemnly proclaimed that such methods used toward a beaten foe were contrary to the standards of British sportsmanship. Yet in all the reparations dispute the British contentions were generally the sounder; nor was British policy more self-centred than French, it was only equally so.

But official action, as contrasted with popular demand, was at all times blocked by the fact that the Germans were not merely resisting impossible reparations provisions; they were fighting the Treaty. Their evasion of reparations clauses was not more determined than of disarmament provisions. To the latter infractions the British government might be willing to turn the blind eye, but not the French. Thus, every British effort to save Germany from the consequences of the absurd reparations terms sooner or later broke down as a result of some political or military action of the Germans themselves.

An admirable example of the divergence of interests of the three nations was supplied by circumstances of the operations of the Anglo-French disarmament commissions. These were charged with the task of destroying German fortifications and dismantling war factories. In dealing with fortresses, the British were only interested in abolishing those which faced the sea. French attention, on the contrary, was entirely occupied with those covering land frontiers.

When these commissions came to dismantle the factories which produced war materials, French interest was exhausted in the destruction of machines which turned out military supplies; British, by contrast, was confined to scrapping those which might be converted to commercial production and thus to competition with British manufactures. But both destructions were at German expense.

As this conflict of Anglo-French interests developed, the world was filled with the uproar of contending national opinions and propaganda. Passionate recriminations were flung back and forth across the Channel. War, too, might have come under other circumstances, but both nations were too completely exhausted to think of new hostilities. Since Britain was seeking peace as the primary condition of her existence, to engage in a new combat would also have been a ghastly paradox and a hopeless folly.

In all this struggle, too, British existence was actually at stake. Britain was not fighting for the right to acquire wealth, but for the chance to live.

"These are my devastated areas," Lloyd George had once flung out passionately in an Anglo-French conference, indicating the paralyzed centres of British industry. The word was just. Lens, Rheims, and St. Quentin were rising from their ruins to normal activity, but

Birmingham, Manchester, and Liverpool, their walls intact, long remained enduring evidences of a destruction quite as complete as that which levelled French cities. And for them the ruin came, not alone in war, but also in peace.

CHAPTER TEN

AMERICAN WITHDRAWAL

RARELY has there been an anticlimax as complete as that disclosed in the relation of the United States to Europe in the war and post-war periods. It begins for America on the high note of making the world safe for democracy. It ends in the drab reality of making allies pay war debts.

For Europe, the United States was the saviour of Western civilization in 1917, and Uncle Shylock ten years later. On both sides of the Atlantic, peoples which had credited each other with the possession of impossible virtue now judged each other guilty of incredible meanness.

Underlying this era of bad feeling, which continues, is the rejection of the Treaty of Versailles and the subsequent withdrawal of the United States from all active participation in European affairs.

This American withdrawal, too, did manifest injury to each of the nations with which the United States had been associated in the war with Germany. French security was compromised. An Anglo-French duel over reparations was precipitated. The whole Versailles settlement was seriously impaired. Even the German people, having surrendered to Woodrow Wilson's programme, felt that they were later abandoned to the vindictive will of their European rivals.

Yet, viewed with the smallest degree of objectivity, it is plain that the course of the American people was no less natural and instinctive than that of all other peoples in the post-war period. After the struggle the French turned inevitably to the question of guarding their own security. The British looked to the restoration of that world system by which they lived. The Italians undertook to realize that dream of unity which had been but partly realized in the great *risorgimento* of the Nineteenth Century.

From the American point of view what had occurred in Europe was patent. Two great coalitions had come to war in 1914. These groups of powers had been on the verge of conflict in 1905, at the moment of the Tangier crisis. The Bosnian affair had brought fresh tension. War was with difficulty avoided during the Agadir dispute in 1911. Finally, the Balkan Wars of 1912–13 had brought new and dangerous hours.

But not in any of the earlier crises, not in the final crisis which led to war, had it occurred to any European state to inquire the American views. In all the dark and desperate days which preceded the ultimate catastrophe, while the foreign offices of all European states were frantically inquiring about the proposed action of the several countries, all without exception ignored Washington, because all with equal certainty and accuracy assumed American neutrality.

And, in precisely the same way, there was not in the United States in the opening months of the World War any difference of opinion as to the policy which the American government should adopt. All the great campaigns for American belligerency came, not with the war, but during it. Any man who had proposed in August or September, 1914, that America should enter the combat would have been regarded by all sections of American public opinion as unmistakably mad.

Later campaigns by champions of the Allied powers did not deeply affect this fundamental American resolve for neutrality. This decision was not accidental or limited; it was instinctive and general. It was not due to any refusal to face the facts. It resulted from a calm, deliberate, and careful examination of the question. The American people had plenty of time to study the problem of the European War, and it arrived at a final conclusion which was disclosed in the results of the Presidential campaign of 1916.

Nevertheless, the United States was brought into the World War. It was involved, not on any European issue, however, but by a direct act of war of the Imperial German government. The submarine blockade, in its relation to American marine rights, was an interference which no great power could tolerate. Therefore, although they had consistently refused to be drawn into the war on any European question, the American people did decide to become belligerents upon an American issue.

Although remote from the field of the combat and in its own mind only slightly concerned with the outcome of this Continental war, the United States sent more than two million soldiers to Europe, undertook an enormous economic and industrial campaign largely on behalf of the European allies, loaned vast sums of money to them, and actually made possible a military decision. The victory of the Allied armies is not otherwise explicable than on the basis of the weight supplied by the fresh American divisions.

When the fighting was terminated, the United States announced and rigidly adhered to the purpose to take neither territories nor money indemnities from the beaten foe. No particular moral elevation was disclosed in this self-denying ordinance, because the United States desired no territory and needed no money. But it might have claimed both, and its claim could hardly have been denied in justice or in reason.

Finally, the United States, having permitted its associates of the war to share the relatively considerable fruits of the common victory among themselves, retired from Europe and adopted a policy which was comprehended in the purpose to assume no further responsibilities of a political or material character in Europe.

In any ordinary circumstances, this decision would have excited no protest and it could have justified no criticism. This is true because, with the breaking of the military power of Germany, the single objective of American belligerency was achieved. The German assumption to regulate the use of the seas by American merchant marine was abolished. This German assumption explained American entrance into the war. Thus, although the European allies had actually profited enormously from American participation in the war, they owed their victory in the first instance to German stupidity. On the other hand, they had no valid claim for further American assistance.

Again, looked at dispassionately, there was no material or political interest of the American people which could be served by further American participation in European affairs. Talleyrand had once said that cooperation between France and Britain was as natural as between Man and Horse. But he had added, that did not warrant France to assume the rôle of the Horse. Yet, in Europe, after 1919, no other rôle was open to the United States.

So far, then, the facts might seem to be perfectly clear. America's reason for retiring from Europe was, after all, identical with Europe's reasons for wishing the United States to remain. The American people judged their material interests best served by withdrawal. The European people quite as accurately saw the profit to themselves in American presence in Europe permanently. Both conceptions were, perhaps, equally selfish, yet in reality both were similarly natural and human.

But at this point one comes in contact with two utterly divergent and highly explosive public opinions. On either side of the Atlantic there is the deliberate charge of a breach of contract. The European peoples offer in evidence the Treaty of Versailles signed in the name of the American people, and allege that, although Europe had paid for this signature by concessions made at the peace table, the American people repudiated the signature, and, as a consequence, imposed grave losses upon Europe.

By contrast, the American people, with a certain measure of vagueness, present Woodrow Wilson's Fourteen Points and allege that it was on this basis that they made their great effort in the war and on this platform that they were prepared to assist Europe in the post-war period. But, they declare, although pretending to accept these principles, Europe violated them all and sought to bind the United States to perpetual servitude to European ends which were selfish and not in the least peaceful.

On cross examination, moreover, both disputants, with equal appearance of sincerity, deny the contract. The Americans, with utter legal justification, point out that the President's signature had no binding power for them. The Europeans argue that the Fourteen Points could not have meant for them what the Americans assert. In fact, they insist that since the President signed the Versailles Treaty, they must have satisfied all reasonable demands in this direction, since Woodrow Wilson was, after all, the author of the Fourteen Points.

Thus, in the final analysis, each party to the controversy bases its case upon a contract which it alleges valid and its opponent asserts was invalid or imaginary. Why, then, did both the European and American peoples actually believe that neither would take that line in the post-war period, which under all normal circumstances would have been natural and was in fact the line both took?

The explanation for this otherwise unintelligible muddle must be sought, not in the policies actually adopted by the respective peoples, but in the relation of Woodrow Wilson to the public opinions of both European and American peoples in the years during which the United States was actually a belligerent, and indeed in all the years of the war. Sooner or later, in any rational analysis of this dispute between continents, it is to the Wilsonian phase that one must return.

In fact, it was Woodrow Wilson who undertook to prevent Europe from returning after the war to its secular and normal political condition. It was the American President, too, who strove to persuade the people of the United States to abandon their tradition of isolation and become active and permanent participants in European affairs. What occurred resulted primarily from this double endeavour.

Mr. Wilson's relation to the events of the whole period from 1914 to 1919 was based, not upon any estimate of physical facts, but upon interpretations and assumptions of the moral values and meanings of these facts. He lived steadily in a world, not of realities, but of idealities. And he undertook to impose his conceptions, not merely upon the American people, but also upon the European.

From the outset of the war until the proclamation of the submarine blockade, the President had held his country to a policy of neutrality. He had gone much further and demanded that the American people should be neutral in thought as well as in act. He had also proclaimed that the issues of the European conflict had not the smallest interest for the American people.

In this policy of neutrality, however, Woodrow Wilson was not in any degree influenced by any thought of the material advantages incident to his policy. For him, neutrality was a primary and essential circumstance in later intervention. For his country and for himself, he always conceived the mission to end the war by mediation and to impose upon both sets of belligerents that form of peace which satisfied his moral principles.

It was this purpose which explained his frequent irritation and occasional bursts of anger, when various Americans urged intervention on behalf of either belligerent. Such partisanship quite obviously compromised the policy which he was seeking to establish. If the United States clearly sympathized with one coalition, the other would naturally reject its mediation.

The German submarine blockade surprised Mr. Wilson in the midst of one of his periodic soundings of European sentiment in the matter of mediation. The necessity to enter the war demolished all of the President's previous plans for mediation. It did more than that, it forced him to find a new point of departure for his whole programme of idealism. He had refused to recognize the war, and it had now compelled recognition. He had rejected every European issue of the conflict, and now the United States was in the war.

In this crisis, the President did not modify his main conceptions. He still held to the major idea that America must mediate. But he postponed this mediation to the close of the war. Germany had to be beaten, but once this was accomplished, then the United States would go to the peace table and compel both groups of belligerents to accept that programme which Mr. Wilson thought of as American, but which was, in fact. Wilsonian.

Meantime, the President set out to bind both the American and the European peoples to his programme. All the enormous resources of official propaganda, all the influence of the press, the pulpit, and the public oratory of the day, so far as these could be enlisted, were harnessed to the task of creating the stupendous illusion that the presence of the United States in the war had moral, not material meanings, that America was fighting for idealistic and not material purposes.

Thus, for millions of people, there was fashioned the faith that, as a result of the great sacrifices and incredible efforts of the American people, not only was the German to be beaten, this was a detail, but that the war was to end war. Europe was to be regenerated.

Mankind was to be turned to other and better pathways, and America and Woodrow Wilson were to lead the way.

For the President and those who followed him, the United States did not enter the war; it annexed it. There had been one kind of a struggle before the Germans made us belligerents; it was a totally different affair when we began to fight. And, in fact, before the United States entered the war, it had not existed for Mr. Wilson, and when we entered, it instantly became a crusade.

To a degree this campaign met with little opposition because the United States had no material interest at stake in the war. The country was not invaded. It could not be invaded, and the peril to American security was remote, if real at all. Nor could victory itself serve any important national interest. Finally, the German interference with American marine rights was, after all, a rather trivial excuse for an enormous national effort.

Moreover, if the invasion of Belgium, the devastation of northern France, the sinking of the *Lusitania* had each in its time offered moral justification for American intervention, these were not now available. Not only had they been passed over at the moment, but the President of the United States had publicly proclaimed that these were not of interest to the American people.

Therefore, the people of the United States had now to accept European reasons for fighting Germany, thus tacitly admitting that they had been mistaken in not accepting them sooner; to fight over the technical legal question of the blockade, or to find some American explanation for the war. And the President undertook to find the last.

President Wilson's basis for America's belligerency was discoverable for himself in his idealistic conceptions which centred in the League of Nations. He also easily and naturally concluded that what he felt, the majority of the American people also felt. He believed that, if Europe permitted America to assume the moral leadership of the world, the American people would be willing to bear the material burdens which even he saw must result.

It was this assumption which in the end totally deceived Europe. If the British, French, and Belgian peoples, if Europe itself, later came to expect almost unlimited aid and contribution from America, it was because the Wilsonian propaganda in Europe always affirmed that, to establish American idealism, the American people had not only made the prodigious effort of the war but were ready to continue.

But along with the American assumption went the European. If the President believed the American people were fighting primarily, if not exclusively, for his ideals, he also quite as completely believed that the European peoples had accepted these. Whatever doubts he may have had about the leaders, he was always sure about the people. In fact, he was always sure of the people, everywhere and under all circumstances. This was the corner stone of all of his political faith.

If the President's presentation of the state of the American mind deceived Europe, his similar interpretation of the European mind wholly misled the United States. On his statement, they very generally accepted his conclusion that the people of Europe had embraced the Wilsonian platform and programme; that they had put away all their traditional aspirations and conceptions; that, under the shock of American idealism, they had seen a new light and adopted a new faith.

In point of fact, however, the President was fundamentally wrong in his diagnosis of the European situation. While all the moral upheaval incident to the Wilsonian propaganda was going on in the United States, the Allied peoples were continuing with the war. Actually, American entrance coincided with some of the worst moments.

Thus in April, 1917, the French army was beaten at the Aisne and a mutiny followed. Russia collapsed and disappeared during the summer. The British offensive in Flanders came to nothing in the mud and storm of an early autumn. In the following March in Picardy, and in May at the Chemin des Dames, Allied arms suffered colossal disasters. The first half of the campaign of 1918 was thus unfortunate.

In all this time, the Allied peoples were fighting for their lives. They were always under the shadow of ultimate disaster. The entrance of the United States promised new aid. But in the face of the military situation, the arrival of this aid seemed agonizingly delayed. The people of the Allied countries were not thinking of moral issues or of the idealistic programmes. They were, in fact, sick to death of words, promises, programmes. They were exhausted physically and morally. Such strength as remained to them after nearly four years of war hardly sufficed to enable them to exist and to face the strain of each day, which brought fresh casualty lists and new privations.

Just before America became a belligerent, President Wilson had made one of his characteristic speeches which delighted his American admirers but puzzled and irritated all Europeans. Commenting on it, Clemenceau had written, "Yes, these are beautiful words, but *we* are being assassinated." The contrast between American and European points of view in the war period is all disclosed here.

For the American people, the war was a revolution, when they entered it. It aroused enthusiasm, national pride; it stirred us as nothing had stirred us since the Civil War. In fact, it was something without precedent in American national life. It was always possible to attach ideal values to the result, too, because the approach to the end was glorious without being either difficult or terrifying.

After the United States entered the war, as before, the American people continued to live comfortably in their homes. They were not invaded, as were the

French people. They were not hungry, as were the British during the submarine blockade. If the Allied lines broke in Flanders or the Île-de-France, neither Washington nor New York was imperilled. No air raids at night interrupted rest or threatened death.

No one who was not actually in Europe in the last eighteen months of the war could or can realize the contrast between the conditions, the mental conditions of the peoples of Europe and of the United States. To imagine that in these terrible hours the European peoples were capable of examining and weighing the utterances of Woodrow Wilson, the proclamations of high purpose and moral intent, by which American intervention was explained, is to believe that people plunged in a river by some accident, could listen to exhortations pronounced from the bank by those who were not able yet to throw out ropes.

For Woodrow Wilson, the war did not exist as a physical fact; it was an unfortunate prelude to a noble drama. For the people of the United States, the realities of the war were meaningless because there was no possible way of translating to a people living in security and prosperity the effects upon human minds of the years of agony which the war had imposed upon every European human being.

Thus, the President and his followers utterly, the mass of the American people measurably, accepted a totally American view of the war and of the imaginary transformation which had been produced by the American enlistment. From first to last, the combat was in the main a spectacle for the American people. It was a gigantic show, it was never an utter reality. They watched but while American soldiers did finally fight on European soil, the millions of the American people remained remote, uncomprehending, detached. Neither an enemy nor yet hunger nor misery was ever at the American door. The largest touch of reality was the preposterous pursuit of imaginary spies.

Yet Mr. Wilson and his followers were convinced that peoples which were actually in the last extremity of human agony and of physical danger were capable of accepting or even listening to the calm, dispassionate, and concededly lofty sentiments which he was uttering, and every engine of publicity and propaganda in the United States was broadcasting. He believed that in the days when the invading armies advanced miles over French territory and British armies fought with their backs to the sea, that the French and British people were listening to the proclamation of the principles of the Fourteen Points. He was convinced that through the lines of the casualty lists and over the maps of enemy invasion they saw the promises of a new charter for mankind.

Supreme and paralyzing misery lasted in Europe until almost the last days of the war. It was not until October that there was even the hint that there would not be a military campaign of 1919. The hope of an armistice was hardly accepted by the millions of soldiers, who saw it as a delusion and a German trick almost up to the moment when the last shot was fired. Yet, two months later, the Peace Conference was assembling.

To this Europe, Woodrow Wilson came, assured that his moral precepts had already found universal popular understanding and acceptation. In fact, for the masses of the European people, the Fourteen Points did not exist at all; nothing had existed for four years except the war. Millions of French people were now beginning to adventure into the wilderness where they had once lived. England still ate by meat cards, and only the sick could have fires. Milk was almost unknown, and the taste of butter forgotten in the British Isles.

The sound of the guns was still in the ears of millions. They still unconsciously looked to the clouds at night to reckon the chances of a new air raid. And, beneath all the débris of four years and more of conflict, all the little people were undertaking fearfully to resume their lives, to exist amidst the ruins and miseries which the war had brought to them. The memory of death was in every home. The physical evidences of war's afflictions were in all streets and on millions of faces and bodies. Fathers, sons, brothers, the favoured few who had survived, were returning to those who had counted them lost and now saw them safe.

When upon this Europe the President of the United States sought to impose American views of what should be the rewards of all the sacrifices, sufferings, sorrows which all had suffered; what should be the return for all the losses; when the President undertook to speak with the tones of objectivity to people who had spent their final penny and their last remaining ounce of strength to win the victory which brought them at best only meagre salvation, no more than the chance to resume life in the midst of the desolation and destruction of the conflict, not the leaders but the people rebelled.

Thus, there was in Europe before the Paris Conference was two months old, a general and well-nigh universal revolt against the American interference with European rights. America had come late to the struggle. America had suffered little or not at all. It had pocketed the capital of Europe before it became a belligerent. Europe had fought America's battle for four years. But now America undertook to limit Europe's victory. Claiming payment for its own contributions from its allies, it undertook to hamper and forbid collection from the German foe.

When, however, the European statesmen, at the price of concessions which seemed to their peoples excessive, and after delays which had been costly and dangerous, had at last obtained Woodrow Wilson's signature to the peace settlements, American ratification appeared a matter of ordinary honesty and elementary decency.

The President went to Paris, however, followed by a vast army of American journalists. Most of these correspondents shared the President's views as to the European problem. All of them were dependent upon the

American press bureau for their information. No deliberate campaign to influence the American correspondents is disclosed in this fact. The machinery which surrounded the Executive Department in Washington was simply transferred to Paris.

But these correspondents had not the smallest notion of European conditions. They were unfamiliar with European history, with the circumstances of race, religion, and geography which underlie all European conflicts. They saw the thing as the President and his followers saw it, as a struggle between European egoism and American idealism. And they had no other sources of information than those which were official.

This total unfamiliarity with European affairs was not in the least surprising. Had a similar group of European journalists been suddenly transported to an American National Convention or a National League baseball game, their situation would have been identical. All the domestic significance of the events which occurred before their eyes would have been meaningless. The reports sent back to Brussels, Paris, or even London, would have been as ridiculous in American eyes as the reports from Paris appeared in European.

This Paris Conference was, in fact, the first encounter on any considerable scale between two worlds each equally ignorant of the other. It was the first meeting between peoples who were without any standard of measurement to apply to the contiguous realities of each other's lives. They not only spoke different languages, they thought incredibly different things about the same facts.

Inevitably, too, the American journalists dramatized events into a struggle between right and wrong, between America and Europe, between Woodrow Wilson, on the one hand, and Lloyd George, Clemenceau, and Orlando, on the other. Inescapably, too, they saw all circumstances through the eyes of the President and his spokesmen, and transmitted these interpretations to an American audience for whom the Conference was unintelligible on any other basis.

For these American journalists, for all the President's followers and spokesmen at Paris, the inevitable resistance of European statesmen and peoples to the application of the Wilsonian principles instantly took on the appearance of a breach of faith. Europe had accepted American idealistic conception. It had adopted the Fourteen Points during the war, because it needed American aid. Now, after the battle, with victory in hand, Europe was evading the contract.

At the same moment in Paris, European journalism was working at the same problem. Collectively, it knew Europe from the Golden Horn to North Cape, from the Urals to the Channel. For it the problem of peace was definite, concrete, practical, and technical. Nearly all the questions were those of territory and all these were details in the complicated history of Europe, which it knew perfectly. There was nothing new, everything was old and familiar. Nothing had changed except the temporary modification of the balance of power. The settlement was to give a fresh adjustment to questions as old as Cæsar and Roman civilization.

For Americans, the Fourteen Points were a fixed and rigid system of morals, as immutable as the Ten Commandments themselves. For Europeans they were a vague and meaningless formula. What was actually involved in applying the doctrine of self-determination to bits of European territory like the Banat, Macedonia, or the Polish Marches was understood by European journalism and ignored by American.

Between American and European journalism, as between Americans and Europeans at Paris generally, there was little contact and less mutual comprehension. The conceptions of each were, in fact, without meaning to the other. Moreover, while the Europeans looked down upon the Americans as incredibly naïve and grotesquely ignorant of Europe, the Americans pitied the Europeans for their total lack of capacity to understand American idealism.

It is necessary to have lived in Paris during the months of the Peace Conference; it is almost a condition *sine qua non* to have brought to the spectacle the objectivity of another planet to appreciate this astounding absence of tangency between two worlds. Each moved confidently and naturally on its own plane. Each preserved unshaken its conviction that it saw the situation whole and understood its meaning completely. Each looked down upon the other with utter assurance in its own superiority, and neither at any moment had the smallest inkling of what the other actually thought.

As for Woodrow Wilson, he was always suspended between two imaginary worlds. He undertook to interpret an unreal America to Europe and a non-existent Europe to America. There was no America ready to bear vast European burdens or undertake unlimited European responsibilities to insure ideal solutions for practical problems. There was no Europe prepared to abandon all the consequences of a millenary history, all the traditions of peoples, all the aspirations of races either because of the fact of past American aid or of the promise of future American support.

It was due to Woodrow Wilson that Europe imagined the existence of such an America. It was his statements, too, which established in the United States such a conception of Europe. There was not the smallest thought in Europe of evading an American contract, just as there was no appreciation in America of what the President was doing in Europe, or of the promises he was making in the name of the people of the United States. Neither people undertook to deceive the other, but Woodrow Wilson deceived himself about both and thus each about the other.

Meantime, the situation in the United States was changing. The President's partisan political proclamation on the eve of the November election had instantly deprived him of the support of a very large part of the Republican party. His course at Paris seemed from the outset to all American friends of the Allied countries unreasonable and impertinent. Those Americans, who in their hearts still had sympathy or even pity for Germany, resented the degree to which Mr. Wilson seemed to accept the Allied programme. The mass of the American people, who were still violently anti-German, were angry at his apparent tenderness for the recent and still unrepentant enemy.

But beyond and beneath all this, the fundamental instinct of the American people to keep out of the European mess was plainly beginning to reassert itself. The American people were uneasy, apprehensive. They had no confidence in the President's capacity to deal with international questions. They were increasingly suspicious of the future responsibilities he might let them in for. While, in Paris, Woodrow Wilson seemed to speak for the United States with full authority, he had already lost the support of a majority of the American people.

It was at the moment when this mood was beginning to be general in the United States that there came from Paris the vast flood of press comment which had its origin largely in the Wilson entourage. Inspired by the President or his press bureau, but going far beyond the original, these news dispatches emphasized, with increasing force, the idea that European pretensions had been dishonest, that high professions had only covered low cunning. Thus was created the fatal impression that, not only had the Allies deceived America before the

Peace Conference, but that at it they had duped Woodrow Wilson.

As a result, a revolt of the American people against any contract which bound the United States to permanent responsibilities in Europe, as they now saw Europe, was bound to be immediate, far-reaching, and in the end complete. Moreover, it was equally certain that the American people would justify their repudiation of the contract Woodrow Wilson had signed in their name at Paris, on the basis of the prior breach Europe had made in its alleged contract with American idealism.

For Europe, by contrast, the subsequent American rejection of the Versailles settlement, which was for the British, French, and Belgian peoples a supreme disaster, necessarily seemed to give the complete lie to all American idealistic pretensions. To satisfy American wishes, Europe had resigned many of the things actually paid for in blood on the battlefield. American repudiation of the contract in these circumstances was not only a betrayal, but demonstrated that all American claims to higher moral standards were sheerly hypocritical.

When, after American withdrawal, the United States was prosperous and Europe impoverished, the American course seemed at once sordid and contemptible. When, notwithstanding American action, the people of the United States continued to preach to Europe, when they still arrogated to themselves the right to give moral instruction to nations, which felt their present material misery to be due largely to American betrayal, when, last of all, the United States appeared with a bill, the measure was full.

Yet, concomitantly, the American people were satisfied and remain convinced that their withdrawal from Europe was the direct consequence of European bad faith. They believe that they saved their European associates in the war, unselfishly sought to serve them after the close of the conflict. They are satisfied that all their generosity, all their prodigious and unmistakable contributions to the common victory, were in fact seized upon by Europe as materials with which to advance its own selfish ends.

Thus the break was complete and it remains complete. But while the American people, as a consequence, suffered an enforced and unpleasant moral deflation, Europe had to endure immediate and continuing material evils. As a result, while American feeling is scornful, that of Europe is bitter and passionately resentful.

Nevertheless, if the American withdrawal was an immediate calamity for many European peoples, it was just as certainly, although not by an American design, the first step toward the solution of the European problem. For as long as the United States participated in European affairs, the illusion that peace could be made in the spirit of Versailles would have endured. And the German people would still have resisted, for no other course was left to them.

While the political quarrel at Washington doubtless hastened the American withdrawal, it is also impossible to believe, in the light of American traditions and material interests, that the United States would long have continued an active participant in European affairs. Everything which has happened since the Armistice gives the lie to any such assumption. Between peoples which misunderstood each other so profoundly, continued coöperation under existing conditions was impossible.

Since the United States was bound in the end to go home, the sooner it retired and permitted the European peoples to deal with their own problems in their own way, the better for all concerned. If our coming had saved the Allies from very grave dangers, it is at least arguable that American presence in Europe after the close of the fighting was at all times a misfortune, if not in fact a curse. In any event, on the road to Locarno, American withdrawal from Europe was an unmistakable milestone.

PART FOUR

THE ANGLO-FRENCH DUEL

CHAPTER ELEVEN

LLOYD GEORGE

THE decision of the German people to resist the application of the Treaty of Versailles was instant, unanimous, and promptly disclosed. Thus was posed for the conquerors of Germany much the same problem which confronted the Allied sovereigns of a century before, when Napoleon returned from Elba.

All the conditions, however, were different. In 1815, the same community of interest still bound all the recent allies equally, since for all the Napoleonic restoration had a similar menace. In 1920, on the other hand, the German threatened only France directly. America was gone, Italy was absorbed in the Adriatic problem, and bitterly resentful of her recent experience in Paris. As for Britain, all her material interests were far more advantaged by the recovery of Germany than they were affected by questions of French security or payment.

Thus, at the very moment when the Treaty of Versailles came into force in January, 1920, there began that clash of Anglo-French interests which endured for three years and culminated in the occupation of the Ruhr. Moreover, while the World War had been a struggle between two coalitions, the new battle was triangular.

For British, French, and German interests were always divergent and frequently mutually exclusive.

Any study of this period of Anglo-French conflict must necessarily begin with the examination of the relation to it of the man who in all stages dominated the international conferences and filled the European world with his fame. From the signing of the Treaty of Versailles to the eve of the Ruhr occupation, David Lloyd George is the largest figure on the stage. With Raymond Poincaré, too, he must share equally the responsibility for this final catastrophe.

Personally, in his great period, Lloyd George had every charm. Nor did he lack any grace save that ultimate gift of sincerity. Politically, he had all the resources of the Celt, and from his equipment as a statesman there was missing nothing save that solid and somewhat heavy circumstance which the British describe as character.

He could improvise lifelong convictions and discard passionately professed faiths with equal ease. He changed his political principles, not as men put off their clothes, but with the frequency of a woman of society making her daily rounds. He could desert a leader, disrupt a party, intrigue against an associate, or undermine an ally with equal unconcern and with no apparent consciousness of the moral implications of his actions.

As a leader, he had always the qualities of a medium. When his incredible instinct illuminated his mind as to the public will, he could direct the mob in the pathways it desired to tread with an authority which was beyond challenge. But when public sentiment was hidden from him, even momentarily, his agony and terror were unbelievable. Thus, although publicly Lloyd George always adopted the manner of a lion, privately his instinct was that of the rabbit. His moments of supreme audacity were, in fact, brief interludes between periods of utter and childish panic.

With him, any end justified all means. But, in fact, he had no end in view ever. His conception of a solution of any problem was to postpone that crisis which seemed inescapable. He lived by inspiration, acted on intuition, relied upon improvisation. There was always about him the suggestion of the necromancer. He was, in fact, ever the "Welsh Wizard."

But if, for the moment, Lloyd George could make an audience, an associate, every ally believe anything, if under the magic of his personality and the genius of his touch the most awkward of facts seemed transformed, in reality nothing was changed, modified, adjusted. Those who left his presence still under his spell promptly came to believe themselves deceived or even betrayed. In the end, he fell beneath the combined consequences of the crises which he had postponed and the improvisations by which he had achieved the postponement.

While his own countrymen or those of Allied nations still trusted him, he could perform miracles. But each miracle, while it momentarily excited admiration, ultimately reduced the number of believers. He was invariably able to make his colleagues about the green table see their interests through his eyes, but for this momentary illusion they paid with their political heads immediately and Lloyd George ultimately in the unanimous distrust of their countries.

Clemenceau, who despised Lloyd George and more than once declared that but for Woodrow Wilson he could not have endured the enforced contact of the Paris Peace Conference, records a characteristic Lloyd Georgian detail. Called to England to receive a degree from Oxford long after the peace-making, Clemenceau encountered Lloyd George at the House of Commons.

"What do you think of it all now, Mr. President?" was Lloyd George's greeting.

"I think you have been an enemy of my country ever since the Armistice," was the uncompromising reply of the "Tiger."

"Well, you know our British tradition," was the swift and smiling retort.

Sir Robert Horne, once Chancellor of the Exchequer, has preserved a similarly illuminating incident. In the 1923 election, which brought Labour to power briefly, Lloyd George approached Horne and asked his advice.

"As a matter of principle," said Horne, "I think you should keep away from Labour entirely."

"You are right, as usual," Lloyd George replied. "I agree with you perfectly and give you my word that is what I shall do. Besides, I have seen 'Jim' Thomas and he tells me there is nothing doing for me with Labour."

"Jim" Thomas, of course, was MacDonald's lieutenant, who later became Minister of Colonies.

A French secretary at one of the innumerable international conferences of the post-war period observed Lloyd George occupying the time while Cambon was speaking in covering a sheet of foolscap with writings. Sensing the fact that this unconscious performance might have psychologically significant results, he later rescued the sheet from the floor, and discovered that on it was written in a hundred different forms the same word: "Votes, votes, votes."

At the Paris Peace Conference, Lloyd George publicly supported President Wilson in opposing the French effort to annex the Saar Basin. When, however, a compromise had been agreed to which provided a plebiscite for the district, Lloyd George intervened and occupied an hour of one session warning Clemenceau against the terms of this plebiscite. From a wealth of apposite and personal experience, he explained how impossible it would be for the French under the proposed terms to manipulate the election in 1935.

"And I want you to have the Saar," he concluded with touching emotion. Clemenceau, it may perhaps be added, rejected the advice and accepted the proposed terms.

But if the personal phase of Lloyd George cannot be ignored, what is after all most challenging in his career is the fact that, not only was he at his best the greatest parliamentarian of his day, but that in all his foreign negotiations he inevitably made use of the technique which long gave him a mastery of the House of Commons that remains without precedent.

In that forensic field his triumphs were incredible and are now become legendary. He bewildered, dazzled, overcame his opponents by the sheer brilliance of his attacks. Never, however, did he address himself to the principle invoked, the issue raised, the question involved. The charge might be true; he demolished it by an irresistible half truth or by a magnificent and daring untruth. All fact and form in the original question were forgotten in the progress of the debate. What had seemed a matter of principle, became under his touch the ineptitude of a fool or the unsuccessful adventure of a dullard. He destroyed his opponent and no memory remained of the cause the opponent had advocated.

Inevitably he brought all this method and manner to international conferences. Always he undertook to demolish his opponent by a similar *tour de force* or to charm him by those arts which the House of Commons never could resist. There was the same brilliance, the same rapidity of action, the identical and bewildering *volte-faces*. And abroad, as at home, he triumphed over every opponent.

There is, however, a vital difference between conflicts within a national legislature and those between nations which take place at international gatherings. At home, the clever parliamentarian may in debate surprise, confound, rout his opponent. The success is then personal, but it is also political. It not only benefits the victor, it fortifies his party. Popular applause is immediate but votes will come later. The opponent, on the other hand, not merely suffers personally; he drags his party down with him. Both suffer equally.

All such debates, however, take place within the four walls of a national life. Both contestants are equally the servants of the same national will. Both are acting with full knowledge of this national will. Both are, indeed, bidding for the same national support on the basis of greater capacity and ability to do what the people desire.

When, however, Lloyd George, as Prime Minister of Britain, encountered Clemenceau or Millerand or Briand in an international meeting, the conditions were totally different. These Frenchmen represented another national will. Nothing that Lloyd George could do would convince the French constituency that he was in fact a better Frenchman than Briand or Clemenceau.

In this situation, when Lloyd George outwitted Clemenceau, overpersuaded Millerand, or actually convinced Briand, this success was entirely limited to the council chamber. The French will remained unchanged. The French people were simply convinced that their representative had failed them: that they must get a better advocate. Thus, briefly, Lloyd George would meet a new man representing the old principle.

In fact, this process was frequently repeated. Each time the Georgian success was unmistakable. But when the French people had concluded that Lloyd George had been equally triumphant in deceiving Clemenceau, Millerand, Leygues, and Briand, ineluctably they turned to Poincaré. Him, they knew, Lloyd George could not conquer, because in advance, Poincaré had promised to refuse to go to conference at all.

In reality, while he had fancied himself triumphing over an individual antagonist, Lloyd George had triumphed over France. And it was the people of France who resented the defeat saw in the triumph a betrayal of the cause of the Allies, presently identified Lloyd George himself as an enemy of their country. Once this moment was come, however, Lloyd George was lost. All his incidental successes had merely prepared for an ultimate defeat.

In the parliamentary arena victory has no evil consequences. The decision is established by the division, the vote testifies to the triumph. All begins anew tomorrow. Internationally, however, until one nation has obtained satisfaction for its purposes, it will continue. And each denial of what seems to it just and right will not merely arouse passion, but will also harden determination.

In conference, Lloyd George was never unhorsed, but his successes in international meetings finally made all such assemblies impossible. While he still spoke with every assurance as a friend of France, there had developed in France a universal hatred of him which equalled if it did not exceed the detestation felt for the Emperor,

William, in the war period. Thus each effort of Lloyd George to restrain French coercion became in fact an incitation to action.

Moreover, for the French, Lloyd George and his country became largely identical. What Lloyd George did was put down to British purpose. He was regarded in all things as the complete expression of a national will and a national purpose. Therefore, the passion which he aroused against himself extended to his country and as Frenchmen distrusted and hated Lloyd George, they came to distrust and hate Great Britain. The country which had been an ally came in all French eyes to seem an enemy.

Yet always British policy was condemned to seek to restrain French military coercion of Germany, which was dangerous for all British economic and political interests alike. But France could only be restrained by persuasion; power lay completely in French hands. When the French people would no longer listen to British words, the end was in sight.

Here, too, was the profoundest blunder of Lloyd George. He always talked of the balance of power. He frequently felt himself under the shadow of Castlereagh. But while he knew everything about balance, he never had the smallest conception of the bases of power internationally. He knew absolutely nothing about the realities of Europe, and each of his improvisations to meet immediate emergencies had fatal final consequences.

Thus, to forestall the Italian seizure of Smyrna, he

hurried Greek troops to the Asiatic port. But in the Greco-Turkish War which resulted, British support of the Greeks aroused all the millions of Moslem subjects of King George from Palestine to India. It had violent repercussions in Cairo and in Bagdad. It ultimately cost Britain the support of Italy, the single available ally on the Continent. When, too, the Greeks were defeated and the Turks arrived at the Bosporus, British troops stood alone and not only the Allies of 1918 but the British Dominions themselves declined to enlist in a new war of Lloyd George's creation.

In moments of expansion, Lloyd George talked of placating Russia by the retrocession of Bessarabia and Volhynia. He showed concern publicly for the situation of German minorities in Bohemia. But as a consequence, Rumania, Poland, and Czecho-Slovakia stood solidly with France in every international conference. He denounced French militarism, but since the French army was the single guarantee of Belgian security, the Belgian voice was ever on the French side.

This very issue of militarism which Lloyd George exploited against France in all the period of acute controversy was the most dangerous of all questions to raise. He might and did create widespread British resentment of French military strength, but all this criticism, all this denunciation, could not arrive at persuading the French people to reduce their establishment by a division or lessen their garrisons of the Rhineland by a regiment.

Too late, at Cannes, Lloyd George did perceive the

truth. Always, until the failure at the Washington Conference, he had believed in the eventual return of the United States to Europe. In embarking upon his quarrel with France, he had relied upon his ability to cast the American vote and to exploit the American power. After Washington, recognizing the miscalculation, he went to Cannes and offered the French a British guarantee.

But the British guarantee then offered by Lloyd George had ceased to have value in French eyes because the French people no longer trusted the Prime Minister or his country. For them the guarantee seemed one more trick and the Cannes Conference another demonstration of the Lloyd Georgian genius to deceive and to beguile. Therefore, Briand was flung from office by a political *coup d'état* in Paris, and European readjustment was postponed for two terrible years.

All this disaster of Cannes, too, is chargeable to Lloyd George. It was his conduct of the Washington Conference from London which had made that session a final humiliation for the French people. Since Briand was premier, he was responsible and he paid the price. Yet Briand was later to be the man of Locarno, of Thoiry. He was to be the Frenchman of whom a German Chancellor would one day declare in the Reichstag, "We trust the France of M. Briand." And it was the France of Briand whose "militarism" Lloyd George and his agents for more than two years denounced *urbi et orbi.*

Clemenceau, Millerand, and Briand were all in turn potential allies of Lloyd George. In the minds of all three was the same fundamental conception that the future security of France depended upon the preservation of the closest and most friendly relations with Great Britain. All were prepared to make and did make great concessions to this end.

But for Lloyd George each sacrifice consented to was in reality the evidence of a personal triumph in negotiation. Every international meeting was, in fact, a trial of wits, a conflict of mentalities, a battle for points. Thus he destroyed Clemenceau and Briand at home and but for the Polish accident would have demolished Millerand.

In 1921, Briand was the last considerable French champion of the policy of entente with Britain. His failure was certain to doom the whole conception in French eyes. Yet, in pursuit of American support, which was always beyond the limits of possibility, Lloyd George inflicted upon Briand that crowning humiliation of the Washington Conference, which destroyed him.

When, as a consequence, Poincaré came, as he was always bound to come if the policy of entente failed, all was finished for Lloyd George. His own political ruin came promptly. Great Britain was presently condemned to sit helplessly by and watch French and Belgian troops march into the Ruhr; German economic and financial collapse followed swiftly.

In these consequences, the utter failure of the parliamentary method when applied to international relations is fully disclosed. And, in reality, the similar failure of precisely the same method underlies the Versailles episode itself.

Nor is it quite possible to ignore the circumstances of Lloyd George's own domestic political situation in observing his conduct of foreign affairs. He had attained power during the war by a course which seemed to Mr. Asquith and most of his colleagues utterly treacherous. At the end of the war, as a consequence, the Liberal party had divided and one faction had followed Mr. Asquith into the wilderness of the opposition.

Henceforth, Lloyd George depended for support upon a rump of the Liberals and the mass of the Tories. Yet, not only was he not a Tory, but before the war his very name had been anathema in Conservative circles. He was, therefore, always threatened by some revolt within the ranks of the Tory party which would overturn him.

All his political future depended upon his ability to create a new political party, a party of his own. To do this, however, he had to intrigue against the Conservatives, upon whom he depended for his majority. Permanent success could only come with a disruption of the Tory party as fatal to it as that which in his own interest had already destroyed the historic Liberal party.

Thus, in all the period from 1920 to the final disaster which Chanak brought to his political fortunes, Lloyd George was seeking to create a new political party on the ruins of the traditional British parties. This new political group was to be moderate, a middle party. But, in fact, it was to be a Lloyd Georgian party.

To establish himself at home, therefore, he had to succeed abroad. Time and again, too, some of Lloyd George's maddest and most provocative proposals, viewed from the Continental standpoint, had their origin in domestic political circumstances. By a gesture made in Paris, he undertook at home to placate a newspaper, purchase the approval of a group, satisfy a school of economic or political thought. Invariably, his foreign operations were inspired by domestic concerns without the smallest regard for the European realities of the hour.

In sum, although his popularity at the close of the war and in the first year of peace was almost beyond exaggeration, his political position was always difficult. He held power only at the will of those who had been his political foes. He depended each day upon the votes of a party the majority of whose members retained a measure of pre-war distrust. And the price of consolidating his own position was always the ruin of the party which thus maintained him.

When, therefore, he was finally defeated abroad, his situation at home was instantly impossible. But it was the clear perception of this fundamental condition which explained much which Lloyd George did in the days of his greatest influence. It is this, too, which illuminates his bitterness against France, when finally he fell. All the mass of anti-French propaganda which he crowded into his American writing is only thus intelligible. For it was defeat in his great duel with France which ultimately produced his ruin at home. And he never forgave or mistook this fact.

CHAPTER TWELVE

THE BOLSHEVIK CRISIS

SINCE Anglo-French interests were so completely divergent, open collision could not long be postponed. Before the breach came, however, British opinion had been profoundly influenced by the publication in the first days of 1920 of the famous volume of John Maynard Keynes, devoted to the Treaty of Versailles. Describing this document as a "Carthaginian Treaty," Keynes argued for sweeping reduction in all the reparations clauses.

Together with the constriction of reparations totals to figures which at that hour seemed microscopic, Keynes advocated a process of mutual forgiveness of Allied debts. But, at the end of the line, in his programme stood the United States, which was, in fact, to bear the whole burden of this cancellation. Britain and Germany were to benefit, France and the United States to pay for this remaking of the Treaty.

The book had an enormous British success. The Dawes Plan later produced the revision of the reparations figures, although by no means to conformity with Keynes's proposals. But although the United States consistently and frequently refused to accept the cancellation programme, the Balfour Note later repeated it, and British public opinion has never abandoned it. Nor has steady American opposition failed to arouse enduring British resentment.

The immediate political effect of the Keynes book was, however, even more considerable. It caught the ready fancy of Lloyd George. He enlisted at once in the campaign for revision. Moreover, he saw in Keynes, himself, and in the group of young Liberals about him, valuable material for the construction of his new political party.

But at the precise moment when Lloyd George was converted to the revisionist programme and British public opinion was stirring against a treaty which had such obvious dangers for British prosperity, events on the Continent precipitated a grave crisis. In mid-March two German brigades declined to obey demobilization orders, revolted, and seized Berlin. A provisional government, headed by Kapp, was created. Ebert and the legal government fled to Dresden.

For a week the situation in Germany was at once uncertain and to the last degree threatening. The German revolt against the Treaty had now become nationwide. The army was facing the immediate threat of dissolution. All the material for a counter revolution, for a real monarchist *coup d'état*, existed. The whole Versailles settlement, the very results of the military victory of the war were put in jeopardy.

In the end, the Republic was saved by the general

strike of the working men, who responded to the appeal of the President. Meantime, the mass of the civil and military followers of the old order refrained from action. Presently the Kapp divisions marched out of Berlin, firing on the crowd as they passed through the Brandenburger Thor. Kapp himself fled to Sweden. In fact, with little bloodshed, the whole Kapp Putsch fizzled out. Ebert returned to the capital and the Republic continued.

But there now followed Communist risings in the Ruhr. Essen was occupied by Red forces. Thus the first task of Ebert was, not to punish the rebellious military elements, but to employ the army against the people who had wrecked the Kapp Putsch itself. This suppression involved the dispatch of troops to the demilitarized Rhine Zone, which in turn constituted an open violation of the Treaty terms.

When this violation occurred, however, Millerand, who had now succeeded Clemenceau as Prime Minister, promptly sent French troops to occupy both Frankfort and Darmstadt. This occupation, too, led at once to a bloody collision between French soldiers and the citizens of Frankfort.

French action had been precipitate and had been taken without regard to British opinion. As a consequence, there was an immediate and general protest in Great Britain. Lloyd George, with equal haste, dispatched a letter of protest by the hands of his secretary without regard for the Foreign Office or other diplomatic machinery. In this letter, he publicly threatened the dissolution of the Anglo-French alliance.

In the end, this initial breach in the Entente was momentarily closed at the San Remo Conference, the first of those meetings which were henceforth to follow in rapid and bewildering succession. Millerand there agreed that French evacuation should immediately follow German return to the conditions of the Treaty of Versailles. He also gave specific pledge that no territorial sanction should be made the basis for any annexation project. While the French agreed not to act alone again, the British were compelled to agree to joint action under similar circumstances.

But although Lloyd George, after San Remo, issued the rosiest of accounts of its success, Anglo-French relations had been subjected to a strain which left permanent weaknesses. In fact, the real collision of interests and policies was notified to the world and to the Germans first of all.

Moreover, within Germany, a general election following closely upon the Kapp Putsch resulted in a victory for the opponents of the Republic. All the gains went to the extremists, to the Communists and the Monarchists. Henceforth the Republicans governed as a minority. The prestige of the Republic was shattered and the power of the military element was fortified.

San Remo was followed by a new conference at Hythe, where at last Lloyd George had the opportunity to present the views of Keynes and advocate the policy of revision. But the result was the resignation of Raymond Poincaré from the reparations commission, to which he had come on leaving the Presidency. Henceforth, Poincaré's great influence and powerful pen were employed in the French press to fight the British thesis of revision and to establish and defend a policy of integral enforcement of the Treaty of Versailles.

Hythe was followed by another and even more serious collision at Spa. Here the Germans came to meet their conquerors for the first time in discussion. But although disarmament was one of the chief subjects for adjustment, Fehrenbach, the new German chancellor, came without his War Minister and pleaded inability to act. The result was a deadlock and an ultimatum. Allied troops prepared to occupy the Ruhr. French divisions were concentrated.

To this show of force, the unhappy Fehrenbach was forced to surrender, although his yielding insured his immediate retirement from power. In the end, there were German promises to hasten disarmament and to fulfil pledges of coal deliveries. But all appearance of achievement was in the main without reality. Germany had bowed to force, but no government could comply and live. And, in fact, Fehrenbach gave up office shortly after the Spa meeting.

At this precise moment, too, Europe was suddenly confronted with the gravest crisis since the close of the war. Almost without warning a Bolshevist invasion of all of Middle Europe seemed inevitable, and this danger found all the allies of the war in complete disarray and utterly divided as to the policy which should be pursued.

For more than two years Allied fleets had blockaded Russian ports. The effort to employ French and British troops against the Soviet forces had broken down, alike because of public protest at home and mutiny among the soldiers and sailors themselves. At last the Allied effort had been reduced to munitioning and financing the various Russian generals, Yudenitch, Denikine, and Kolchak, who had sought, at the head of Russian forces, to restore the Romanoff régime.

Thus the Allies of 1920 repeated all the mistakes of the foes of the French Revolution. And the result was the same. Every attempt at restoration broke down before the refusal of the peasants to assist in the overturn of the revolutionary régime which had given them the land. Each failure of one of the Monarchist armies, too, bestowed upon the Soviets a vast wealth of military material. Thus, in the end, they were able to create a formidable military force.

In the spring of 1920, the Poles, acting undoubtedly under Allied inspiration, but also influenced by the dream of restoring that greatest Poland which once extended from the Baltic to the Black seas, undertook a wide-swinging invasion which brought victorious divisions to Kiev. In all the early spring days, Europe was filled with the reports of the successes of Pilsudski and his Polish partisans.

Suddenly, however, all changed. Polish disaster was

followed by a retreat which degenerated into a flight. By July, victorious Russian armies were operating on a wide front from the Dniester to the Niemen. City after city fell, Grodno, Lemberg, and Brest-Litovsk. Russian armies approached Warsaw, and the guns of the enemy could be heard from the palaces overlooking the Vistula in the Polish capital.

But with this Russian advance, the problem became instantly European. Beyond the crumbling Polish *cordon sanitaire* was all the shaken and flimsy Central European structure. The recent German election had disclosed enormous Communist strength. Hungary had lately been in Red hands. In fact, the whole European system was now in deadly peril. If Poland fell it was impossible to know what might survive east of the Alps and the Rhine.

At this moment, Britain and France agreed that Poland must be saved, the Red advance arrested. But while Britain proposed negotiation with the Soviet leaders, France favoured fighting. Thus from London were issued proposals to Moscow which, in effect, promised a cessation of Allied attacks upon the Bolshevist state, recognition for it, and advantageous commercial treaties. Any thought of the transportation of British soldiers or war material to the Polish front was abolished by the threat of a general strike made by British Labour.

All the British proposals, however, fell upon deaf ears. The great moment, the supreme opportunity for which Lenin and his associates had been working, was now come. Europe seemed to lie helpless before their feet. They already saw Bolshevist revolutions sweeping Poland, Hungary, Germany, Italy, all of Europe. Proletarian mastery of the entire Continent seemed to be assured by victories which still continued.

In this crisis, France undertook to send military aid. But at the German frontiers all troops were stopped by the threat of armed German resistance. At Danzig, too, the threatening attitude of the German population forbade the landing of supplies. Poland seemed doomed to fall while her western friends stood idly and helplessly by.

In the end, however, France was able to send a large military mission, headed by General Weygand, Foch's ablest lieutenant, and a civil mission led by Jules Jusserand, French Ambassador at Washington. Under the very walls of Warsaw, Bolshevist advance was at last halted. Clever counter offensives were planned and delivered. Old men and boys went to the trenches, even women volunteered. The spirit of Poland in this hour of utter peril was that of France at the Marne.

Thus, as suddenly as it had come, the Soviet invasion disappeared. Victorious armies melted into panic-stricken mobs. As the Poles advanced, they captured men by the thousand and all the artillery and equipment of the Red armies. The rout was complete, and, in fact, the westward thrust and the expansive power of the Russian Revolution were decisively broken. The armistice which followed promptly was the prelude to that

Peace of Riga which gave Poland vast territorial areas in Volhynia and Polesia.

Thus, as a consequence of victory, Poland emerged potentially a great power. But even while the Polish armies advanced eastward, there came from London emphatic demands that they should pause at that point, vaguely described as the "ethnic frontier." From Paris, by contrast, came incitations to continue. And while Britain opposed, France approved the terms of the Riga Settlement, while the later seizure of Vilna similarly evoked French approbation and British protest.

This renascent Poland was now become the natural and powerful ally of France. There was henceforth on the eastern boundaries of Germany a state of thirty millions of inhabitants. Under French guidance, a powerful Polish army could be developed. Since Germany would always continue to seek to suppress the Polish Corridor and regain Danzig, Poland and Germany would remain, as Prussia and Poland had ever been, hereditary enemies.

But the new Polish army would be for France what the Russian armies had been before and during the war. No Frenchman forgot that it was the advance of Russian divisions into East Prussia in August of 1914 which had compelled the Germans to detach divisions from the western front before the battle at the Marne had been joined. Any new German attack would be crippled by similar eastern dangers.

In reality, the thing went deeper. France was beginning to abandon hope of obtaining either British or American guarantees for her security. But here at last was the basis for an alternative policy. Poland, Czecho-Slovakia, and Belgium were equally menaced by German power. All were natural allies of France, because, for each, the French army was the ultimate insurance of independence and territorial integrity. The armies of these three countries, combined with the French, insured military superiority even in the face of German evasion of disarmament terms.

Here, too, was the basis of political as well as military power. All three states had precisely the same interest as France in preventing German evasion of the Treaty. Belgium, like France, was directly concerned in German reparations. These four states acting together in Europe could dispose of decisive military strength.

Thus, if under the walls of Warsaw Polish troops had repeated the achievement of Sobieski before Vienna and broken the thrusting power of an invasion which threatened the whole European structure, the ultimate consequence was to reëstablish the compromised position of France. The French share in the victory gave to France the credit of having saved Europe despite British hesitations and compromises. Millerand became President of the Republic as a result. Much of the injury done to French position in Europe as a consequence of the failure of the Guarantee treaties was now repaired.

There was, in fact, left to the British only one useful ally in Europe. An Anglo-Italian association might still restore some semblance of a balance of power on the Continent. But at this moment British prospects in that quarter were gravely compromised. Lloyd George had enthusiastically hurried Greek troops to Smyrna to forestall Italian occupation. These Greek troops were now organizing a colossal offensive which was designed to reach Angora and break Turkish resistance to the Paris settlements. But Greek success would raise Greece to the rank of a considerable state, and all Greek gain would be at Italian expense. For it was in the Ægean and the eastern Mediterranean that Italy now dreamed of establishing a colonial empire.

Italy was bound in the end to support the Turk against the Greek. Anglo-French quarrels over Syria were moving France in a similar direction. If Franco-Italian relations were far from cordial and Italy would still for a moment support Britain in international conferences, this Greek adventure of Lloyd George was certain in the end to place too great a strain on Italian complaisance.

Thus, two years later, when the French determination to occupy the Ruhr took definite shape, the Italian vote was cast with the French and the Belgian. Italian endorsement covered the Ruhr occupation, and British opposition was unsupported and therefore impotent.

At the same moment, the Little Entente was taking form. This association of Rumania, Czecho-Slovakia, and Jugo-Slavia was mainly concerned with the preservation of the *status quo* in the Danubian area. But Rumania shared Polish dangers on the Russian side, and Germany was a similar menace to the Poles and Czechs. If Jugo-Slavia was less concerned with extraneous issues, two of the three members of this new alliance had sound reasons for French association. And, in fact, French influence was shortly complete within the Little Entente. French military missions, too, undertook the task of refitting and establishing the armies of all three of these countries, while French factories furnished the arms and the French Treasury financed these operations.

In November, the American Presidential election completed the ruin 1920 had for British interests in Europe. Up to the very end of the campaign, the British public and press had cherished the hope that the American people would rally to the support of the principles of Woodrow Wilson and insure the ratification of his treaties. As a consequence, the colossal size of the Republican majorities was a staggering blow. If it did not quite abolish British hope, which endured until the Washington Conference, it was, nevertheless, a heavy blow.

This defeat of the treaties and denial of American interest in Europe, in fact, left Britain unsupported in the face of France. Moreover, this followed closely upon the Polish events which had raised French influence upon the Continent to very real heights. And it abolished any restraining influence which might flow from French expectation of eventual American return. In the very nature of things, it was bound to harden French determination to seek security by the Continental method.

Nor was it less evident that the American decision would hearten German resistance already encouraged by Anglo-French differences. Again and again, during the current year, German evasions had provoked incidents and precipitated crises. The troops had been on the point of moving at the moment of Spa. German violations of the disarmament provisions of the Treaty were open, flagrant, and beyond palliation.

But all this resistance had patent repercussions in France. French opinion was becoming suspicious, resentful, impatient. The French Treasury was beginning to feel the strain incident to financing the reconstruction of the devastated areas without German aid. The French people had accepted the fact of German resistance and evasion as definite and enduring.

In this situation, French opinion was not only hardening against Germany, but was becoming bitterly resentful of British restraints. The book of Keynes, which had made such a strong appeal to British opinion, excited all French wrath and passion. And, despite everything, the Treaty of Versailles was still the public law of Europe. It could not be modified without French consent. And all modification seemed to the French people no more than the deliberate sacrifice of their rights to British interests.

British campaigns against alleged French militarism,

which were provoking American echoes, were equally unfortunate in their French consequences. They were accepted as the evidence of a deliberate British purpose to disarm France in the presence of Germany: to deprive France of the means by which reparations could be collected, because reparations were no longer a British interest.

In Great Britain, the rise of French influence on the Continent, the expansion of French military power, the creation of a new system of alliances, all these circumstances were viewed with increasing disapproval and growing alarm. In many British minds, the war itself had been a consequence of the systems of alliances which had covered the Continent in 1914. But now all the old evil was being repeated.

Nor was there less apprehension arising from the reappearance of France as the dominant Continental state. In the long past, the British had fought many wars to restrain French power. But the overthrow of Germany and the consequent disarmament had in reality restored France to Napoleonic proportions. If the Tory faction of British public opinion remained sympathetic with France, the Liberals and the Labourites, now rising to prominence, were not only critical but publicly hostile.

Moreover, what was actually taking place on the Continent was in every detail inimical to British interests. Economic and financial chaos continued and increased. Germany, despite all outward appearances, was actually sinking steadily. All the Succession States which had risen on the ruins of the Russian and Austro-Hungarian empires were disclosing exaggerated nationalisms. Fresh causes for new wars seemed to the British public to be developing daily.

Tariff barriers between states which had recently been vital portions of homogeneous economic units shocked and alarmed the commercially minded English. On the Continent, there was neither political peace nor economic recovery, Middle Europe was being Balkanized; all Europe was going down hill. Nevertheless, although every British interest was at stake, neither British power nor influence could accomplish anything.

French purpose was immutable; French position becoming increasingly impregnable. The promise of American aid was at least fading. The British public opinion rapidly accepted the view that the United Kingdom was now condemned to complete isolation in perilous proximity to that colossal madhouse which was the Continent. But the very sense of impotence, new in British experience, roused angry recriminations.

More and more, in this first year of the Treaty, too, British opinion consolidated in the conviction that the responsibility was exclusively French. All French policy, every French act, easily came to be translated in traditional terms. Imperialism and militarism were the ready reproaches of the Liberal and Labour journals and orators; and while the French still found loyal defenders on British soil, the number, on the whole, diminished visibly.

If the Entente endured, if there was no open break in the partnership, this had a single explanation. On all sides, it was perceived that the actual dissolution of the alliance would in fact free France from the last restraint upon her course. While the French people still cherished any hope of an ultimate British guarantee, while there endured the belief that the old association which had saved the war could be restored, French action would naturally be moderated.

But, concomitantly, the opposition to bestowing upon France that British guarantee which alone made the British association valuable in French eyes continued to mount steadily. And, in fact, by the close of 1920, the Anglo-French alliance had become of little practical value. It was no more than a nominal tie between two peoples who saw their vital interests as conflicting and felt them fast becoming irreconcilable.

CHAPTER THIRTEEN

THE WASHINGTON CONFERENCE

IF THE first year of the Treaty of Versailles had been stormy, the second promptly became tempestuous. Moreover, while the struggle of 1920 had been mainly between France and Great Britain, in the following year German action momentarily, but only momentarily, restored the Allied front. In fact, German intransigence compelled the British to share in a policy of active coercion which was at once inconsistent with their material interests and out of harmony with their post-war state of mind.

The new crisis arrived rapidly. In January, a Paris conference, which was but a continuation of a December session at Brussels, established an Allied agreement as to reparations totals. All Europe had watched this Paris meeting with intense interest, because Anglo-French relations had again become difficult. Leygues, who had succeeded Millerand, had quickly fallen, Briand had come to power, but Poincaré was now and henceforth in the background.

All the world understood that, if Briand were to survive, if the Anglo-French Alliance were to continue as anything but an empty fiction, Briand would have to obtain substantial results. When he accepted $21,000,-000,000 as the permanent total of German payments, France assailed him for his sacrifices. But the size of the sum created consternation in London. In reality, it was at least twice as large as most experts now regarded as possible, and more than four times the now-familiar figures of Keynes.

In February, the scene shifted to London. The Germans were now called upon to make their proposals for meeting the Paris requirements. But instead, the Foreign Minister, Dr. Simons, presented to the astounded Allies what was in reality little more than a free translation of the Keynes programme. Insignificant payments were offered, and even these were conditioned upon certain political advantages, of which assured possession of Upper Silesia was the most important.

Upon the British, this German offer fell like a bombshell. Prepared to argue for moderation, Lloyd George found himself silenced in advance by proposals which the most friendly British critics described as derisory. What had happened, of course, was that the extent of Anglo-French differences in recent months had encouraged German hope that these could be exploited. But the attempt was as stupid as it was significant.

For Lloyd George now the choice was clear. He must break with France outright or join France in action. If he separated, Briand, or more likely Poincaré, would march into the Ruhr alone. But should he support France, British troops would have to accompany French.

If to break was, in the circumstances, impossible, to march was to arouse angry British protest.

Nevertheless, action was inevitable. On March 7th, Allied troops marched into Duisburg, Dusseldorf, and Ruhrort. The gateways of the great Ruhr industrial region were now in Allied hands. French artillery commanded Essen, the centre of the whole Westphalian district. New customs barriers were also erected to isolate the Rhineland from the Reich and fresh export taxes were imposed. But while Paris applauded all these reprisals, London watched with grim disfavour.

Following this action, London sessions in April and May led to a report of the commission appointed under the Treaty to establish the sum of German liability. The figure fixed was $33,000,000,000. New ultimatums, together with fresh threats of military sanctions to cover the whole Ruhr, accompanied further demands that the Germans now undertake to meet the immediate Allied requirements under this report.

Thereupon, one more political upset took place in Berlin. Wirth, a member of the Catholic Centre, came as Chancellor, proposing a policy of fulfilment. He was accompanied by Walter Rathenau, distinguished as an industrialist, thinker, and writer. But although both Wirth and Rathenau were sincere, for both the policy which they advocated was fatal. Wirth presently fell; Rathenau was later assassinated.

The utter collapse of this policy of fulfilment followed closely and surely after the solution of the Upper Silesian crisis in the autumn. The Treaty of Versailles had provided for a plebiscite in the industrial region, which lies in the southeast corner of Silesia and in the upper valley of the Oder. The vast majority of the inhabitants of this region are Slavonic by race. But the territory had not been Polish for six hundred years. Frederick the Great had stolen it for Prussia and from Austria in the Eighteenth Century.

The discovery of vast coal seams in this Upper Silesian district had been followed by an enormous industrial development. Next to the Ruhr, Upper Silesia was the greatest coal and iron centre in Germany. Kattowitz, Beuthen, and Hindenburg were flourishing cities. A vast network of railways bound factories and mines together and the Oder had been canalized to the sea. All this development, too, had been the work of German brains and German capital.

Originally, the Treaty of Versailles had bestowed all this district upon Poland. German protest, backed by Lloyd George, had produced the compromise of a referendum. But, after the vote, there had broken out a bitter Anglo-French dispute as to how the territory should be distributed. In the whole district, the German had prevailed, polling 705,000 votes against 473,000 for the Poles. But the Treaty had provided that the settlement should be based upon the majorities in the communes.

Thus, while in the north the German success had been overwhelming, in the south the Polish advantage had been decisive. But the real dispute was over the centre where the vote was close, the Germans carrying all the cities, the Poles dominating in the country. Here, too, was the great industrial prize for which both were fighting.

France backed Poland without reservation or restraint. The British supported the German. But the policy arose out of the British hostility to the further expansion of Poland, now become a French ally, while the French, for similar reasons, fought for every possible Polish advantage. Moreover, the entire situation was complicated by an insurrection headed by Korfanty, a German Pole, who recruited partisans from across the Polish border.

Briand and Lloyd George met in Paris in midsummer to settle this dispute. But no amicable settlement was possible. For Briand, to sacrifice Polish interests meant ruin politically. Against the Polish claim, British sentiment was enormously excited. In the end, the matter was referred to the League of Nations. But when in October the League decided in such fashion as to give Poland the larger portion of the industrial and mineral area, British wrath was instant. In British eyes, the League was gravely compromised. As for the Germans, to them the decision appeared utterly unjust, the League an instrument of oppression, and the loss of the Silesian coalfields a crowning disaster.

German resentment thus roused doomed any policy

of fulfilment. Nor, after years, has German determination to recover the Upper Silesian areas diminished. The battle between Polish and German populations is a detail of every election. Like that of the "Corridor," too, the Silesian question remains one of the more serious dangers to the peace of Europe, even after Locarno.

Viewed objectively, it is clear that, early in 1921, the political situations in Europe closely resembled the military condition five years earlier. Between France, Germany, and Britain, a state of deadlock had arrived. German will to resist the Treaty remained unbroken; French determination to enforce it hardened steadily. Although British interest increasingly demanded that European chaos should be ended, British policy could accomplish nothing.

In Europe, generally, too, the perception of this fact had led to a recrudescence of desire to bring the United States back. During the protracted March crisis, the German government had appealed directly to Washington. The new Harding Administration had just taken office. Berlin obviously believed that, with the change, the German cause might find a friendlier hearing.

This was a miscalculation. Woodrow Wilson's policies had been repudiated, but only for American reasons. Popular sentiment was still bitter against the German. The resistance to the Treaty seemed a deliberate and wilful attempt to destroy the Allied victory to which American arms had contributed. Thus, presently, the

German government was advised to approach its European conquerors and admonished to meet its reparations obligations.

Almost at the same time, René Viviani, who had come to Washington with Balfour at the moment the United States entered the war, returned to sound American feeling in respect to French policy. On the whole, his mission was successful. French interests still commanded general American sympathy. Nowhere was there discoverable any considerable support for either a German or a British thesis of treaty revision. American troops remained on the Rhine. The Harding Administration was prepared to keep them there. It was planning a separate peace with Germany, but not with any unfriendly thought to the Allies of the war, who were now themselves at peace with Germany.

It was, however, in Britain that the desire for an American return to Europe took the most definite form. The full extent of the disaster incident to American withdrawal was now appreciated. Not only was France out of hand, but Briand had to be supported in coercive measures as the single means of preventing the arrival of Poincaré and the catastrophe which that would involve.

Only American support could in the end prevent a general European disaster: this was the universal British conclusion. And at this moment the question of naval armaments seemed to offer a possible bridge. While still neutral, the United States had embarked upon a great programme of naval expansion. Now the moment was at hand when the programme would be realized and, with it, the passing from Britain to America of naval supremacy in the world.

Every question of prestige, if none of practical policy, moved the British to desire to avoid such an eventuality. Yet, if the United States chose to continue, the financial condition of the United Kingdom forbade any attempt to build ton for ton. And, of course, there was no thought, as there had been in the German case, of resorting to force. The American fleet did not threaten British safety. It was not a menace, although it was an unpleasant reminder of the material consequences of the recent struggle.

On the other hand, London was informed that there was a growing protest in the United States against the enormous expense of a naval expansion which had no basis in the national policy or interest. Presently, too, diplomatic hints began to arrive that the United States would welcome an international conference at which naval rivalry might be abolished and American and British naval strengths adjusted on the basis of equality.

Such a proposal found enthusiastic hearing in London. Nor was there objection to the further hint that the United States would also ask the dissolution of the Anglo-Japanese Alliance. An Imperial Conference in the summer disclosed the fact that several of the Dominions were equally unfriendly to the perpetuation of an alliance which had been useful before the war, but with the disappearance of the German High Seas Fleet had lost its value.

London then took up the American suggestion promptly. Italy and France, as well as Japan, agreed. But beyond the immediate business in hand, Lloyd George readily perceived the larger possibility. After Europe had consented to come to Washington to satisfy an American desire, was it unreasonable to hope that America would return to a European conference? Thus, at last, Britain might find the American associate, missing since the Peace Conference, but now ready to support measures which looked to the restoration of economic peace in Europe.

And, naturally and inevitably, Lloyd George, like all Britons, saw in the American return the promise of support against France. So far, in all the European conflict, during the entire Anglo-French duel, American sympathy, while passive, had been visibly with France. But at Washington all might be changed.

It was, then, to recapture America that the British dispatched to Washington, not only Mr. Balfour, their ablest negotiator, and Lord Lee, who in the older days had been with the American army in Cuba, but also a body of distinguished journalists, whose writings, contracted for in advance, were destined to set forth the British aspects of the European controversy to millions of American newspaper readers.

In fact, although the mass of the American people saw the Washington gathering as a new peace conference, while it was opened with prayer and accompanied by an emotional outburst hardly paralleled even in American history, it was predestined to be the battleground between French and British policies. This fact was as patent to the Dutch, Belgian, and Italian delegations, which came also, as it was hidden from the American public and government alike.

The French, on their side, perceived the danger. But they came convinced that, in reality, the Conference would develop into a battle between the United States and the Anglo-Japanese Alliance. Briand, Viviani, and Sarraut all journeyed to Washington satisfied that they would strengthen the unmistakable American affection for France by supporting the American representatives against a British offensive.

For Charles E. Hughes, who, as Secretary of State, now undertook to succeed in the field where Woodrow Wilson had failed nearly three years before, the problem was double. The United States had prospective supremacy in battleships. Britain had actual advantage in cruisers. Equality, which was the American objective, would only be attained if the two circumstances were balanced. He had, also, to get rid of the Japanese alliance, but in this, beneath the surface, British and American desires were identical. The larger problems of the Pacific were vitally important circumstances of the agenda, but these lie outside the field of the present study.

On the whole, however, power was in Mr. Hughes's

hands. Both Britain and France had set out to enlist American aid. But since both were equally interested in obtaining this, just as long as he held the balance even between the two nations, he would have equal claim upon the support of both. His single real danger lay in the possibility that he might at some moment be put in the position of the ally of one against the other, and in practice that he might come to assume in French eyes the appearance of a British champion.

Always, however, Mr. Hughes's necessity was to keep in mind the fact that, in Europe, France and Britain were diplomatically and politically engaged in a desperate struggle and that inevitably the battle would continue in America. Unfortunately, Mr. Hughes chose to assume toward the European circumstances in Washington precisely the attitude he had adopted toward the Hiram Johnson detail in California in 1916. That is to say, he ignored it completely. And the result to his conference was as fatal as it had been to his Presidential campaign.

At the outset of the sessions, Mr. Hughes startled all his hearers by announcing in advance of negotiation a programme of battleship adjustment which instantly abandoned all prospective American supremacy in the battle line. This was a magnificent gesture, but it left British, and even Japanese, advantage in cruisers unaffected. Nor did there remain to the American negotiator any further resource to trade against cruiser reduction. Thus, on the first day, all the naval advantage desired by the British was assured to them without cost.

Secret negotiations now followed inevitably. But in entering upon these, Mr. Hughes easily fell into the error of weighing nations by their naval tonnage. Thus, while France and Italy were great powers measured by all European political standards, they were hardly third-class powers judged by tonnage tables. Accordingly, Mr. Hughes confined his discussions to Britain and Japan, while France and Italy remained isolated and ignored. And inevitably the representatives of both countries felt humiliated.

In due course of time, agreement was reached between the United States, Japan, and Britain, but agreement involved fixing French and Italian naval strength also—because British strength would inevitably have to be based upon French and Italian. But when Mr. Hughes approached M. Sarraut with the results of his discussions with Mr. Balfour, not by design but in fact he seemed to be imposing a British thesis upon the French Ambassador.

By this time Briand had returned to Paris, having made one speech upon land armament. Viviani, quick-tempered and deeply resentful of treatment which he regarded as a deliberate insult, was about to go. Sarraut had to remain, but he, too, was indignant. Accordingly, he at once began to make objection to Mr. Hughes's proposals, which, in fact, were for him British proposals.

"The voice is the voice of Hughes, but the hand is the hand of Balfour"—this *mot* of a clever Dutch journalist had instant and immense vogue and perfectly represented the view of all the Europeans as to what had happened.

But the resistance of Sarraut imperilled the whole Conference. In this situation, Mr. Hughes took the momentous step of appealing to Briand in Paris over the head of Sarraut in Washington. Had he been in the least familiar with French domestic political conditions, Mr. Hughes could hardly have turned to Briand. For Sarraut's brother was not only owner of one of the most important newspapers in southern France, but also actually controlled a group of members of the Chamber of Deputies upon whom Briand depended directly for his majority.

Mr. Hughes had then invited M. Briand to choose between suicide at home and a quarrel with the American people abroad. From this situation Briand escaped by asserting that, in the matter of battleships, he had passed his word to Mr. Hughes while he was in Washington. It was a lame excuse at best, and in point of fact it left him with a fatal weakness in his Cabinet which contributed to his fall a few weeks later. But to balance his concession to Mr. Hughes, Briand was obliged to give Sarraut the private assurance that henceforth he would have a free hand in Washington.

Sarraut was now personally humiliated. As a Frenchman, too, he felt that his country had suffered as a consequence of Mr. Hughes's open adoption of British views. The Conference was becoming a British success. All credit in American eyes would now go to Britain. All permanent political advantage would inure to the Republican party, which M. Sarraut well remembered had been responsible for the rejection of the Treaty of Versailles, to the grave disadvantage of France.

Before he came to Washington, Sarraut had been Governor General of Indo-China. He had enjoyed rare opportunities to observe the Oriental methods in diplomatic affairs. He knew now what had to be done, but he was also willing to bide his time.

Nor did he have long to wait. For now Mr. Hughes embarked upon a final venture which precipitated the catastrophe. At the outset of the Conference, an American Naval Advisory Committee, appointed to make recommendations, had turned in a report advocating the retention of the submarine as a naval weapon. Mr. Hughes had supported this thesis in the first session. Mr. Balfour had protested because the submarine was the one real threat to British security. The war had recently demonstrated its potency.

In Europe, as in America, the British had argued for the abolition of the undersea craft. But, for the French, submarines had a distinct political value. They set a limit to British sea power, otherwise absolute. They gave France an admirable basis for bargaining. Thus France had ostensibly planned a considerable programme of submarine construction. This programme, too, had been the subject of angry debate between the Paris and London journals. Briand, embarking from New York, had ironically explained French submarine expansion as disclosing a purpose "to explore the flora and fauna of the sea." The jest had called forth passionate British protest.

Now, however, rumours ran round the Washington Conference that Mr. Hughes had abandoned the American thesis and gone over to the British. It was reported that, yielding to the campaign of certain American newspapers, cleverly reinforced by the writings of British journalists and by the charming words of Mr. Balfour, the Secretary of State had accepted the principle of banning the submarine.

At this moment, the American Secretary of State approached M. Sarraut. He did not, to be sure, propose abolition. But he did suggest that French strength in this submarine arm be reduced to the 5-5-3-1.75-1.75 ratio, which had been fixed for battleship tonnage for America, Britain, Japan, Italy, and France, respectively.

For Mr. Hughes, a submarine was only a submarine. Its relation to the general scheme of limitation of naval armaments was patent to him. But its value in the great diplomatic game which was being played in Europe for unlimited stakes he never even suspected. He saw the undersea craft as a child might see the chips of a poker game. For him, the chips are only celluloid disks. But for the players, the dollar values are always evident. Thus, no matter how innocent the child, its attempt to transfer the chips from one player to another invariably arouses protest.

To every Frenchman, therefore, Mr. Hughes's proposal was instant and complete proof that the American Secretary of State had "gone British." Smarting under what all felt was the humiliating treatment French representatives had been compelled to endure in Washington, this final circumstance had immediate repercussions both in Washington and in Paris.

The moment for which Sarraut had waited was now come. At home he was assured of unanimous support for any step he might take to resist this apparent Anglo-Saxon combination. In it, the French people would see the effort of nations which had evaded the promise to guarantee French security, to limit French means of defence.

Accordingly, Sarraut struck swiftly, surely, and with great cleverness. France, he explained, in her desire to contribute to the success of an American conference, had consented to accept permanently the rank of a third-class naval power. This was in itself unfair, because, while, during the war, Britain and the United States had been expanding their navies, France had been consuming her steel in shells fired against the common enemy. The limit of concession had, however, been reached. The battleship was the weapon of the rich; the submarine of the poor. France, by reason of her great sacrifices in the war, was now unhappily poor. But she had still to maintain communications with her great colonial empire. On this point, therefore, French opinion was fixed, the French programme immutable. France had accepted the view of the American advisory committee. She continued to adhere to it. The French refusal to Mr. Hughes's proposal was irrevocable.

There, then, was a limit to all further naval limitation. The British, on their part, now came forward and gravely explained that, since the French retained submarines, they must keep on their cruisers. Thus, while the United States had surrendered potential battleship supremacy, it had not obtained equality in fleets. Five years later, President Coolidge would seek a new conference to repair the consequences of the failure. But for the moment all was lost.

Following closely upon this final and disruptive crisis, there now arrived from London the polite suggestion that the United States should come to Europe. Mr. Hughes was invited to return the visit of Mr. Balfour. An economic conference was proposed at Genoa. Up to this moment, everything at Washington had proceeded according to British plan. French performance had exceeded British hope. Mr. Hughes divided the honours with Mr. Balfour. American anger with France was general. If America should come now, a British ally was assured.

But Congress, on its side, was becoming apprehensive. The American navy looked with utter dismay at what had been flung away for nothing at the Conference table. The Republican Irreconcilables of the Senate, whose campaign for isolation had been endorsed by a seven-million majority at the polls, had no wish to be dragged into a repudiation of all the principles which they had professed in their fight against Mr. Wilson. So, presently, there emerged from the White House a categorical refusal. America would not go to Europe. And immediately, almost overnight, Europe went home. The battle of Washington was over. No diplomatic battle had ever been better fought. None less than Mr. Balfour, shortly to be disguised as Lord Balfour, deserved the disappointment which it brought.

For Americans, the Washington Conference has certain unmistakable lessons. It was the second, as Paris had been the first, considerable contact of America with Europe about the green table. In both cases, the causes of failure were identical, although the differences in personality were enormous.

Mr. Wilson at Paris and Mr. Hughes at Washington were ultimately shipwrecked because both refused utterly to recognize European realities. The President imagined that Britons, Belgians, Italians, and Frenchmen would think internationally when national interests were at stake. The Secretary of State believed that Europeans coming fresh from diplomatic battlefields, where they were fighting for their lives, would easily assimilate the cool and complete detachment which he had adopted toward all foreign matters.

Wholly unconsciously, Mr. Hughes walked between the firing lines of two quarrelling European peoples.

When, inevitably, bullets began to whistle about his head, he was amazed. One day in Paris, Mr. Wilson had awakened to discover that he was in Europe. On another day, Mr. Hughes similarly perceived that Europe was in Washington. Both were similarly overwhelmed.

The conferences of Washington and Paris were equally illustrative of the fundamental weakness of America's dealings with Europe. It is not the innate wickedness, superior cunning, or ultimate trickery of European diplomacies which explain the unvarying American confusion at the end of each experiment.

Always, at bottom, American disaster proceeds from the enormous initial assumption that the question at issue has only American aspects. Thus Woodrow Wilson could lead his country in a war which had endured for years and was being fought on issues centuries old, and yet imagine that, with American entrance, everything had been changed. Mr. Hughes, on his part, could invite a Europe, actually in conflict, to come to America, with no thought that the battle would be resumed on American soil.

Mr. Wilson saw Paris as a gathering to create a League of Nations. Mr. Hughes accepted the Washington Conference simply as the meeting place of foreign diplomats who felt about naval disarmament as he felt. All his thought was concentrated upon the preparation of tonnage tables. He knew the battleships of the world by name and by number. He lay awake nights balancing strengths down to the last remote submarine chaser.

No fact escaped him. Nothing that the encyclopædia, the naval almanacs, the Statesman's Yearbook, could tell him was overlooked.

Not only did the Secretary of State think in terms of tonnage, he even measured great nations by their naval displacements. He studied every material factor. No man ever laboured harder, worked more sincerely, strove more wholeheartedly to arrive at results than the Secretary of State at the Washington Conference. No public official ever gave more of his time to the press correspondents, and all of his explanations were mathematically perfect.

Only one thing was lacking. Never for a single moment did he stop to consider how a Frenchman might think because he was a Frenchman; what British interests must be because Britons represented them. No material element was ignored, but all the moral values, all the imponderables, all the European circumstances were dismissed. Inside the Volstead territorial limit, examination was microscopic; beyond, nothing was considered.

When the final hour came and with it ruin for all but the battleship detail in his limitation programme, Mr. Hughes had every alibi and no defence. He knew himself to have been innocent of any intent to offend, any design to humiliate, any purpose to wound French pride. What he was unable to perceive, then or thereafter, was that he had done all these things.

Thus, at a later time, he could go to New Haven and

solemnly warn the French people against that invasion of the Ruhr upon which they were already resolved. In doing this, he felt that he spoke as a friend of France, and he believed that his words would have a restraining influence. But, in fact, France remembered Washington, held Mr. Hughes as enemy, and found in his words incitation to that very action against which he was solemnly protesting.

When, too, in February, 1927, President Coolidge proposed a new naval conference, it was M. Briand who promptly vetoed the proposal. For France the Washington experience was a conference to end conferences, and Coolidge reaped where Hughes had sowed.

In the progress of the European settlement, however, the Washington Conference is primarily important because it marks the destruction of the last European hope of an American return. With President Harding's refusal to send representatives to Genoa, the European problem became exclusively European. Moreover, on November 11th, one day before the Washington Conference opened, Germany and the United States exchanged ratifications of the separate peace. Thus, the United States, having entered the war on an American issue, made peace in its own way.

CHAPTER FOURTEEN

CANNES—THE FRENCH REVOLT

IF THE Washington Conference in its naval aspects was a disappointment for the American people and in the future destined to be the cause of general disillusionment, for Europe it was a disaster pure and simple. The apparent combination of the United States and Great Britain, the unmistakable intimacy of Mr. Hughes and Mr. Balfour, created the conviction in the French mind that M. Briand had been the victim at Washington, as they regarded M. Clemenceau the casualty of Paris.

American criticism of French military establishments, the battle over the submarine, profound and universal resentment at what seemed a deliberate and successful campaign on the part of the British ally to destroy France in the eyes of the people of the United States, all these circumstances combined to provoke in France the fatal revolt which had long been preparing.

German resistance to the disarmament provisions of the Treaty was notorious. In the first days of the new year, notice came from Berlin of inability to fulfil the reparations promises of London. Every hour the French financial situation was becoming difficult. To the bitterness which had already been aroused by the sense that France had been abandoned by her allies of the war, there was now added the conviction that, in fact, the Allies had become enemies.

Hatred of Lloyd George passed all conceivable limits. Every music hall and theatre performance included some bitter and violent reproach. The Paris press was filled with attacks not only upon Lloyd George but upon his country. Washington had, in fact, been the crowning humiliation and the ultimate incitation.

For Briand, the end was already in sight. In the first week of January, he set out for Cannes to meet Lloyd George. On this conference the whole future of Anglo-French relations depended, and the immediate hopes for European reconstruction were equally issues of the discussion which was to take place amidst all the beautiful surroundings of the French Riviera. But although Briand went reinforced by a reassuring majority in the Chamber of Deputies, he visibly negotiated with a noose about his neck.

Nor was Lloyd George's position in the least secure. British public opinion was becoming alarmed over the steady failure of British statesmanship to provide any solution for those international problems which were in reality matters of domestic concern. More than two million unemployed drew doles from the British Treasury. Although the war had now been ended more than three years, economic recovery was far distant.

Politically, Lloyd George was in trouble. He had dreamed of turning the first successes of the Washington Conference into the pretext for another election like the Khaki affair following the Armistice. On the basis of reënlisting the United States for European service, he planned to obtain a new mandate, and the members elected would be his followers first and members of political parties only secondly.

All this plan was blocked by a sudden protest within the Tory party. Sir George Younger, manager of the Conservatives, promptly vetoed the Lloyd Georgian programme. Younger, like many other Tories, saw that Lloyd George was patently aiming at the creation of a new political party. They realized that a new mandate would give him a further lease of power and an extended opportunity to break down the Conservative party.

In an outburst of temper, Lloyd George denounced the Younger revolt as the insubordination of a "cabin boy" against the discipline of the "captain." But the will of the "cabin boy" prevailed. The disclosure of this "Die-hard" insurrection followed Cannes, but for the first time Lloyd George set out for a European conference with a clear limit place upon his power. His prestige was becoming impaired at home, if not abroad. Such success as had been achieved at Washington was credited to Mr. Balfour. He had now to win a new victory abroad to save his domestic front.

Yet victory was difficult to achieve, because he was faced with the plain fact that, unless he were able to make concessions to M. Briand, concessions which must now include the much-feared British guarantee of French security, Briand would fall. Thus Lloyd George could no longer hope for any personal or political advantage incident to triumphing over Briand. On the contrary, the very situation compelled him to present the French premier with a victory.

In the hour of adversity, Lloyd George's marvellous imagination flashed forth dazzlingly. He dreamed a great new European conference. It would assemble at Genoa, where he would be assured the aid of Italy. Russia would be invited, and thus the Liberal and Labour elements in Britain placated. America would come, for he was still unaware of the imminent American refusal.

At this conference, with Germany, Russia, and the United States present, with Italian support assured, the French influence in Europe, based upon the association of the Succession States, Poland and Belgium, with France, would be neutralized. Every kind of revision of European frontiers and readjustment of economic conditions lay in the background. His own unrivalled and unimagined skill in the conduct of conferences would have unlimited scope.

British instinctive objection to the French guarantee would be temporarily silenced by the brilliant prospectus of Genoa. After success, this minor price would be forgotten. With achievement abroad, too, would come sure reward at home. The election now vetoed by Tory opposition would be easy to obtain and certain to bring a new lease of power.

All that was necessary now was to placate France. Such appeasement was easy because the long-withheld guarantee would at once consolidate M. Briand's position and win his consent for the great Genoa enterprise. On this platform Lloyd George took his stand and with this programme already privately approved by Briand at a London meeting, he set out in the first days of January for the Supreme Council Meeting at Cannes. At the moment, his fame still filled Europe, his confidence in himself was unshaken.

At Cannes, too, briefly, he unfolded his plans to Briand, and a few days later Paris, London, and the world were informed that at last the Anglo-French breach had been repaired permanently and that France was now promised that British guarantee, the loss of which, after Paris, had explained all subsequent quarrellings and misunderstandings.

Then, suddenly, disaster without limit came. And it came as an immediate consequence of one of the most grotesque episodes in all diplomatic history. In the genial sun of the Riviera, Lloyd George persuaded Briand to try the fascination of golf. Paris newspapers promptly contained reports and presented pictures of the French Premier essaying with not too much grace to play the game which was the chosen pastime of the British Prime Minister. Briand was pictured and described in his attitude of becoming attention while the adroit Welshman gave him first instruction.

And irrationally, but instantly, Paris, France generally, rebelled. Lloyd George was the enemy. Briand had but yesterday been the victim of the present guest of Cannes. French prestige and popularity in America had been destroyed by the skill and the chicane of the British statesman who was now leading Briand, not down the primrose path, perhaps, but certainly across the slippery greens.

Without warning there came from Paris alarming messages. A split in the French Cabinet had developed, a split to which Mr. Hughes had already contributed materially by his battleship gesture. Briand abandoned the sunny tees and hastened to Paris. By a brief cabinet meeting, he seemed to have succeeded in restoring unity. In a speech in the Chamber, he apparently reasserted his mastery of that tumultuous body.

But, in fact, it was too late. Emerging from the session in which his eloquence appeared irresistible, Briand suddenly resigned. For a moment it was believed that a new Briand Cabinet would be formed. But Millerand, President of the Republic, sent for Poincaré. All had been planned in advance. Poincaré accepted, the Chamber rallied to the former President. His majority exceeded that of Briand's a few days before. For his part in this conspiracy Millerand would be flung from the Elysée Palace two years later, but in his hour he had done the will of France.

Thus briefly expired the hope of Cannes. Years later, Briand would say that Cannes had been the promise of Locarno and that what had been postponed in 1922 was realized in 1925. But for the moment the disaster was complete. The British guarantee lapsed. The break in sympathy between France and Britain was instantly and continuingly absolute. If Cannes was a remote promise of Locarno, it was the immediate prelude to the Ruhr.

And in the events of Cannes and of Paris one must see clearly the revolt of a whole people. In French eyes Briand represented the last hope of successful association with Great Britain. All France had felt that he and not Clemenceau should have made peace at Paris. He was, quite as much as M. Clemenceau, a champion of the principle of Anglo-French coöperation. As Prime Minister during the war he had learned the value of the British alliance in the terrible experiences of a doubtful struggle.

In the year in which he had been Prime Minister, Briand seemed in French eyes to have made all the sacrifices and all the surrenders. Each reduction in reparations totals, which was in fact a concession to reality, appeared to the French people an abandonment of French rights in return for illusory benefits. While Briand had been assailed in the critical press of Britain and the United States as the convinced spokesman of a militaristic France, all his fellow countrymen recognized him as the sincere advocate of a policy of moderation and of a course of coöperation.

Always, however, in his brief and troubled premiership, Briand had been caught between two forces. Abroad, the realities of the French political situation and the depth of French convictions were unappreciated.

At home, the facts in the world outside were ignored. Great as was his skill, supreme as was his charm, Briand was very far from being able to dominate a tempest or control a storm. His strength, after all, lay not in force but in manner. If he was later to achieve far-shining success in restoring French position in the world and peace in Europe, he was, in fact, utterly helpless in the whirlwind of 1922.

The bitter irony of the Cannes episode lies in the fact that the French Premier was the victim of two countries, each of which was vitally interested in seeing prevail the ideas and the methods for which M. Briand was fighting desperately in France. If the arrival of Poincaré was not an immediate disaster for the United States, as it certainly was for Britain, American material interests were no less certainly affected by peace or war in Europe.

Yet the British, in pursuit of American assistance, the American in search of the totally insignificant detail of a submarine limitation, had combined to destroy at home the single French Premier who could even conceivably restrain the storm which was gathering. In so far as the Washington Conference was a peace conference, it made war in Europe inescapable. For Poincaré did bring war, and the Washington Conference placed power in his hands.

Briand was certainly Prime Minister of a country which was armed. But Briand was also the Frenchman most opposed to the use of these arms as a means to international settlement. Seeking to disarm his country, the statesmen and the people of Britain and the United States successfully thrust power in the hands of a man who was constantly preaching force as the single means of attaining his country's ends.

In the winter of 1921–22 the problem was, not to reduce the number of divisions or submarines France possessed, but to find a way by which to prevent France from using them. And there was in power in France at the moment a man who, measured by every fact of his public life before and since, was opposed to French use of arms. Yet, at Washington, Briand was destroyed in the name of peace and Poincaré established in power as a consequence of the campaign for disarmament.

The fall of Briand following the Conference of Cannes marks a moment in the period in European history which we have been examining. At the Washington Conference, the determination of the United States to remain outside of Europe was clearly established. The consequences of Cannes finally doomed the Anglo-French partnership which had been a decisive factor in the war and had survived in principle if not in practice as the basis of European order.

Moreover, the failure of Cannes carried with it the doom of the conference method, by which Europe had been controlled from the moment of the Paris Conference onward. No circumstance contributed more to Briand's disaster than the premature publication in the Paris press of reports of the proposed Genoa meeting. With the memories of Washington in every French mind, the prospect of a renewal of the struggle on the chosen ground of the British Prime Minister roused instant protest and immediate apprehension.

For the French people, conferences meant assemblies convoked to impose new sacrifices and place fresh humiliations upon France. Washington had been the most unfortunate, but all had been equally without profit. Each had been marked by French discomfiture. The new Premier would neither play golf with Lloyd George at Cannes nor take tea with Chicherin at Rapallo.

CHAPTER FIFTEEN

POINCARE—LA RUHR

IN MAKING way for Poincaré, Briand left a stage on which his hour was not yet come. For his successor, by contrast, the opportunity seemed to have been long preparing. His shadow had been over Anglo-French negotiation for more than a year. His coming had already been forecast as a promise of violence. Yet, although in the end he did all the things which the world had expected of him, no man ever played a part which seemed natural with greater reluctance or with less skill.

Clemenceau had once described Lord Kitchener as a "symbol" and added the definition—"a symbol is a public man about whom some people still believe what was never true." In this sense, no man was ever more completely a "symbol" than Raymond Poincaré, for more than seven years President of the Republic and three times in fifteen years President of the Council.

Thus, while to every foreign view Poincaré is the incarnation of the imagined militarism of France, in reality, so far from suggesting the martial circumstance of the soldier in every detail he recalls the conventional portrait of the country lawyer. To think of him as the proverbial "man on horseback" is, moreover, utterly absurd. Those who have examined his writings or studied his once notorious Sunday "sermons" may have found there echoes of the Bismarckian gospel of "blood and iron." But in French political circles, where Poincaré is best known, if his obstinacy is recognized, his caution, stretching to intellectual timidity, is legendary.

Those who follow Poincaré, follow reluctantly. The votes of confidence which he obtains frequently, while in office, are always given grudgingly. He never arouses enthusiasm or enlists loyalty. In office or out, he is always a lonely figure, remote and isolated amidst his books and papers. He never played a game or shared a sport. Even the necessary excursions to the country are made by train rather than motor, so that he may have a steady table on which to write his inevitable *dossiers*.

Yet this man has three times been master of France in moments of great stress. After Agadir, after Cannes, and again following the *dégringolade* of the franc in 1926, his fellow countrymen turned to him, and his name was the foundation of a union of men of many parties. Thus, those who have denounced him personally with the greatest violence and opposed him publicly with the last degree of bitterness have invariably ended by serving with him in a ministry of national safety.

Speaking of Poincaré and Briand, Clemenceau once said, "Briand knows nothing and understands everything. Poincaré knows everything and understands nothing." In this *mot* of the "Tiger" there is at least a hint of the strength as well as the weakness of the former President. In fact, if statistics and tabulated data were the sum of human existence and the rules of geometry and algebra the bases of all human knowledge, Poincaré would certainly be the greatest public man of his generation.

Whether as a publicist, statesman, or lawyer, no man ever speaks with greater authority, none ever displays more tireless energy in preparing a case. Concerning all questions which he touches, Poincaré is, in the phrase of his countrymen, "documented." Always, too, he is first of all the attorney. He approaches his problems from a legal point of view. Not only has he all the legal qualifications to the highest degree, but he also discloses every limitation of the judicial mind to a similar extent. Those who compared him with Field Marshal von Hindenburg were simply stupid, but his resemblances to Charles Evans Hughes are striking.

Yet this timid, suspicious, provincial barrister twice played an important rôle in the onset of a European conflagration. He is still to-day, even for millions of his fellow countrymen, *Poincaré-la Guerre* and *Poincaré-la Ruhr*. And the explanation of this circumstance, as of much else which is otherwise inexplicable, is to be discovered in the fact that he is also *Poincaré-le lorrain.* "Prudence Lorraine," Sisley Huddleston, author of the best biography of the ex-President, explains that fellow students called the future Prime Minister in his academic days.

Raymond Poincaré was born in Bar-le-Duc, hard by the frontier as it existed before the Eighteenth Century and again after 1871. Two marshals of Napoleon first saw the light of day in this same gray provincial capital with its stiff old town and towers set high above the Ornain valley. One of these was also military governor of Berlin. Through this city marched two invading armies, in 1814 and in 1870, and Raymond Poincaré, as a boy, saw the latter.

Frontier peoples have a peculiar mentality, and that of the Lorrainer is proverbial throughout France. Had he been born in Brittany or Dauphiny, Poincaré might have been nothing more than an attorney who, rising by degrees and deservedly both as a publicist and an attorney, arrived at last at Cabinet rank. But, having been born in Lorraine, he is a patriot first, and all else second. For him, the humiliation of his youth, the defeat of 1870, the loss of Metz and Strasbourg, excited the passion of his maturity.

By instinct, by profession in all the other circumstances of his life, Poincaré is a man of peace. He is a convinced Republican—and a Republican of the Left, an uncompromising constitutionalist. His personal ambition, which is great, has always been rigidly confined within conventional limits. He is not in any sense a Militarist, just as in ordinary sense he is far from being a reactionary. He is, however, a Nationalist, because by birth he is a Lorrainer.

Called to power first in 1911 to liquidate the Agadir mess, after the fall of Caillaux which followed the humiliating sacrifices of the Congo, Poincaré set out to order the affairs of France for the trial he believed at hand. For what he did in these two years he stands indicted by an increasing number of students of contemporary history as one of the authors of the supreme tragedy, which was the war. Yet nothing is more difficult to visualize than this insignificant bourgeois figure, with his inevitable cotton umbrella, this country lawyer with the manners and lack of manner of the province, deliberately undertaking to set the world in flames.

And, of course, no such purpose ever entered Poincaré's head. He has met his critics and accusers in a defence which has already extended to several volumes and bears the significant title, "In the Service of France." In these volumes he easily refutes every specific charge. He did nothing to precipitate the war because of any desire for war. He did nothing to hasten it because he believed it would be profitable for France. He did not "will" the war. But at all times, in all things, under all circumstances, he only prepared for that war which he always believed had already been "willed."

Come to the Presidency in 1913, he disappeared instantly and completely into the obscurity which the office insures. He was actually travelling in Russia when the storm burst. He touched French soil before the declaration of war. But he was then, as always, without hope of peace. What seemed to most of the world a terrible calamity, appeared in the eyes of the Lorrainer as a simple and natural event, long expected, delayed rather than premature.

At the very outset of the conflict, Poincaré was guilty of an incredible and completely characteristic blunder. When the German armies approached Paris, the government retired to Bordeaux. Obviously, the machinery of administration had to be removed, but Poincaré went out with the baggage of the Viviani Cabinet. He went, not because he was a physical coward—he has never been that. But he did go because he fancied that the majesty of France was in some fashion invested in his person. He saw himself in German hands as Francis I had been a captive after Pavia.

That journey to Bordeaux was a mistake which was long unforgiven by the French people. It deprived Poincaré of all influence during the war. Clemenceau ruthlessly suppressed him in the treaty-making time. In 1920, he left the Élysée Palace far less important politically than when he had entered that sterilizing plant. Even the place which he took upon the Reparations Commission seemed insignificant. And, in fact, he resigned this with great promptitude, after Hythe.

But in 1922, and in his early sixties, Poincaré was actually at the prime of intellectual life. The situation was, too, made to order for his legal mind. To the defence of the Treaty, which he had begun by denouncing, he brought all the resources of a really great lawyer and a not less distinguished journalist. For him, all the parchment provisions of the enormous document were sacred rights, just as the whole Treaty had become the law of Europe. It was something to be applied, not to be modified. All things therein contained were property: integral enforcement was more than a phrase, it was a solemn duty.

For the methods of Lloyd George, Poincaré had every contempt of an orderly mind. For the diplomacy of the cinema, the international conference done to jazz tunes, he had utmost scorn. He saw German evasion as the contemporary expression of an enduring will to injure France, the present evidence of what would one day be a new explosion of hate and vengeance. He interpreted British policy as the latest revelation of a national egoism which was traditional. The Treaty, itself, was insufficient, but it was still something, all that was left of the victory—it must not be *saboté*.

So, daily and weekly, in all the influential press, Poincaré built up the case of France. He reinforced the double conviction that France was being defrauded and that in the Treaty there still lay the basis of military security and of financial salvation. To the discussion he brought a wealth of facts, a mastery of logic, a power of lucidity which defied refutation. Each surrender, at San Remo, at Hythe, at Spa, the humiliations of Washington, the prospective perils of Genoa, pointed his text and fortified his sermon.

Called to power, ambitious to repair the accidents which had kept him in obscurity in the period of the great conflict, convinced of the critical character of the times, profoundly moved in all his patriotic sentiments, Poincaré arrived at the moment when France had been converted to his arguments. But inexorably he was thereafter the captive of these arguments. As Lloyd George at the Peace Conference had been committed to the principle of the "last farthing," Poincaré was similarly bound to that thesis that Germany could be made to pay everything.

And the eternal paradox in Poincaré is disclosed in the fact that while he preached what was in fact violence, he never wholly accepted the programme himself. He believed implicitly that his arrival would in itself break down the German will to resist. He regarded British policy as only a device used against a weak and opportunistic Briand. He was satisfied that it would be abandoned before his own established firmness.

Even when, with patent reluctance, he set out to occupy the Ruhr, he never dreamed of German resistance. He imagined that he was sending a sheriff to execute a writ. When the whole German people rose passionately and violently, when passive resistance came promptly, he was utterly amazed. The military occupation which had to follow was totally improvised and therefore was carried out with the clumsiness of a national guard manœuvre. In all that happened subsequently, he was the victim of his own utter and complete misconception.

When Great Britain was alienated, America chilled, Europe alarmed; when in Germany there grew up instantly a bitter, violent, and vindictive passion which had not before existed in all the centuries of strife between the two races; when France itself was shaken by the growing sense of this unlimited and threatening hate, Poincaré was helpless and in the main blind and deaf.

He had prepared everything legally and nothing materially. He had made allowance for every juridical circumstance but none for any moral consequence. National opinions in the face of legally constituted authority seemed to him irrelevant if not impertinent. They were like manifestations of opinion in a courtroom, to be silenced by clearing the court. The fact that he had the letter of the law with him left him unimpressed by the spirit of any people.

When the Ruhr occupation developed into actual war, his very timidity and obstinacy left him unable to end victoriously what he had begun blindly. When, in September, 1923, the German surrendered, he had no plan. The news of the capitulation reached him at Sampigny, where he was meditating amidst the ruins of his villa, wrecked by German cannon. From Sampigny, the Quai d'Orsay was warned by telephone to do nothing. The victory, dearly purchased at best, was thus without advantage as a consequence. "Even when Poincaré catches the right train, he misses the right station," an Italian diplomat remarked—and the jest was fair.

Moreover, intent upon the Ruhr, Poincaré forgot the financial situation of his own country. On the morrow of his failure to collect German reparations with bayonets, he was forced to ask Frenchmen to pay in taxes for the policy which he had guaranteed to produce revenues. But the people who had accepted his logic, easily and instantly repudiated the logician when he led them into the most complete of all fallacies.

In the popular sense, Poincaré is the last villain in the drama which begins at Sarajevo and ends at Locarno. He is the last public man to satisfy the universal craving for a criminal statesman or a guilty people as a simple and easily comprehensible explanation for an international tragedy. But, like all the other figures which for a few months or years have performed this necessary service for the credulous millions, he is in all respects inadequate for the rôle.

In the public life of Poincaré, it is the Rhineland episode which is at once the most significant and the most revealing. Following the occupation of the Ruhr in the summer and autumn of 1923, there broke out in the occupied area a series of disturbances which disclosed the Separatist conspiracy.

If the local authors of this "affair" were German renegades, it was nevertheless planned in Paris. It was a movement which had no real or spontaneous basis in the wish or will of the millions of German people living in the region dominated by French bayonets. It was no more than an effort to translate into reality, by the use of thugs and blacklegs, that Foch plan which had been proposed at the Paris Peace Conference itself.

The effort to give it the character of a local struggle for autonomy was futile. For, if Maurice Barrès and a few romantic French patriots still capitalized the welcome which had greeted the soldiers of the French Revolution, when they had arrived at the Middle Rhine a century and a quarter before, in the Rhineland itself that memory was no more vital than that of the legions of Cæsar which had once patrolled the same region. Mangin had tried the same thing in the days of the Peace Conference, and Clemenceau had savagely repressed him.

What was undertaken was neither better nor worse than what the Germans had attempted, when they strove to separate the Walloons and Flemings in the period of their occupation of Belgium. It was the same form of violence inspired by a similar purpose. But in the Rhineland and the Palatinate there was not even a difference of race to supply an outward warrant for what was in fact without justification in both cases.

Nothing that France did in all the post-war period is so completely lacking in all possible justification as this Separatist operation. The "Black Horror of the Rhine" was by comparison only a stupidity without really evil effects, despite all the propaganda explosion it precipitated. Had the Separatist plot succeeded, even temporarily and in outward appearance, the evil precedents of Alsace-Lorraine would have been far outdistanced.

Yet in all the months when this mean and wretched conspiracy was going forward, Poincaré in Paris closed his eyes to it. He would not receive Dorten, the chief French tool, but he permitted the French military and civil authorities to become accessories to the crime. When, at last, the operation degenerated into mere violence and the "liberators" plundered banks to obtain funds to finance the sinking cause, the soldiers who intervened in the name of order and decency were criticized from Paris. Always, too, Poincaré, the man of action, was in reality busy constructing his alibi.

"If we did for ourselves what we do for our country, what would people say of us?" This word of Cavour applies to Poincaré. But while the former President was always willing to do for France what Cavour had done for Italy and Bismarck for Germany, he had neither the vision of the one nor the strength of the other. Accordingly, when the Separatist movement collapsed and the German populations took bloody toll of the traitors in the shambles of Pirmasens, not only had the reputation of France suffered, but its prestige had been lowered.

Thus when one comes at last to analyze the fact of Poincaré, nothing is more necessary than to perceive that, while he is universally denounced by all liberal-minded men and women as a man of violence and an exponent of force, he is, in reality, far more accurately appraised by those who actually believe in the principle of the strong hand. "He is a lath painted to look like iron," was the bitter word of André Tardieu, and the comment is illuminating.

Had Poincaré actually been what millions still believe him, had he been strong, ruthless, inflexible, as in the legend, while he might have done his country and Europe incredible and enduring harm, the history of the period would have been far different. France and Europe were saved, not because a strong man failed in pursuing a policy of violence, but because a timid man was driven at last by the logic of his own words and against his own will to play a rôle for which he had not one single qualification.

All the inner meaning of the Ruhr, all the realities of this great explosion, are unintelligible, unless it be perceived that, while Poincaré used the words of a dictator, in fact, so far from being a man of force, his timidity was beyond exaggeration. Thus he brought discredit upon a method which, in stronger and abler hands, might have led Europe to utter and enduring ruin.

Napoleon, Bismarck, even Mussolini might have made the Ruhr a tragic reality; thanks to Poincaré, it was never more than a ghastly farce. To portray Raymond Poincaré as a master criminal in this final scene is as grotesque as to equip Mrs. Partington with the trident instead of the broom.

CHAPTER SIXTEEN

GENOA AND CHANAK

OF ALL the years which separate Versailles from Locarno, none is more difficult to visualize in retrospect than 1922, because none seems so simple and unmistakable and yet none was more confused and marked by so many indirections. Viewed on the surface, all things seem to march steadily toward the inevitable tragedy which was the occupation of the Ruhr. Yet in reality there was neither order nor sequence.

For the world at the moment and thereafter, the coming of Poincaré seemed the sure preface to violence. Yet Poincaré himself arrived satisfied that his mere presence would make coercion unnecessary. But in one thing he always saw eye to eye with his fellow countrymen. France had called him to break the power of Lloyd George in Europe. To this task he addressed himself instantly.

The first encounter was at Boulogne in February. Poincaré had endeavoured to prevent any meeting. For him, an exchange of notes was always preferable. But Lloyd George, who accomplished everything at close range, insisted upon a personal encounter. At the meeting, however, Poincaré coldly and a little roughly laid down his terms. Briand, at Cannes, had pledged France to attend a conference at Genoa; Poincaré at Boulogne acknowledged the obligation.

But at the same time he imposed conditions which were, in effect, fatal for all Lloyd George's grandiose plans. Neither reparations nor Paris treaties were to be discussed. The presence of Russia was not to constitute a *de jure* recognition of the Soviet government. Thus, from the outset, Poincaré had done much to make Genoa futile; he continued on this line after Boulogne as before.

Having temporarily disposed of Genoa, too, Poincaré opened the question of the British guarantee. For France he rejected the Cannes proposal, the unilateral guarantee which placed his country in the position of a protected and therefore of a dependent nation. He proposed, instead, a formal alliance, extending not for ten years, as in the Cannes proposal, but for a generation. Two great powers were to unite as France and Russia had combined long before the World War.

But such an alliance was totally foreign to all British instinct and tradition. Nor was it less unpopular in the present circumstances of Europe. Many if not all Englishmen felt that, in view of what had happened at Paris, Britain was morally if not legally bound to guarantee French security. The project was unpopular, but public acceptance was possible. On the other hand, a partnership which bound Britain to all the consequences and responsibilities of French Continental policy was utterly out of the question. Thus the Cannes proposal lapsed. But Lloyd George was left with no hold upon France, and at Chanak he would presently need French military support.

Postponed by an Italian Cabinet crisis, for Italy was now sinking into that incoherence which a few months later launched Mussolini upon his march to Rome, the great Genoa Conference assembled only in April. No international gathering was ever more widely advertised and none less carefully prepared. It was, in fact, Lloyd George's last bid for European leadership, and as such Europe recognized it. But the refusal of Poincaré to attend in person was an opening blow. Barthou, who did represent France, lacked both authority and importance. From Paris, Poincaré directed everything.

In Lloyd George's brilliant forecasts, Genoa was to be the launching of a concerted programme of European economic reconstruction. Backed by Italian Socialism and spurred on by British Liberal and Labour elements, the British Prime Minister planned to bring Russia back into the economic and financial world. Germany, too, was to be received on something like a basis of equality. A mutual pact of non-aggression was to crown the economic achievements.

But at the very outset of the Conference, Russia and Germany suddenly confronted the astounded delegates with the accomplished fact of a treaty of alliance, done at Rapallo, near Genoa, in the first days of the gathering. No bolt from the blue ever fell more unexpectedly or more fatally. Panic followed the first rumours of the agreement. France, Poland, Czecho-Slovakia, Rumania, and Belgium were all equally alarmed.

For France, the alliance became instantly a military compact. It was a double threat to French security, since it menaced France directly and Poland as well. Indeed, the whole territorial system of Middle Europe, created at Paris in 1919, seemed placed in jeopardy. No protestations of Wirth and Rathenau, representing Germany, no assurances offered by Chicherin and Rakovsky, speaking for Soviet Russia, could enlist credence or diminish apprehension. Instantly and permanently Poland, the Little Entente, and Belgium took sides with France.

Thus, actually, in the second week, the Genoa Conference was wrecked. The Germans, who had thought to fortify their insecure position by this diplomatic *coup*, were henceforth barred from Russian discussions. Although Lloyd George never showed greater skill or more amazing genius than in the days which followed the disclosure, he had in fact been ruined by the countries which he had undertaken to restore to European standing.

Nor was the spectacle of Genoa invested with greater dignity, when, presently, the scandal of oil crept into the discussions. The French and Belgians alleged that the Germans and British were actually seeking to obtain, at Russian hands, lands which had before the war been Belgian. However preposterous the charge, in the poisoned atmosphere of Genoa it found credence, and in America it achieved acceptance.

Finally, in the midst of all other incoherencies, Poincaré, speaking in his native Bar-le-Duc to "Frenchmen of the frontier," solemnly warned Germany that, if performance did not precede the arrival of May 31st, one more ultimatum date, France would act. While he expressed the hope that the British would march with the French, Poincaré clearly indicated that France would, if necessary, act alone.

This was, in reality, the final blow. Genoa did not exactly die, it flickered out. Absolute failure was covered by the programme of a reconvening at The Hague. But this pretence deceived no one. At Genoa a battle had been fought between France and Britain, between Lloyd George and Poincaré. Victory belonged to the French Premier who from Paris had reduced the Conference to futility.

From Genoa, Lloyd George returned as Napoleon from Moscow. His prestige was fatally shaken. His country was becoming alarmed at the incoherence and chaos of foreign relations. It was wearying of never-ending conferences which ended nothing. It felt keenly practical isolation and increasing impotence in Europe. If the Liberal and Labour elements had encouraged Lloyd George in his negotiations with the Bolshevists, the Tory "Die Hards" had never ceased to condemn them. Finally domestic conditions continued to worsen, unemployment endured, trade did not improve.

On his return, too, Lloyd George met an American refusal to go to The Hague far more precise and pointed than the original refusal to attend the Geneva meeting. Neither the American government nor the American people were prepared to deal with Russia. They regarded the sacrifice of principles incident to the Geneva conversations with the Soviet as both wicked and futile. In all things Russian, Washington "saw red," and in America Geneva had been counted a Russian triumph.

Thus to the final disappointment of a definite Amercan refusal to share in European economic reconstruction there was added the sting of an American condemnation of the method by which reconstruction had been undertaken. And although probably not by design, the note of Mr. Hughes, which was reinforced by a public speech of Mr. Hoover, at once gave American endorsement to the Russian policy of Poincaré and to Tory criticisms of Lloyd George's course.

Moreover, Lloyd George's position was further complicated by the arrival of the first clear and unmistakable hints from Washington that the Harding Administration purposed to insist upon the funding and payment of the debts incurred in the United States by the Allies during and immediately following the war.

No appearance of a debt collector could have been more unwelcome than in the existing circumstances. Germany was now sinking rapidly in the fatal bog of inflation. British economic conditions were unspeakably bad. France was approaching bankruptcy as a result of the enormous expenditures incident to the reconstruction of the devastated area without German contribution. And French threats to seize the Ruhr were steadily mounting. Italy was on the verge of revolution.

In the face of the American demand, Lloyd George first permitted the publication of a proposal that Great Britain should cancel all of the debts owing it from its allies, and that, at a London Conference, the whole debt and reparations question should be settled. Debts were to be abolished, reparations reduced. But while this proposal aroused no American counter proposal of generosity, it fell dead in Britain.

Now, for the first time, Lloyd George was face to face with the fact that the United States meant to be paid. Neither he nor any other European statesman had ever before believed this. All had counted upon ultimate cancellation. Keynes had preached it in his book. Even in the Paris Peace Conference it had been suggested, and Tardieu in his description of the making of the Treaty of Versailles had asserted that at Paris Americans had encouraged the hope. Although this statement has always been denied by American representatives it is at least significant of Allied expectations.

In this situation the British Prime Minister had recourse to a step which was at once supremely clever and completely fatal. Lord Balfour had recently been in Washington. He had been equally successful in enlisting popular applause and official confidence. It was believed in England that his voice and his opinion would carry enormous weight in the United States.

Accordingly, Balfour prepared and the British government issued in July that note which at once and continuingly bedevilled the whole debt question. Never was a document prepared with greater dialectical skill, yet never did any public paper more completely fail in its purpose. What the Balfour Note actually aimed at procuring was American cancellation. But the major proposal was arrived at by an indirection which aroused all American wrath.

Transmitted to the European states which owed Great Britain money, this Balfour Note announced that while Great Britain would prefer to share in a policy of general cancellation, the American policy of collection made this impossible. Therefore the British government would restrict its claims upon its allies and Germany to sums which would just meet the American claim upon Britain.

Obviously this was another way of announcing that while a generous Britain desired to cancel its claims, a rapacious America made this impossible. European resentment was thus directed at the United States. American responsibility for all the chaos and misery in Europe was similarly established by inference and innuendo. And the purpose was patently to shame the United States into a resignation that it had been impossible hitherto to obtain by direct appeal.

The effect in the United States was, however, quite different. The Balfour Note roused a resentment nationwide. It met instant official rejection. Popular indignation was immediate and universal. Those who had favoured cancellation were as angry as those who had insisted upon integral payment. General opinion, which was hitherto unformed, took definite shape, and cancellation ceased for years to be a practical possibility.

As a result, a few months later, the Baldwin Commission had to come to Washington to arrange terms for the funding of the debt. And the Commission found America prepared to be just but with no inclination to be generous. What British diplomacy had gained in American regard at the Washington Conference was utterly sacrificed in the Balfour Note.

But if the American repercussions were ultimately disastrous, the immediate European consequences were even more serious. A conference had been called in London for July to deal with the now inevitable German default. Poincaré had promised to come. He had accepted the original British suggestion of a European cancellation and adjustment as a basis for negotiation and had prepared an elaborate plan, based on this assumption.

But the Balfour Note changed everything. Accordingly, Poincaré answered the British gesture by a violent and hasty reprisal directed at German residents of Alsace-Lorraine and German funds in French banks. The first were roughly sent across the frontier. The latter were suddenly seized. And, in fact, Poincaré's domestic position was becoming difficult because, as he had once preached action while out of power, Tardieu and other critics were now taking up the parable.

The London Conference failed, as it was always bound to fail after the Balfour Note. In fact, the American insistence upon the payment of the debt was the first of the decisive steps leading to the occupation of the Ruhr. The second was the British decision to call upon the Continental debtors to pay in accordance with the principles of the Balfour Note. For if the United States insisted upon British and French payments, if Britain in turn insisted upon French payment, nothing was more inevitable than that France should look to Germany for payment in her turn.

Since, moreover, it was now clear that German inflation, begun deliberately to escape reparations payments, had passed all control and a moratorium and a foreign loan were inevitable, Poincaré demanded that France should have productive guarantees, which meant in reality control of the earning power of the Ruhr and of German state forests. On such a programme British and French disagreement was certain, and on this issue the London Conference broke up.

In the events of this summer, too, must be clearly perceived the profound change in American opinion toward Europe. American sympathy with a Europe which was visibly peaceful and patently striving for reconstruction and conciliation was still possible. But in American eyes Europe was now engaged upon a new competition in armaments, a fresh construction of alliances. Cable dispatches emphasized all the circumstances which found expression in the Anti-French press of Britain.

Thus, for millions of Americans any remission of the Allied debts seemed the final encouragement to Europe to pursue policies which, to the American mind, had led to the World War. The billions which might be forgiven European states at the expense of the American taxpayer were bound to be turned to use in new militaristic and imperialistic adventures. Moreover, as the charges and counter charges of British and French journals had found equal credence in the United States, the implications of the Balfour Note had demolished sympathy and stimulated suspicion.

Nor was American feeling modified when Lloyd George, on his part, publicly criticized American policy, and French and British newspapers, in "leaders" and by cartoons, assailed American action. "Uncle in name and Uncle in nature" was one British jibe that travelled widely and bit deeply. But if it foreshadowed the day when "Uncle Sam" would be "Uncle Shylock," it did not promote good feeling or encourage generosity.

The London Conference failed in the first days of August. By September, the attention of Europe and the world was concentrated upon a Near Eastern crisis which for several weeks seemed to threaten a new war.

Between the Russo-Polish War of 1920 and the Greco-Turkish conflict of 1922 there are many points of resemblance, and at bottom the same incoherence in the policy of the great powers is discoverable.

Turkey had been an ally of Germany, and at Paris there had been passed upon the Turkish Empire what was in fact a sentence of death. The European lands of the Osmanli had been bestowed upon the Greek. Allied troops occupied Constantinople, and the feeble Sultan was actually a prisoner of his conquerors. By the Treaty of Sèvres, too, Britain had, under a mandate from the League of Nations, acquired Mesopotamia, Palestine, and the general control of all of the Arab lands save Syria. This fell to France. Even Armenia was marked down for an American mandate. Italian spheres of interest were recognized in the area of the Gulf of Adalia.

Following the making of the Treaty of Sèvres, at the inspiration of Lloyd George and with the consent of France, Greek troops had been hurried to Smyrna to forestall Italian occupation of this great seaport. All the territory immediately back of Smyrna was consolidated into a Greek mandate. A large Greek army was established on the Asiatic shores of the Ægean. To the Turk there was left nothing but an undefined territory lying inland in the great peninsula of Asia Minor. And at the moment Turkey was crushed, helpless, seemingly at last abolished as a factor either in European or Asiatic questions.

Lloyd George, moreover, under the spell of Venizelos, the great Greek statesman and patriot, had adopted the vast and shining programme of the Greater Greece. From the Crimean War until the first years of the Nineteenth Century, British influence had been supreme at the Golden Horn, and British power had saved the otherwise doomed empire of the Sick Man of Europe. The formation of the Triple Entente, which drew Russia and Britain together, inevitably destroyed the British position in Turkey, since at the bottom of the Russo-British association lay the tacit renunciation by Great Britain of the policy which had long forbidden the Russians to seize Constantinople and thus to obtain an outlet on the open seas. Russia, on the other hand, became a comrade of Britain in the struggle with Germany, already close at hand.

Turkey, on its part, naturally and inevitably turned to Germany. Thus, before 1914, German influence had replaced British at the Sublime Porte, and when the war came, Turkish armies fought beside German. The unhappy Gallipoli campaign had been a desperate but unsuccessful effort to open the Straits and thus restore communication between Russia and her western allies. One of the causes of the ultimate Russian collapse was this failure at the Dardanelles.

The collapse of Russia had abolished the British agreement to Russian possession of the Straits. But there was no British forgiveness for the Turk. Instead, British diplomacy and statesmanship adopted the "bag and baggage" policy of an earlier day and conceived of making Greece at once the soldier and sailor of Britain in the Near East. The new Greece rising on either side of the Ægean was to become a considerable nation. Italian and French aspirations were to be checked by British support of Hellenic territorial claims. Even Constantinople, in the end, was to fall to the country of Venizelos.

Thus, in a very real sense, Greece was to play for Britain in the Near East the rôle which Poland played for France in the north. And as Pilsudski, under French inspiration, had undertaken to reëstablish that greatest Poland, which belonged to the period of the Jagellons, Venizelos, with British support, now set out to restore the Byzantine Empire. But exactly as Britain had opposed Polish aspirations for French reasons, France and Italy were now hostile to Hellenic ambitions for British reasons.

Thus, from 1919 onward, the Turkish question became the battleground between rival purposes of the nations which had been victorious allies in the World War. Thanks to incoherence and intrigue, Turkey rallied. Mustapha Kemal Pasha seized the power from the feeble hands of the Sultan and reëstablished the Turkish capital at Angora in the heart of Anatolia. Making peace first with the Soviets, who resigned territory and transferred munitions of war, that the Turk might do battle with the western foes of the Bolshevists, Kemal then turned to France and Italy.

At the moment France had no available troops to defend the Syrian mandate and the long disputes over frontiers with Britain both on the side of Mosul and of Palestine had angered French opinion. Accordingly, in 1921, Franklin-Bouillon, a conspicuous French parliamentary leader, made terms with the Turks at Angora. France retired from Cilicia and south of the Bagdad Railway, surrendering certain war material to the Turks. Kemal, on his side, recognized the frontiers of Syria thus amended.

At that very moment when Italy was supporting Britain at Genoa, in the following year, the Facta Cabinet made a similar treaty with Kemal. Italian forces were withdrawn from the mainland of Asia, the Adalian Sphere was abandoned in return for certain commercial and mineral concessions. Italy, moreover, followed the example of France in assisting Kemal in acquiring arms for his approaching battle with the Greeks.

Meantime, in Athens there had been a new revolution. If a game of golf had transformed the course of events in the west of Europe, a monkey bite now revolutionized history in the Near East. After Constantine had been exiled Venizelos had placed a younger son on the throne. But the bite of a pet monkey was fatal to the latest Alexander to reign in Macedon. Thereafter, the supporters of Constantine successfully overthrew the Venizelos régime and Constantine returned as king.

Constantine had been an ally of Germany. French

marines had, on his urgings, been murdered in the royal park in Athens in the critical days of 1915. Therefore, French hostility to any extension of Greece was instantly strengthened, and French support of the Turk similarly extended. Hitherto, the French had opposed Greece because of their quarrel with the British; now there was a German reason.

Meantime, in two campaigns the Greek armies had just missed seizing Angora. At the moment of their farthest advance, Greek soldiers were almost in sight of the last remaining citadel of the Osmanli. But just as Pilsudski had failed at Kiev, because the undertaking was totally beyond the resources of Poland at that hour, Greek commanders were compelled to abandon a similarly grandiose adventure.

By the winter of 1921–22, it was plain to all military observers that the Greek armies, which remained far inland at Eski Sher on the railway line which comes south from Constantinople, could not long hold their ground. Kemal's armies were growing daily, and from Russian, Italian, and French sources were acquiring war material. British support of the Greeks was growing less and less adequate.

Actually Greece was becoming exhausted. The country had been at war almost continuously since 1912. Many of the soldiers now doing duty in Asia had been under arms for ten years. The country, the people, the army were worn out. An appeal to the great powers to permit Greek occupation of Constantinople, as a sign of western support, was approved by Lloyd George but vetoed by the French and Italians.

Salvation for the Greek army was now dependent upon immediate retreat. But instead it was encouraged to hang on for a few months. A new conference at Venice was planned, and Lloyd George calculated that there peace might be made and Turkish acceptance of the Sèvres Treaty obtained in return for the Greek abandonment of Asia, which was now universally perceived to be inevitable.

Kemal, however, anticipated the Venetian affair by a swift and deadly offensive. In a few days the Greek troops were in wild flight which ended only when Greek transports had transferred them to European shores. Turkish troops pursued rapidly. Smyrna fell and disappeared in a fearful conflagration. Presently Kemal's army arrived at the Straits, and Turkish patrols approached Chanak, on the south side of the Bosporus, where British troops covered Constantinople itself.

Flushed with victory, Kemal now demanded the immediate and unconditional evacuation of Constantinople and all of Thrace up to the Maritza River. An attack upon the insignificant Allied garrisons in and about Constantinople was threatened if evacuation were not immediate. British and even European prestige was instantly threatened, and behind Kemal, all Asia, all Islam observed with wonder and delight the incredible resurgence of the Osmanli.

In this critical moment, Lloyd George lost his presence

of mind. He appealed to Paris and to Rome for military support. He even invited the Jugo-Slavs and the Rumanians to send troops to the Straits and undertake a new war for British advantage. He flung forth a frantic appeal to Canada, Australia, and South Africa for colonial contingents to share in a new Gallipoli adventure.

But Paris and Rome responded by ordering their troops to quit the Asiatic shores. The French Prime Minister had offered Lloyd George a military alliance after Boulogne and it had been rejected haughtily. As for the Italians, they could not forget that the whole struggle had its genesis in Lloyd George's hasty decision to let Greek troops and not Italians hold Smyrna. Rumania remembered that, at Genoa, Lloyd George had at least hinted at the return of Bessarabia to Russia. Jugo-Slavia recalled Lloyd Georgian denunciations of Balkanization in Middle Europe. As for the Dominions, they greeted the invitation to a new European war coldly, and the memory of the appeal had evil consequences later. At the same moment, too, all the British Mohammedan subjects in India, all the Islamic populations in Mesopotamia, Palestine, and Egypt espoused the Turkish cause. The loyalty of Britain's Mohammedan subjects was instantly shaken.

In this situation there was nothing for it but to surrender to the Turk. For days the danger of actual hostilities was very great. General Harington, commanding the British troops, faced the Turks boldly, and British naval resources were mobilized. But in the end the Armistice of Mudania confirmed all the demands of Kemal. Within a month, Turkish troops were to occupy all the Greek territory up to the Maritza. Constantinople was to be restored to Turkish control.

At the same time, Kemal proclaimed his purpose to expel the Hellenic populations from Asia. Thus a million and a half of Greeks, whose ancestors had lived on the Asiatic shores of the Ægean and the Black seas since the remote age of the Persian invasions, were suddenly uprooted and exiled. The unhappy Sultan fled for protection to a British battleship. Kemal promptly executed the Turkish public men who had proposed surrender to the Christian and acceptance of the Treaty of Sèvres.

No more humiliating surrender of Europe to Asia was ever made. No more striking example of the weakness of the recent victors in the World War could be imagined, for Kemal never commanded a hundred thousand troops. Moreover, from one end of Asia to the other, this exposure of western weakness had immediate and continuing repercussions. The Bolshevists were encouraged to resume their offensive, this time on the Asiatic front. Later, Chinese events were evil reminders of the significance of Chanak, and even to the present hour the consequences of the ignominious surrender endure.

And on the morrow of Chanak, Lloyd George fell. A revolt within the Tory party culminated in the famous meeting at the Carlton Club where, by a decisive vote, the Conservatives decided against continuation of the

Coalition government. Balfour, Birkenhead, and Austen Chamberlain stood with Lloyd George, but Andrew Bonar Law turned against him, and this defection was fatal.

"We have been waiting for you for three years," a contemporary cartoon described Clemenceau and Woodrow Wilson as saying to Lloyd George as they greeted him at the gateway to Oblivion. And, in fact, he was the last survivor of the Paris Peace Conference; all the other considerable figures had already left the stage. But for none was the disaster so complete.

Nor did any public man quitting office ever leave to his successor a more unattractive inheritance. America had been alienated by the Balfour Note. France was embittered by the whole Anglo-French duel. Italy had been lost by the Smyrna manœuvre, and as Kemal triumphed in Asia, Mussolini entered Rome. Henceforth, for a time, Italian policy would take another direction. The Mohammedan world had been roused. British influence throughout Asia had been shattered. The Dominions had been disturbed by the Chanak appeal.

Moreover, in Europe, Germany was now in the last stages of economic and financial disintegration. French action was impending, and French power in Europe was now beyond British restraint. At home, British economic prostration continued; abroad, British prestige had sunk to the lowest point since the far-off days of the Stuarts.

CHAPTER SEVENTEEN

THE OCCUPATION OF THE RUHR

THE deadlock in London in August was the prelude to an open breach at Paris in the first days of January. Moreover, a break between France and Britain had always been the certain preface to violent French action in the case of Germany. Compromise was no longer possible between the British and French policies, because four years of Lloyd George had destroyed the confidence of the French in the loyalty of the British ally, while less than a year of Poincaré had been equally disastrous to British feeling for France.

From the morning of the Armistice, the material interests of France and Great Britain had been not only divergent but essentially opposed. There had survived on both sides of the Channel sentiments which had naturally developed as a result of the long struggle against a common foe. There remained even now in Britain not a little real sympathy for the justice of French claims, but there was a double perception that the means by which France was now seeking to satisfy her legitimate demands were at once doomed to failure and destined to have evil consequences alike for British prosperity and European peace.

Bonar Law, who succeeded Lloyd George, might have

been in other circumstances the man for the hour. He was a devoted friend of France, and the fact that he had lost a son in the war was a circumstance never without importance across the Channel. In his position as an important Cabinet officer during the war, he had many times rendered valuable service to the alliance. He was, moreover, simple, loyal, and straightforward. If he was not in any sense a great man, he was a public servant of long experience, sound judgment, and wholly worthy of the confidence he had always inspired at home and abroad.

Unfortunately, not only did Bonar Law take office at a moment of vast confusion, but also, he was already stricken with a mortal malady which was destined to compel his retirement and bring his death shortly. He was therefore physically unfit for the great task which came to his hands. Moreover, his attention was diverted by the crisis in the Near East, peculiarly menacing to the British Empire, the drudgery of a General Election, and the aggravations of the American debt question.

As a consequence, when at last he did come to Paris, in the first days of January, he brought only a memorandum prepared by the British Treasury. On its technical side, the proposal doubtless had much merit. But the situation at the moment was political before it was financial. As a consequence, not only was the British proposal rejected by the French, but by the Belgians and the Italians as well. All were equally indignant at its content.

Thus Bonar Law immediately faced a combination of three Continental states which had already, through the Reparations Commission, united in declaring Germany in technical default. This declaration prepared the legal ground for the later occupation of the Ruhr. Against participation in this adventure, the British Prime Minister set his face firmly. But he had now no alternative policy to propose. Accordingly, he wished Poincaré success in an undertaking which he believed doomed to failure, and returned to London. The press at the moment described the break as a *rupture cordiale*, but in fact it was a rupture, and cordiality could not last.

Poincaré had now no choice but to act. In France, he was assailed on one side by Briand and the moderate elements, whom he had driven out of control in the spring. He had denounced their weakness, but, in fact, where Briand had actually collected millions, he had taken in nothing. On the other side, he was assailed by Tardieu and the Nationalists, because while he had threatened force continually, he had never employed it. He had, moreover, convinced the French people that Germany could be made to pay. His strong words, which he had conceived as an end in themselves, had been accepted as a prospectus.

On the threshold of this Ruhr operation, which is, in reality, the final convulsion of the World War, it is essential to perceive the situation as it existed in fact and not as it was presented then and thereafter by the propaganda of the several nations immediately concerned or later translated by ready sympathy stirred by the operation itself.

In the first place, the French case was strong not alone in law but in justice. While France had expended upward of $6,000,000,000 for the reconstruction of the devastated area and was now on the verge of bankruptcy, Germany had paid little in the aggregate and nothing on account of reconstruction. She was now asking for a moratorium, and if this were granted, France could hope for no money payments for years; even further coal deliveries were problematical.

Germany was not now seeking a moratorium because she had been compelled to pay unreasonable sums. It was perfectly true that the figures fixed by the Reparations Commission as the total of German liability were fantastic. But what had been actually required of Germany in 1921 was only $250,000,000, plus an export tax of 26 per cent. What was demanded for 1922 was $500,000,000 plus the same tax.

Measured by the standards of the Dawes Plan, which followed German economic and industrial collapse incident to the Ruhr, these demands were not extravagant. For 1927, the Dawes requirement was $300,000,000 and the total rose thereafter sharply to $625,000,000. In fact, in the long struggle between 1919 and 1922, the actual requirements of Germany had been deflated to approximately reasonable amounts.

German inability to pay in 1922 arose from the fact

that the German government had deliberately embarked upon a policy of inflation. By this device upward of $1,000,000,000 had been raised by the sale of paper marks abroad. Inflation deprived this paper of value, and the German profit was obvious. This sum was, too, in excess of all Germany had paid in reparations, both in money and in kind, in these two years.

But in 1922, German inflation was entering the later stage. In the beginning, German manufacturers had been able to undersell rivals in the world market. The domestic debt had been practically eliminated. A fictitious prosperity had been general. But now collapse was at hand. The "flight from the mark" was general. It was no longer possible to pay reparations and it was necessary that Germany should obtain a foreign loan to enable the adoption of a plan of stabilization.

Nevertheless, inflation had been at bottom a device to avoid reparations payments and spare the German people from taxation to the extent to which both the British and the French people were taxing themselves. In the situation, Germany did not come with clean hands into that court from which she now demanded relief. Only on the assumption that Germany was wrongfully held to pay any reparations could her actual case be held sound. And the Germans themselves had never disputed the legality or justice of the claim against themselves in the matter of French reconstruction.

In the existing situation, too, Poincaré did not propose to send an army into the Ruhr. All his several proposals and the final programme which was notified to Germany in advance, envisaged nothing but the dispatch of a certain number of civilians, engineers, and other experts. Their mission was precisely that of the representatives of a court sent to supervise the assets of a fraudulent bankrupt. Only a few squads of soldiers were to be sent along to protect the civilians.

The essential vice of the Poincaré proposal lay in the assumption that the German people would submit to this operation passively. In the existing state of the German mind, no one properly outside of Bedlam could have believed this. But Poincaré did and his action was based on this assumption. Every soldier in France warned him against it. The military authorities prepared for him an elaborate scheme of real military occupation. But Poincaré rejected it.

Thus, different as it was in many essential characteristics from the German invasion of Belgium, the French occupation of the Ruhr, as Poincaré devised it, had one thing in common with the earlier operation. The authors of both schemes totally failed to reckon with the same factor. Both left out of account the possibility of resistance by the population and the effect of this resistance upon the public opinion of the world.

Morally, no people ever had a better case against another than the French against the German in January, 1923. But the difficulty always lay in the fact that a resort to force would infallibly, if wholly irrationally, destroy the moral advantage. Thus the military occupation of any territory, the use of military weapons against unarmed and helpless populations, is always a stupid affair. The spectacle of thousands of soldiers, provided with machine guns, supported by artillery, reinforced by tanks, patrolling defenceless cities, breaking popular resistance by musket fire which kills innocent and guilty alike, occupying schoolhouses for barracks, expelling hundreds of civilians, resorting to petty aggressions and minor oppressions, can, in the nature of things, excite but one feeling in the outside world.

Poincaré did not plan this sort of operation. When inevitable resistance immediately transformed the character of the occupation, he was totally surprised. Because he had not foreseen resistance, the military operation was badly executed. Thus, the German people, who are a military nation with a genius for organization, so far from being impressed by French force, watched French blundering with utmost contempt. But, by contrast, the world outside at once accepted the fact that what happened had occurred "according to plan."

Poincaré's responsibility for what took place in the Ruhr is beyond denial. But if the episode itself is to be intelligible, it must be seen that his responsibility is not to be compared with that of the assassin who sets out deliberately, gun in hand, to commit murder, but only with that of the proverbial bungler who kills because he does not know the gun is loaded.

When one turns to the German aspect of the case, it is equally essential to perceive that the Ruhr was the logical and inescapable consequence of the will to resist the Treaty of Versailles, which had been disclosed steadily, from the moment when German signature was forced under the threat of immediate invasion by Allied armies. The question of the reasonableness or unreasonableness of the Allied claims was beside the point. The German people had refused to accept the Treaty.

Viewed with the calmer judgment of a later period, it is difficult not to sympathize with the German resistance, just as it remains impossible not to recognize the justice of the French demands. No great people could conceivably accept the position of moral and political inferiority which, by the Treaty of Versailles and in the manner of its application, had been imposed upon the German people.

But German resistance was in the end bound to provoke French coercion. If the original demands of the Treaty in the matter of reparations had been beyond reason, German determination to evade all conditions, financial and military, equally overpassed the limit. Sooner or later, collision was inescapable. British efforts had achieved much in reducing French demands, but they had never made real progress in modifying German purpose.

When, moreover, the German government undertook to resist the Ruhr occupation, that was open war. Had the resistance been successful, Germany would have escaped from all financial consequences of her defeat, and France would have lost the war. Moreover, the possibility of such an outcome was always in the German mind, after the battle had been joined. At bottom there was absolute justice in the underlying objective of each people; the supreme tragedy of the Ruhr was that for both people; it insured ruin without advancing the legitimate aspirations of either.

Bonar Law had shared Poincaré's delusion that Germany would not resist. He promptly recognized, when resistance came, that mediation was impossible. Thus he stood aside. His successor, influenced by Curzon, was less well advised. Once entered upon, the struggle of the Ruhr was in the nature of things bound to go to a decision.

Following the Anglo-French rupture events moved rapidly. The Reparations Commission again voted Germany in default, this time generally. France, Belgium, and Italy associated themselves with the decision. Sir John Bradbury angrily dissented. He also protested against the legality of the proposed action in the Ruhr. Henceforth, this issue was a subject of dispute between jurists of the several powers. The British argued that action could only be taken after unanimous decision. The French, Belgian, and Italian governments insisted that each power was authorized to take action and pointed to the fact that Lloyd George himself had threatened separate action on one occasion. Lloyd George's explanation that his threat was a "bluff" did not materially strengthen Curzon's contention.

This dispute was, however, of little actual importance. France and Belgium were determined to act, and Italy consented to send engineers, thus giving moral support. In the second week in January, Paris notified Berlin that a civilian mission was to be sent into the Ruhr. It was expressly stated that neither the population nor the industries were to be disturbed provided there was no resistance.

Thus, at last, the long-threatened Ruhr excursion was undertaken. As far back as 1920 it had been a subject of daily discussion, and in 1921 French troops had moved into Dusseldorf, Ruhrort, and Duisburg, where they still remained. Always, too, it had been recognized on every side that the Ruhr was the very heart of German industrial existence. If it passed to foreign control, Germany itself was at the mercy of the occupying power.

Meantime, changes had taken place within Germany. Wirth had fallen. In his place had come Cuno who was neither a politician nor a diplomat but a plain business man. Having recently visited both the United States and Great Britain, Cuno had reached the conclusion that neither country approved of a Ruhr occupation and that both would intervene officially to prevent it. The rupture at Paris had confirmed this impression as to Britain. Mr. Hughes's New Haven protest had similarly strengthened his American hopes. The resolution in the United States Senate calling for the repatriation of the American troops on the Rhine seemed a further straw. Cuno was, therefore, resolved to fight.

Thus when Poincaré began his "invisible" occupation, resistance was immediate. The Coal Syndicate, which directed the vast mine fields, retired to Hamburg. The miners were called from the pits. A general strike paralyzed the whole Ruhr district. Presently it extended to the railways and transport and communication were similarly brought to a halt. From Berlin, Cuno proclaimed an end of coal deliveries under the Treaty and appealed to London, Washington, to the world at large.

German resistance, however, with equal promptitude transformed the French operation. In a few days 40,000 troops were in the Ruhr. The number rose rapidly to 100,000. Martial law was proclaimed. Disorders in Essen led to violent repression and blood was shed. The Ruhr was isolated and the coal supply of Germany interrupted. Further sanctions were later taken in the form of occupations of railway junctions on German territory facing Strassburg.

Thus, with no further disguise, began the siege of Germany. French military power had seized the vital elements in the industrial life of the country. Slowly but surely the whole German machine was now destined to run down. As in the case of every other siege, the end was always assured unless the garrison were relieved. But in this hope Cuno fought on.

In the early weeks, however, Bonar Law deliberately stood aside. In the summer, Baldwin replaced the dying Prime Minister. Then began a long-range duel between the British Foreign Office and the Quai d'Orsay. Curzon in London and Poincaré in Paris showered each other with notes. Baldwin, after a friendly visit to Paris, from which much was expected, drifted into a hostile attitude. There was even a threat that Britain would deal directly with Germany.

But once more British efforts were paralyzed by German policy. Advised from London to make a peace proposal, the Germans came forward with terms as impossible as those which had fatally compromised Lloyd George in the days of the London Conference of 1921. Under British scolding, the offers were revised, but British public opinion was affronted by this performance. Always, too, there was strong sympathy for France in certain British quarters, and nowhere was it more marked than in that Die-hard corner of the Tory party whence had come the revolt which had overturned Lloyd George.

In the duel between Curzon and Poincaré, the former was fatally handicapped because he lacked power to enforce his threats, while the latter had behind him the strength of 750,000 bayonets. Conceited, pompous, easily appearing arrogant, Curzon presently became ridiculous in the eyes of the world, because he was unable to support his strong words by even the feeblest of actions. In the actual exchange of notes, Poincaré invariably scored. Instead of shaking French resolution, the British Foreign Secretary only compromised British prestige.

The battle endured to the end of September. During its progress, the German misery mounted rapidly. If the working men and the farmers suffered comparatively little, the mass of the middle class were fatally afflicted. All who lived on fixed incomes or had placed their savings in government securities and war loans were totally ruined. Misery and starvation were general. In the last stages, the inflation phenomenon passed all belief.

But, after midsummer, it was no longer to be questioned that Germany must surrender. Relief was not to come either from Washington or London. Only war could break French determination. The attempt to finance the struggle, to maintain a population of six millions in idleness, was totally beyond German capacity. Not only the Ruhr industries, but those of all Germany were paralyzed. The ruin which had now overtaken the country has hardly been paralleled in modern times, and the suffering of masses of the German people were great enough to have satisfied even the sternest of Germany's judges.

Presently, Cuno fell, and he was replaced by Gustav Stresemann. Of the great figures of Locarno, Stresemann was thus the first to take the stage. But although Stresemann at once began to make peace proposals, Poincaré long remained unmoved. His obstinacy was never more clearly disclosed. Now he demanded unconditional surrender, witnessed by the withdrawal of all government encouragement of the Ruhr resistance. As the

Ruhr had been war, so he insisted upon capitulation as complete as that which had terminated the struggle of 1918.

Meantime, at the same moment, the attention of the world was directed toward the Separatist movements taking place in the Rhineland and the Palatinate. Momentary success seemed to insure destruction of German unity. British indignation was outspoken. Curzon ordered an official investigation by a British diplomat and made the Clive Report a basis for bitter indictment.

In the closing months of 1923, the completeness of the French victory was thus disclosed on all sides. Germany now seemed absolutely broken to the wheel. But never was a harvest of hate more terrifying. It was to find expression in the May Election of 1924, when all moderate and Republican parties opened to right and to left, and on the one hand the Communists, and on the other the Monarchists, took political toll for Allied performances in the Ruhr. Moscow and Potsdam rightly celebrated the victory Paris claimed.

Moreover, if Poincaré had won, his triumph was wholly Pyrrhic. If victory without peace had come in 1918, success without profit was the result of 1923. Germany was now industrially, economically, financially ruined. If, after long months, the French and Belgian occupying forces had been able to reorganize operation and to restore coal deliveries during much of the time French as well as German plants had been closed down, and the economic life of France had suffered correspondingly.

But, beyond all else, Poincaré had not found reparations in the Ruhr. He had won a political victory, so far as the French public opinion was concerned, but, by the close of 1923, the French people had no stomach for new conflicts and no appetite for additional glory. While the battle lasted, national pride and patriotic spirit had been roused. But when it was over, the French people calculated their losses, not only in the sympathy of the world, but in the March panic in the collapse of the franc.

There was no actual ending to the Ruhr conflict. Timidity and obstinacy prevented Poincaré from seizing upon the surrender of September 27th alike as the evidence of complete triumph and the opportunity for a direct settlement with Germany. After that, the situation drifted out of his hands. The occupation forces remained, but gradually the character of the occupation changed. Not, however, until a year after the adoption of the Dawes Plan did Essen, Dusseldorf, and Duisburg see the last of the "horizon blue" uniforms.

While the siege of Germany progressed, too, at Lausanne, Europe was forced to consent to humiliations at the hands of the victorious Turk which were utterly destructive of the prestige of the West in all of the Near and Far East. By the treaty signed on the shores of the Lake of Geneva, Turkey escaped from all the servitudes of a century of failing power. Thereafter, breaking with all tradition, Kemal at one moment adopted the political forms of Europe and successfully expelled Europe from the westernmost regions of Asia.

The withdrawal of the American troops from the Rhine, following the French entrance into the Ruhr, formally terminated all American participation in European affairs. When General Allen hauled down the Stars and Stripes from Ehrenbreitstein, the first American chapter in European history came to an end. Moreover, American departure at one time cleared the way for the futile French Separatist operations and encouraged German resistance, which was equally hopeless.

Finally, to complete the story of the year's misfortunes for Europe, the murder of an Italian general serving on a commission to fix the Greco-Albanian boundary led in September to the famous descent upon Corfu, the bombardment of the ancient citadel, and thus to the first of that long series of demonstrations by which Mussolini was now to disclose the fact that Italy could no longer be counted negligible in European affairs and that the Mediterranean Question had resumed its place on the agenda of European discussions.

PART FIVE

TO LOCARNO

CHAPTER EIGHTEEN

THE BANKRUPTCY OF NATIONALISM

THE closing weeks of 1923 were beyond question the darkest since the termination of the actual fighting in the war. In the Allied countries they were the gloomiest since the German successes of March and April, 1918. The occupation of the Ruhr and its later consequences seemed to disclose, not merely the bankruptcy of European statesmanship, but the prelude to a decline of European civilization itself. On all sides there was the rapidly mounting belief that the great conflict had produced evils and wrought destruction which were irremediable.

From Versailles to the Ruhr, Europe had, on the whole, moved with even and steady step toward political and economic disintegration. Each year and every month had added to the extent of political disarray within national frontiers, and international incoherence equalled national disorder. Hope aroused in the first hours of calm following the long conflict upon the battlefield seemed now well-nigh extinguished.

The mere record of the passing years discloses the direction of events. Thus, in 1920, Bolshevism was only checked before Warsaw by a miracle as complete and unexpected as that of the Marne. The long duel between France and Great Britain over the application of the Treaty of Versailles began. The Kapp Putsch gravely threatened and permanently compromised the weak German Republic. The American election, following the rejection of the Versailles Settlement by the United States Senate, abolished most of the hope of American coöperation in the reconstruction of Europe.

In 1921, German intransigence at London provoked partial occupation of the Ruhr. The decision of the League of Nations in the Upper Silesian dispute at one time aroused German resentment and British distrust of the League. After this decision no party and no public man in Germany could safely support any policy of fulfilment under the Treaty.

In 1922, Cannes destroyed Briand. The Washington Conference accentuated Anglo-French quarrels, while it finally extinguished hope of American return to Europe. Genoa demolished the most ambitious programme for European construction which had yet been formulated. The American demand for payment of the debts precipitated the Balfour Note, and the Balfour Note insured the final Anglo-French deadlock at London. Finally, Chanak threatened a new war, destroyed a considerable portion of the Paris Settlement, and fatally undermined European prestige in Asia and Africa alike.

Nor can it be mistaken that 1923 was the worst year in the unhappy series. The Anglo-French rupture in Paris in January was closely followed by the Ruhr occupation. The long struggle which accompanied this occupation seemed to forecast the complete disintegration of the political and economic life of the Continent. Spengler's *Decline of the West* was just issuing from the press and the title, if not the book, claimed instant attention. Meanwhile, Soviet dictatorship continued at Moscow, and the new Fascisti domination at Rome expressed itself in Mussolini's notorious Corfu adventure.

Thus, five years after the fighting had terminated on November 11, 1918, and nearly ten years after the World War had broken out, Europe seemed visibly threatened by a collective catastrophe as great as that which had overtaken and destroyed Roman civilization. Not only was international strife continuing and growing, but within many countries parliamentary democracy appeared doomed to futility and dictatorship was becoming the dangerously popular substitute for impotent parliamentarism.

Nevertheless, while the bankruptcy of statesmanship claimed universal attention, the actual bankruptcy which had now arrived was that of the Nationalism, which from the outbreak of the war to that hour had dominated in all belligerent countries. In accordance with the spirit and tradition of this Nationalism, the Treaty of Versailles had been made and, in a similar obedience to the same spirit, application of the Treaty had been attempted.

In the latter half of 1923, however, a tremendous revolution was taking place within the frontiers of several

European countries. It would perhaps be more exact to say that in this time it was at last beginning to be disclosed that a revolution had taken place. Nothing is more difficult than to mark the exact moment when a democracy changes cars. The great transformation comes slowly, imperceptibly, in the main without awakening suspicion. It is only as an accomplished fact that it finally achieves recognition.

Such a change had now taken place. The failure of the several statesmen of various countries to make peace had discredited that Nationalism which all had substantially represented. The way was now cleared for the restoration of Liberalism as a force in national political life. In the second place, mob psychology and war mentality, which had persisted since the close of the struggle, were breaking down. Weariness and misery were rapidly bringing masses of people to desire not alone peace, but even peace without victory.

No calamity of all which had followed in the train of the World War was at once so inevitable and so disastrous as that which was comprehended in the sudden and almost complete silencing of all those voices which had hitherto spoken for liberal ideas and liberal policies in all the years before the struggle. Our modern world had come to be directed by political leaders and by political principles which represented the steady shock between conservatism and liberalism. Turn and turn about, each obtained power, corrected the excesses of the other, steadied the march of legislation and of thought.

Lacking either of these mutually necessary forces, only an unstable equilibrium could exist in any country.

At the moment the war broke, Britain was governed by the Liberal party, which was liberal in nature as well as in name. It had controlled since the morrow of the Boer War, and it still expressed the will of the mass of the British people in its long programme of social reform. In France, the Parliament which confronted invasion had been elected to reduce the three-year military service. Even in the United States, Woodrow Wilson had been chosen as a result of a split between "progressive" and reactionary elements in the Republican party and was, himself, a Liberal.

Once the war did come, however, since it was, itself, the negation of everything liberal, the *dégringolade* began. In France it was instant. As the German armies approached the Marne, every voice was silenced, save that crying out for unity and resistance, for defence and victory. In Britain, liberalism lasted weakly for another year, but, as it had been unable to foresee or prevent the conflict, it was now unable to conduct or prosecute it. Therefore, Asquith fell after Loos, and with his fall the spirit of nationalism replaced that of the recent order.

Thereafter, the mass of Liberals, both in Britain and in France, rallied to the nationalistic banners, while a small minority went into outer darkness. Their opposition to the war discredited their principles and brought to them personally every possible form of denunciation and persecution. Lord Haldane, who had once, in an incautious moment, declared Germany to be his "spiritual home," was avoided as a suspect. Ramsay MacDonald, who was an unrepentant Pacifist and Socialist, was exposed to physical violence. Caillaux, who advocated peace by negotiation for France, narrowly escaped the firing squad.

By the end of the war liberalism was smashed. Liberals in all countries had either recanted and were tolerated solely on that account, or had clung to their principles and were now outside the pale. At the close of the struggle, too, the rise of the Russian Revolution brought new and general discredit. In 1917, when the first Russian revolt against the Czarist régime was proclaimed, liberalism the world over had hailed what seemed in its eyes a promise of something which might, after all, justify the destruction and misery of the conflict.

But if liberalism had cheered Russian Revolution in the hour of Kerensky, the arrival of Lenin brought to it infinite discredit. When Bolshevism disclosed its real purpose, when the world was filled with the ghastly reports of murders in Petrograd and Moscow, when Bela Kun came to Budapest, when Bavaria seemed sinking to Red anarchy, then there was born a new fear, quite as enormous as that which had prevailed during the war itself. This fear, too, gave rise to suspicions which were equally directed at the Bolshevist abroad and the Liberal at home.

It was under the double shadow of fear of Russian

Revolution, now become flaming red, and of a war psychology little moderated yet, that the Treaty of Versailles was made. The policy toward Russia and the treatment of Germany were equally determined by a state of mind which was well-nigh universal and utterly prevented effective protest by the weak and scattered remnant of the Liberal world.

Five years later, however, old fears had given place to new judgment. It was at last becoming clear beyond peradventure that the men and the methods which had won the war had proved inadequate to restore the peace. It was no longer the enormous discredit which had come to liberalism as a consequence of the events of 1914, when the war broke, and of 1918 when Bolshevism began its violent phase, that dominated the minds of the masses.

On the contrary, Europe was now filled with the evidences of the incapacity of that nationalism which had failed in every single effort to restore order. No political group had ever been allowed greater latitude in the application of their ideas than was bestowed upon the respective leaders of various countries between 1919 and 1924. Yet the failure first of the Coalition and then of the Die-hard reaction in Britain was as complete as that of the Bloc National which was based upon the Union Sacrée in France. Five fruitless and futile years stood to the discredit of those who, on the strength of their undeniable services during the war, had undertaken to restore peace.

By the winter of 1923–24. Liberalism throughout Europe had emerged literally and figuratively from prison. It was no longer suffering under a discredit which involved complete political exclusion. On the contrary, it had, almost without general appreciation, resumed its position as the natural and necessary opposition. The time had passed when it was treason to criticize the government. Denunciatory voices could no longer be silenced by the charge of Pro-Germanism or Pro-Bolshevism.

Appeals to fear or to passion could not serve to destroy a rising public protest against governmental failure. It is true that this renascent liberalism returned in a violent mood little consonant with its tradition. It had suffered far too much to come back in the spirit which is naturally associated with its name. Its denunciations of nationalism and Nationalist leaders were as violent, bitter, passionate as those other voices which for ten long years had been assailing the enemy abroad and the Liberal at home with equal fury. It had measurably been corrupted by the manners and methods which it instinctively abhorred.

Yet, at last, there was an alternative and an opposition in Europe. And along with the renaissance of liberalism there had come a change in the public mind which made an opposition useful. The people were weary of strife, they were sick of leaders who preached peace but sought it always by violent means. In fact, their actual mood was even simpler—they were tired of failure.

They had given all power to men and parties who had promised to exploit victory, to collect the profits resulting from the incredible efforts and sacrifices of masses of people.

And there had been no profits. There had been nothing but continued misery and growing chaos. Thus, while in 1923 nationalism seemed outwardly triumphant and unassailable, at the very moment when the occupation of the Ruhr appeared to many eyes as the final proof that the passions of the war continued unabated and Poincaré seemed the disclosure of a will which would definitively wreck Europe, the people of all countries had already recognized the bankruptcy of the principles and the futility of the statesmen professing them.

If Woodrow Wilson had lost the United States for the Democratic party while he was negotiating in Paris, Raymond Poincaré had just as unmistakably lost France for the Nationalists while he was occupying the Ruhr. Although to all outward appearance he was triumphing over Germany, he was actually bringing final discredit to an idea which he represented in the eyes, not alone of the outside world, but of the French people themselves.

In the closing months of 1923 in western Europe and in the British Isles, there was nowhere any surviving illusion of victory. Angora was the only capital of any state holding European territories which could display flags to celebrate national triumph. Economic ruin was visible in Britain, French bankruptcy was approaching, Germany was broken as no modern state has ever been broken. Italy had turned to a dictator. Primo di Vera was indicated in Spain and Pilsudski would presently arrive in Poland.

And the peoples of the three Allied countries, France, Belgium, and Britain, which, in 1919, had coupled their demands for peace with their insistence upon the profits of a dictated peace, were, at last, weary of the whole mess. All now desired a settlement more than all else. They were disillusioned, exhausted. Peace was no longer the prospectus of a promised land, it no longer forecast a New Europe or a New Age. It now meant solely and simply a termination of an agony which was no longer tolerable.

There, beyond all else, was the great and real revolution which had taken place in Europe in the post-war years. Idealism and nationalism were bankrupt, the one at Versailles, the other in the Ruhr. If liberalism now obtained a hearing, it was not primarily because men and women at that moment believed in Liberal doctrines; it was because liberalism represented a creed and a party which were hostile to what existed. because it was the opposition.

Thus it was true, at last, that there existed in Europe a state of mind which would permit peace to be made. Or, more exactly, Europe at the end of 1923 was come to a point at which it was possible to end the war. There was a universal perception that the men who had made the war were unable to end it. New men were thus certain now to take control and new ideas were therefore bound to replace those which had been born of the fears and passions of the struggle.

Yet it would be a mistake to see either in the new men or the new ideas which did arrive the underlying explanation of the great change. Thus, Aristide Briand, who was the conspicuous figure of Locarno and welcomed Stresemann at Geneva, was the same Briand who had fallen at Cannes, repudiated by the vast majority of his fellow countrymen. It was not Briand who had changed; indeed, in after years, he would point to Locarno as only the postponed programme of Cannes.

And in exactly the same way the return of liberalism was not itself the decisive factor after the Ruhr. It was the profound and utter change in the minds of millions of men and women of many nations in the years between Versailles and the Ruhr which prepared the way for this Liberal renaissance. Liberalism itself did not create the revolution which it expressed. Power actually came to its hands as a surprise. None was more amazed than Ramsay Macdonald, when, reading the returns of the British election in December, 1923, he saw himself Prime Minister of Great Britain.

In the narrower political sense, the war had destroyed the opposition. The rise of the Bolshevist peril had postponed all possibility of reviving it. But, by 1923, the balance was being restored. Unrestrained nationalism had failed; its failure was no longer disguised. No appeal to real or imaginary dangers in the distance could distract popular attention from immediate evils. Liberalism was not only renascent, but the peoples of many countries, and notably of Britain and France, were now prepared to use the alternative it placed within their reach.

CHAPTER NINETEEN

POLITICAL UPHEAVAL

THE British General Election of December, 1923, supplied the first authentic indication of a change of public sentiment in Europe. The arrival in Downing Street of a Prime Minister who was both a proved Pacifist and a declared Socialist constituted nothing short of a political revolution. Since Ramsay MacDonald had always opposed the war with Germany and steadily advocated recognition of Soviet Russia, his mere accession to power was proof positive that the British people had ceased to be dominated by wartime prejudices against the German and at least temporarily by post-war propaganda against the Bolshevists.

In all British political history, no election ever had results more unexpected or more bewildering. The outcome, too, demonstrated that Tory leadership had been as inept in measuring public sentiment at home as it had been impotent in protecting national interest abroad. For, however confusing the verdict of the ballot box might seem in all other details, it was at least clear that the British people had voted against the Conservative party.

The pretext for the election had been the pledge made by Stanley Baldwin to consult the British people in advance of undertaking any tariff change. But no moment could have been more unfortunate than that in which he chose to appeal to a people disgusted with the Tory record at home and abroad. Nor could any issue have been more unlucky than that which by proposing a change in the traditional free-trade policy of Great Britain, insured the combined opposition of Labour and both factions of the divided Liberal party.

In the last days of 1923, the British people were furiously angry and generally disgusted. They were angry with France because of the Ruhr. They were disgusted with the Tory government because it had not stopped the Ruhr occupation. They were critical of the Liberal party because it had not prevented the war. Affirmatively, they had not in the least accepted the Labour platform; negatively, they welcomed the existence of a Labour party as providing a stick with which to beat both the older organizations.

At this moment the British mood was one of utter disillusionment. War-born sentiment was generally dead. Sympathy with France had largely vanished. The soldiers who had been persuaded to enlist by the promise of a "better England after the war" for the moment saw England as worse and the promise as an empty trick. Confidence in the old leadership was gone; faith in the capacity of that system which had governed Britain for centuries was shaken.

Thus, when the results of the election were published, although Labour remained a minority party, popular sentiment instantly demanded that it be permitted to form a government. The wild and panic-mongering protest of various newspapers, the carefully prepared propaganda for a new coalition, the clever effort to exploit the "red" peril incident to a Socialist Cabinet, not only failed to arouse public apprehension, but hardened public will.

The British people knew that they were not "red." They recognized that a minority Labour government could not act in conformity with the spirit of Moscow, even if it desired. No social or economic revolution had taken place. Neither communism nor socialism, in the Continental sense, had suddenly conquered Britain. The results of the election merely provided a Heaven-sent and utterly anodyne method of punishing two political parties for recent and obvious failures. The British public embraced it.

Never were the maturity and sanity of the British democracy more clearly disclosed than in this instance. Labour had been rising steadily for nearly a quarter of a century. It had become the official opposition in 1922. To have denied it power in 1924 would have been to arm it with a grievance. Nor in the existing state of England and of Europe could any coalition have hoped for achievement which would long postpone inevitable Labour succession.

Only with the support of the Liberal party could Labour take office. Always its programme was at the mercy of the Liberal decision. But since both the Tory and Liberal parties had made a complete mess of foreign policy, British public sentiment was prepared to permit Labour to have its try. The British people wanted peace; they were satisfied that all the old methods to restore it had failed; MacDonald and Labour proposed a new method, within limits and without undue risks to themselves; the British people were resolved that the method should be tried.

Of all the figures who appeared on the stage of post-war Europe, none was more transient nor more important than J. Ramsay MacDonald. His stay in office lasted much less than a year. His actual power was always narrowly limited, not merely because his was a minority government, but also because, within itself, it was sharply split between the moderates and the extremists, between the former Liberals and the "wild men" from the Clydeside. Yet within this period, which was measured by weeks, MacDonald changed the whole atmosphere of European relations. Indeed, his achievement justifies the claim that it was a pacifist who at last led the way to the restoration of peace in Europe.

Personally, MacDonald is, to a degree, a Wilsonian figure, with the same underlying Scotch character. An idealist in fact, he is also, in theory at least, an internationalist, and his relation to the Protocol in the Geneva Assembly strikingly recalls President Wilson's experience with the Covenant in Paris. But unlike Woodrow Wilson, Ramsay MacDonald combines with idealism great practical experience and wide political knowledge. As a journalist and as a Labour leader, he had attended innumerable conferences in Europe. He was familiar with all Continental countries and no Prime Minister since Castlereagh was ever better acquainted with Europe, and none had known the Empire so well.

Of humble and even obscure origin, MacDonald undeniably has the manner of an aristocrat. A Socialist by conviction, he is, nevertheless, essentially Conservative and, in fact, thoroughly Scotch. "It is good to have a gentleman to deal with again," was the comment of a permanent official in the British Foreign Office, when "Romsay Mac" of Lossiemouth succeeded Viscount Curzon of Kedleston. Moreover, both in Egypt and in India, those who expected a Socialist Prime Minister to be hesitating or weak, presently received a rude awakening.

In reality, limited as he was by poor health, by an excessive sensitiveness, and by something of the same inability to associate considerable men with his undertakings which characterized Wilson, MacDonald proved, nevertheless, to be one of the greatest of British foreign ministers. He and not Lloyd George actually followed in the footsteps of Castlereagh. He and not the far cleverer Welshman understood the facts in the European situation.

As Prime Minister, MacDonald was beyond question a failure. As a party leader his record in office was far from brilliant, and he disclosed none of the qualities which made Lloyd George a supreme parliamentarian. But as Foreign Secretary his success was beyond challenge, and although he had long disappeared from power when the Locarno settlement was framed, it may fairly be claimed for him that he was the pioneer who cleared the way for Briand, Stresemann, and Austen Chamberlain.

The key to this success abroad, too, lay always in the honesty, the simplicity, and the gift of sympathetic understanding of Ramsay MacDonald. His feelings toward the German had never been influenced by wartime passion. For him the recent enemy had never been a "Hun." He saw peoples not as "guilty" but as mistaken; for him war was caused by the folly not the criminality of human beings. But if his critics and friends had expected him to display sympathy with the German, the skill, tact, and understanding which he revealed in dealing with the French took all by surprise.

To an American journalist with whom he talked immediately after taking office, MacDonald said, "Until there is a state of mind in Europe in which doubt and suspicion are absent, it is perfectly useless to discuss details. Under such circumstances, discussions become mere battles for points. Until there is an atmosphere of mutual confidence, there is no use in opening conversations."

That was in February, but in July, Herriot and Marx sat around a table with MacDonald in the historic Downing Street home of all British prime ministers.

At this conference, too, were framed the conditions which later insured French and German acceptance of the Dawes Plan. And in these few weeks, all the long-drawn thunder of the press battle between London and Paris had been silenced. Mutual recriminations, which had continued since the days of the Paris Peace Conference, were largely stilled on either side of the Channel.

The British election had taken place in December, 1923, in May of the following year a similar overturn marked a French general election. In Britain, the domestic question of tariff reform had been the nominal cause of the upset; in France, the similarly parochial issue of taxation was the precipitating cause. But in both instances the driving force was popular dissatisfaction with foreign failure.

Even before the Ruhr occupation, Poincaré had been in trouble. The return to war conditions during this struggle momentarily silenced domestic criticism, but the German surrender revived it. The sudden collapse of the franc in March produced a panic and demonstrated the complete failure of the Ruhr policy. In April, an accidental division in the Chamber left the government in the minority. Millerand persuaded Poincaré to continue, and the Premier remade his Cabinet. The new ministry disclosed more liberal tendencies, and notes between Paris and London revealed Poincaré in a changed and chastened mood.

But it was too late. The French people had followed

Poincaré to failure, but they were now aware of the extent of the failure. If the Premier had given France a new victory over Germany and consolidated the French political position in Europe, the victory had been accompanied by a new and terrifying revelation of German passion, while French influence on the Continent had been attained at the cost of British and American sympathy. Moreover, the price of glory was now disclosed in impending tax bills.

Like the British people the French were disillusioned. Everything they had expected from victory seemed now beyond attainment. All the glittering promises successive premiers had held out, all the pledges to make Germany pay, were now disclosed as empty. Taxation, long postponed on the expectation of German reparations, had now to be accepted. Victory had brought neither reparations nor security as the French people had hoped for both in 1918. By contrast, the occupation of the Ruhr had demonstrated to the full satisfaction of the French people that neither reparations nor security could be obtained by that method.

The French people were now prepared to make peace with Germany on conditions which would have been utterly unacceptable to them five years before. They were weary of strife, disgusted with leadership which in recent years had only brought new disappointments. They still insisted that Germany must pay something and that French security should be established. But, in the matter of reparations, they no longer hoped for the billions of 1919. As for security, they at last recognized it was attainable only through a British guarantee. Any British assurance, too, was patently contingent upon settlement with Germany.

The May election, which led to the defeat of Poincaré and the Bloc National, did not disclose any great change in votes. In this respect, it followed the British precedent. Again, while throughout his stay in Downing Street MacDonald was always at the mercy of the Liberals, three successive French premiers were now to depend upon the support of the Socialists for survival, and Léon Blum, who led the Socialist group in the Chamber of Deputies, became the *éminence grise* of the coalition.

Incoherent as was this new majority in the Chamber, composed of a fusion of radical Republican and Socialist parties described as the Cartel des Gauches, it did represent a spirit far different from that of the Bloc National which had been elected on the crest of war emotions and patriotic fears. In point of fact, the new Chamber of 1924 fairly closely recalled that of 1914, which had been in a real sense liberal. Thus, to a striking degree, France reverted to her pre-war political state of mind.

The temper of the new Chamber was promptly disclosed in the refusal to coöperate with the President of the Republic. Briand had not forgiven the Cannes conspiracy; all the Cartel leaders were indignant at Millerand's efforts to assist the Bloc National in the recent election. After a brief resistance, Millerand surrendered ignominiously and departed from the Élysée Palace, to which he had come after the Polish victory. Later amnesties bestowed upon Caillaux and Malvy, who had suffered at the hands of Clemenceau for alleged "defeatism" during the war, were equally indicative of the change in feeling.

As its first Premier, the Cartel des Gauches elected Edouard Herriot, "perpetual" mayor of Lyon and the leader of the largest party in the coalition. While Herriot may very fairly be termed a Liberal, he is a much less considerable figure than MacDonald. Clumsy, personally well intentioned, honestly and sincerely devoted to the policy of conciliation in foreign relations, Herriot is, nevertheless, politically a weak and ineffective man. During all his year of power, he was pulled backward and forward by the divergent interests within the Cartel. His ultimate fall precipitated by the Polish question was chiefly due to hopeless mismanagement of the financial problems.

In 1924, however, Herriot's usefulness lay precisely in the fact that he was both by nature and because of the political circumstances of the moment totally hostile to the foreign policy of Poincaré. In addition, he immediately acquired both the trust and affection of MacDonald. As a result, when, later, French opinion was dangerously roused over false reports of concessions made by Herriot in London, MacDonald in person hastened to Paris to save the French Premier by categorical denial. The innate kindliness and simplicity of Herriot similarly won the confidence of Marx. Thus he played a real, if subordinate, rôle in the London Conference which adopted the Dawes Plan.

Behind Herriot, too, there was always Briand. His party, to which Painlevé also belonged, had joined the Cartel. At the moment, his rôle was inconsiderable and he remained deliberately in the background, but he was, in the French phrase, "indicated." From the outset, it was appreciated that Painlevé would follow Herriot, but after Painlevé, Briand would come quickly.

In domestic affairs, Herriot's failure was even more complete than that of MacDonald. Under the pressure of the more radical elements in the Cartel, he revived the old controversies with the Church, which had shaken France before the war. His handling of the French finances was such as to insure later disaster. National unity which had been created during the war disappeared and political strife and passion were roused. But at the same time, Herriot did restore French position abroad. By his course at London and at Geneva, the unhappy consequences of Poincaré's foreign policy were abolished and the legend of a militaristic France exploded.

"You have seen how we made war, you will now see how we make peace." Jean Giraudoux, the brilliant French novelist also become an official in the Quai D'Orsay, declared in 1924. Within limits, this is a fair statement of what was undertaken by Herriot and continued under Painlevé. But it was only in the far more competent hands of Briand that the policy of conciliation was carried to success. No such success, too, would have been possible but for the political change of May, 1924. Between Poincaré and MacDonald, no real coöperation was possible. Between Marx and Poincaré a meeting could hardly have been arranged.

Almost concomitantly with the French election, another German campaign had produced diametrically opposite results. While the failure of British and French nationalistic governments had been established by the Ruhr occupation and had precipitated Liberal reactions, in Germany the policy of Poincaré had played directly into the hands of both the Nationalists and the Communists. Thus, at the precise moment when moderate men and liberal ideas were triumphing in France and Britain, reaction scored in Germany.

Fortunately, great as was the Republican disaster, the results of the German election just missed compromising the Republic. At the moment of the Ruhr surrender, Stresemann had succeeded Cuno; four months later, Marx had replaced Stresemann. Now, after a period of confusion, Marx and Stresemann were able to reconstruct a ministry, with a slight but adequate majority.

As a consequence, while in France and Great Britain the political upheavals had at one time revealed a far-reaching change of popular sentiment in both Allied countries and an even more revolutionary transformation in political control, the German decision did not disturb those statesmen, who were now prepared to abandon the policy of passive resistance for that of conditional fulfilment. Moreover, the German election returns were a warning signal to the Allied peoples, who were now capable of appreciating their meaning.

Thus, while the German people saw in the fall of Poincaré the defeat of an enemy and in the arrival of MacDonald the coming of a friend, the British and French peoples recognized in the triumph of the German Nationalists a peril which was unmistakable. Both illuminations contributed promptly and materially to the success of MacDonald's great effort to create a new atmosphere in Europe.

CHAPTER TWENTY

THE DAWES PLAN

THE successive failures at Genoa, London, and Paris had discredited conference as a method of conducting European relations. Moreover, while the occupation of the Ruhr had produced a condition closely approximating war between France and Germany, it had at the same time destroyed even the fiction of Anglo-French association.

In the spring of 1924, however, the necessity for another international meeting was perceived on all sides. Although the character of the French occupation in the Ruhr had been modified and had thus become less intolerable, the existing situation could not endure. Solution had to be found for the gravest problem which had confronted post-war Europe.

At this moment, too, there was at last presented to the world that programme which, under the name of the Dawes Plan, was to prove the corner stone of European reconstruction. The proposal for an expert and impartial investigation of German capacity had been made frequently before the Ruhr occupation. It had been urged by the German government in its note addressed to Washington in 1921. It had been repeated by the

American Secretary of State, Mr. Hughes, in his New Haven speech in December, 1922.

Always, however, to the moment when the German resistance in the Ruhr had broken down in September, 1923, French opposition had been constant and unyielding. In French eyes the proposal was no more than another attempt to compromise French rights and to transfer to unfriendly and selfish control the whole question of German performance. It seemed an Anglo-Saxon plant to save Germany and sacrifice France.

From the London Conference onward, not only had the whole question of reparations been lodged with the commission established for that purpose by the Treaty of Versailles, but France, always backed by Belgium and frequently by Italy, had steadily dominated the commission. As Viscount Curzon had charged in one of his bitter communications during the controversial period of the Ruhr occupation, the Reparations Commission had steadily been an adjunct of French policy.

The utter prostration of Germany following the Ruhr occupation put a new face upon the question. Hitherto, the issue had arisen over the question of what Germany should pay. Now, before any German payments could be made, it was clear that the economic life and the financial stability of the Reich must be restored. In point of fact, the question of reparations had at last escaped French control.

An appeal to American and British finance was inescapable, but, in this situation, finance was bound to impose its own conditions. Thus, while French political power had grown steadily from Versailles to the Ruhr, nevertheless, the concomitant weakening of French financial resources had counterbalanced the gain in political influence. Military power had now to capitulate to money power.

Nor was the German situation less extraordinary. In the late autumn of 1923, the rentenmark had been issued to replace the now worthless mark. The new finance minister, Dr. Hans Luther, later Chancellor in the Locarno period, and Dr. Hjalmar Schacht, recently become president of the Reichsbank, were responsible for this operation. But it was, in fact, no more than a daring gamble. "A bridge between chaos and hope," Schacht later described it, and since adequate reserves were lacking, the bridge was doomed to crash unless foreign aid were quickly forthcoming.

In this situation, politics in all countries was compelled to turn to finance. But while a new financial breakdown in Germany threatened both economic and political consequences which could not fail to be disastrous for all Europe, the bankers of the world were unwilling to adventure the money which they must raise from American and British investors in a Germany which was exposed to new French political and military interventions.

Although in November, 1923, Poincaré had consented to the appointment of an expert commission, his attitude was suspicious if not hostile· Convinced that

German will to evade explained the whole reparations trouble, he attached little importance to an investigation of German capacity. In the end he agreed to it only because he was permitted to have a second investigation, undertaken to determine the amount of German capital which had escaped from the Reich, and to recommend methods of bringing this back.

Poincaré also insisted that these two commissions should be named by the Reparations Commission and should report to it, thus maintaining the principle of control which had continued since the London Conference. Despite the hopes of the French Premier, however, the commission named to investigate the flight of German capital, which took its name from the chairman, Reginald McKenna, former Chancellor of the British Exchequer, achieved nothing. It finally reported that upward of $1,500,000,000 had escaped, but it suggested no method of recalling this huge sum.

By contrast, the commission charged with the investigation of German economic and financial conditions almost instantly captured the confidence of Europe. France saw in General Charles G. Dawes, the chairman, who had served with General Pershing in the war, a declared friend. German business and finance, on its side, discovered in Owen D. Young an ability which henceforth entitled him to rank with Herbert Hoover as one of the two great American figures in post-war Europe.

To the task of the Commission, General Dawes

brought the knowledge and experience of a successful banker, but his services on the political side were more important. To Owen Young, whose mastery of the intricate circumstances of a modern industrial state fell little short of sheer genius, belonged the larger share of the credit of authorship. With Dawes and Young was associated Henry M. Robinson, a lawyer of distinction, whose war service had been considerable.

The Dawes Commission was, therefore, to a large extent an American enterprise, although the American members were without official connection with their government. Nevertheless, ultimate success was materially assisted by the American ambassadors in Berlin, Paris, and London, Houghton, Herrick, and Kellogg, respectively. French affection for Herrick and German faith in Houghton were the imponderables, lacking which failure might have resulted.

In the spring of 1924, the Dawes Commission had terminated its job. And by this time, not only had the silent and efficient manner in which the work had been conducted produced a profound impression everywhere, but in France, Poincaré, as a result of the March slump in the franc, impatiently pressed for a speedy report. In reality, the project which he had distrusted and opposed constituted his sole avenue of escape. But, as it turned out, the report came too late to save him.

The Dawes Plan, which issued from the Commission, was necessarily intricate in its actual details. Its main features were, by contrast, perfectly simple. Laying aside all political and national considerations, the Commission had started with the assumption that Germany not only ought to pay but could pay largely. On the other hand, it silenced the German protest against slavery to foreign creditors by citation of the actual situation produced in Germany by inflation.

As a result of this inflation, Germany had wiped out its domestic debt. The victorious nations, by contrast, since they were meeting the costs of their domestic debts, would be unfairly handicapped in the world markets if they were compelled to compete with German production, freed of all domestic taxation resulting from the war. Thus the Dawes Commission took as its basic principle that equality of burdens should be the measure.

As a foreign loan was the primary condition of German domestic recovery, the Dawes Commission provided for the marketing abroad, chiefly in America and Britain, of bonds to the amount of $200,000,000. A portion of this sum was to be retained in Germany to support the rentenmark, the balance was to supply part of the funds necessary for reparations payments during the early period when direct German contributions must be inconsiderable.

There was created a central bank of issue, subject to foreign supervision, which, in addition to issuing currency, was to conduct all the complicated operation of financing the deliveries in kind on account of reparations, receiving from the government the necessary funds. These funds were to come in part from current revenues. In addition, a mortgage of $1,250,000,000 was to be placed upon German industry, and the German State Railways were to be bonded for $2,500,000,000. This latter detail was the basis for the later and famous conversations of Thoiry.

Lastly, the Dawes Plan provided for the payment of reparations on a sliding scale, which started with $250,000,000 for the first year, stood at $300,000,000 for the second and third, and rose sharply to $625,000,000 in the fifth. But to balance all the provisions for payment of reparations, there was established the principle that at no time should any payment in cash or kind be made when such payment threatened to disturb German exchange.

This condition immediately put an end to any possibility of any military coercion based upon German failure to meet reparations charges, when German capacity to pay was inadequate. Joined to this circumstance were a whole series of recommendations which, while carefully avoiding direct reference to the Ruhr, manifestly envisaged its speedy evacuation. In addition, similar recommendations clearly foreshadowed the restoration to German hands of control of all the elements of national industry and all the powers necessary to regulate tariffs.

Broadly speaking, the Dawes Plan thus proposed to fix a scale for German payments based on German capacity and safeguarding German interests. At the same time it established the principle that, subject to honest endeavour and reasonable fulfilment, Germany should be once for all freed from all threat of foreign coercion, assured not only mastery within her own frontiers, but protection against all intervention.

While, technically, the powers of the Reparations Commission were not to be impaired, in fact the administration of the whole machinery created by the Dawes Plan was transferred to an Agent General and by common consent it was agreed in advance that this official should be an American, appointed with the consent and approval of the American government.

The supreme merit of the Dawes Plan lay in the fact that it definitively removed the reparations issue from politics. The German demand for an expert and scientific determination of German capacity to pay was satisfied absolutely. On the other hand, the French contention that Germany could pay and must pay was similarly sustained. Since, moreover, the schedule fixed by the London ultimatums of 1921 had provided that Germany should pay $250,000,000 in 1921 and $500,000,000 in succeeding years the actual reduction was not considerable.

But the moral value of the Dawes Plan actually surpassed the material. For all the complicated and contradictory provisions of the Treaty of Versailles, there was substituted a simple and straightforward programme. Fulfilment of this insured for the German, not only a guarantee against interference, but an insurance of national recovery. Once for all, there was demolished the foundations of the universal German belief that reparations were to be made the pretext for the prohibition of German recovery and the warrant for the destruction of German unity. In place of a vague, unlimited, and unilateral obligation, the German people were now to have a definite contract. Whereas payment under the Treaty seemed merely to insure fresh exactions, payment under the Dawes Plan excluded all possibility of further demands.

Once the Dawes Plan had been published as a report to the Reparations Commission there arose the practical problem of obtaining for it ratification by both the French and German parliaments. And the first step was necessarily a conference in two stages, first, between the British and the French, and, later, between these Allied nations and the Germans. This was the basis for the London Conference of July.

In the Anglo-French stage, all turned upon the question of future coercion. Herriot came to London condemned to insist on behalf of his country that acceptance of the Dawes Plan should not abolish the French right to use force to break any future and wilful German evasion. In France, there still survived the suspicion that the Dawes Plan was only one more device to diminish the French share in the fruits of the common victory and that, once the right to act had been taken from France, German evasion would be inevitable and even encouraged.

MacDonald, on his side, argued for the abolition of the right of coercion. In his stand he followed closely the view of American and British bankers, who were always in the background during this meeting. Thus the world was treated to the delicious spectacle of a Socialist Prime Minister actually defending the thesis of international finance. Always, too, the bankers firmly refused to risk investors' money, while German recovery was at the mercy of French political and military intervention.

In the end the Anglo-French views were adjusted by a compromise which, while it left France the right to act in case of fresh German evasion, limited this right by providing that the fact of wilful evasion should be determined by arbitration. Moreover, since the casting vote in case of division of opinion was to belong to an American, what France retained in theory, she lost in fact.

This point settled, Marx and Stresemann joined the conference. Immediately, however, they presented the demand that acceptance of the Dawes Plan by Germany should be conditional upon the immediate evacuation of the Ruhr by French troops. Herriot, on his side, had come to London pledged in advance to agree to no evacuation until the Germans had both accepted the Dawes Plan and given evidence of a will to fulfil.

From the first meeting of MacDonald, Marx, and Herriot there survives a legend which is illustrative of the European situation of the moment.

"It is useless for me to agree to any programme," the German Chancellor explained. "I represent a minority government."

"Why make a point of that?" rejoined MacDonald. "Do you think there is anything unusual in it? Am I not, also, the head of a minority ministry?"

"*Moi aussi, beaucoup de plus!*" interjected the President of the French council.

Thus three premiers sat down together, each representing a minority government and all threatened with immediate disappearance. But the common danger proved a starting point for a coöperation which endured when Chamberlain, Stresemann, and Briand continued at Locarno what had been begun at London. Moreover, while the three premiers seemed engaged in violent controversy, in fact, from the outset, they actually united to frame conditions which would satisfy the parliaments of all three countries.

Thus, in the end, Herriot agreed for France that the evacuation of the Ruhr should take place one year from the acceptance of the Dawes Plan by Marx in London. He also made many other pledges to soften the character of the occupation and held out the hope that French retirement might be hastened, were German good faith established promptly. This was the outside limit of French concession, and because of it, Herriot very nearly lost his political head.

Marx presently accepted the Herriot proposal, and the Dawes Plan, with the additions agreed upon in the

London Conference, was later ratified by the French Parliament and the German Reichstag. The appointment of S. Parker Gilbert, Assistant Secretary of the Treasury, as Agent General placed the administration of the Dawes Plan in amazingly efficient hands. Thereafter, reparations disappeared as a cause of international dispute and an obstacle to European recovery. All the fears and suspicions of Paris and Berlin proved idle. All the difficulties which at the moment appeared insurmountable, in retrospect seem ridiculous.

On the German side, two circumstances combined to compel acceptance. In the first place, the financial crisis was acute. Without foreign aid, the rentenmark was at the end of its tether. Thus, although they loudly protested, the German Nationalists did not dare to assume the responsibility for a new crash, and in the end supplied the necessary votes for ratification.

Equally important was the fact that the Dawes Plan was, in all its essentials, an American plan, not the work of Germany's European conquerors. The conditions surrounding its application, too, had been framed in a conference in which German delegates had participated on an equal footing. Negotiation had preceded decision, and the proposal came to the German Reichstag backed by no threat. No ultimatum accompanied it, and adoption by the German Reichstag represented a voluntary agreement.

In the French, as in the German Parliament, criticism was general and extreme, but while legislators demanded the retention of the right to employ coercion and to continue the Ruhr occupation until German performance was assured, every Frenchman knew that force had failed and could never again be employed. On a point of honour, France insisted upon certain technical details, but in practice the French people were looking for a way out, not for a warrant for further advance.

In Germany, while ratification was obtained, public opinion was only slowly modified. Hope had been so long deferred that it was not until French troops left the Ruhr and Allied troops retired from the Cologne Zone in the next year that at last a majority of the German people were able to believe that German recovery was to be permitted. Fortunately, while the political benefits were delayed, the financial advantages were promptly realized and Germany at last turned the corner. Henceforth, her recovery, if slow, was destined to be steady.

Yet, in understanding German opinion, it is essential to recognize that no country, either during or after the war, passed through a period of prostration as complete as that of Germany in 1923 and 1924. Nowhere was misery so general, nowhere was suffering so universal. Even in the winter of 1924–25, life was excessively difficult. Students in the universities existed on one meal a day. Books and papers were almost beyond reach. Men still wore their often-patched uniforms of the war. Women turned and re-turned the clothes of their pre-war days.

No city in Europe was more dingy, more depressing, more completely the capital of a beaten and crushed people than Berlin in the winter of 1924–25. Visitors who exclaimed over the paucity of automobiles in the streets and the absence of lights at night were called upon to testify to the intensity of traffic and the restored brilliance. The faces of the throngs on the streets in the daytime showed evidences of the recent strain, while the physical condition of the children was appalling, and from the very young and the very old, death took a terrible toll.

Nor can one fairly ignore the degree to which the sense of moral isolation and the consciousness of a moral blockade contributed to German misery and hopelessness. No proud people had ever been forced to endure greater humiliation. Nothing of physical or mental suffering had been spared the inhabitants of the great cities. Nor is it an exaggeration to say that the limit of human endurance had been reached. Never was a race between ultimate ruin and possible recovery more closely run. Actually, the salvation of the Dawes Plan arrived at the eleventh hour.

CHAPTER TWENTY-ONE

THE PROTOCOL

BRILLIANT as was the success of the London Conference in bringing about a compromise between Herriot and Marx, this was by no means the limit of achievement. On the contrary, while accord between France and Germany made certain the acceptance of the Dawes Plan, concomitant agreement between Britain and France brought to an end the long and futile Anglo-French duel. At one time, therefore, German resistance to the Treaty of Versailles was terminated and a new period of British and French coöperation begun.

The basis of the agreement between MacDonald and Herriot was contained in the mutual promise to make the League of Nations the instrumentality of European restoration. Moreover, not only was German admission to the League accepted in principle by both the British and French premiers, but Marx and Stresemann, as well, returned to Berlin persuaded by their London experience that the road to German recovery led through Geneva.

The results of these London decisions were destined to change completely the whole relation of the League of Nations to European problems. The mere presence of Herriot and MacDonald in Geneva, whither they went almost immediately after the London Conference, invested the Fifth Assembly of the League with a prominence and an importance which had been lacking in all the earlier meetings. And, in fact, this Assembly of 1924 marks the turning point in the fortunes of the League itself. Therefore, if the Geneva organization owes its existence to Woodrow Wilson, it is just as unmistakably indebted to Ramsay MacDonald for its later prosperity, since it was he who led Britain and France to Geneva.

Before 1924, the rôle of the League of Nations had not only been inconsiderable, but utterly inglorious. Designed to become the agency alike for the restoration of peace and for the prevention of war, it had been condemned to sit passively by while European anarchy and disorder spread and new conflicts produced fresh devastations.

To this impotence, the action of the American Senate, by rejecting the Treaty of Versailles, unquestionably contributed. But it is a profound error to conclude that the American refusal to join the League was the main cause of early failure. On the contrary, the reasons for that failure were much more fundamental. Above all, it was the connection between the League and the Treaty of Versailles which paralyzed Geneva precisely as long as the conflict incident to German resistance to the Treaty continued, and, in fact, until Germany joined the circle of member nations.

The same document which imposed upon Germany all the various moral condemnations and material burdens of the Versailles settlement called the League into existence. While the German people resisted the Treaty of Versailles, the League was thus bound to have in their eyes the character of an agency of the victorious countries to oppress the defeated. In their minds, too, it was a detail in the great system of fraud and hypocrisy, which was designed to destroy their physical existence on the pretext of their moral inferiority.

Again, while the United States, Germany, and Russia were absent from Geneva, France and Great Britain, the remaining great powers, whose support might otherwise have contributed to achievement, were from the outset separated by that quarrel over the application of the Treaty of Versailles which continued and developed in all the years from the Paris Conference to the occupation of the Ruhr.

In all this time the League was ignored. Not one of the almost innumerable international conferences called to deal with the problems of peace met at Geneva. No British or French Prime Minister or Foreign Minister attended the Geneva sessions. Lip service was done to the League both in London and Paris. But while Lloyd George, Millerand, and Briand praised the noble ideals which the League was supposed to express, this praise was empty and, measured by the treatment which the League suffered at their hands, better calculated to excite derision than to carry conviction. Not from Geneva, but from London, Paris, Brussels, and Rome came the decisions which were controlling in Europe.

Two wars of considerable magnitude, that between

Poland and Russia in 1920 and that between Turkey and Greece in 1922, directly confounded the claims of the friends of the League of Nations that it could preserve peace. Moreover, not only was the League powerless to prevent these conflicts, but it was also utterly unable to give aid or protection either to Poland or to Greece, although both were member nations.

In precisely the same fashion a long series of acts of aggression of relatively lesser magnitude were equally disastrous to League prestige. French performance in the Saar District, where League of Nations supervision was provided by the Treaty of Versailles, left Geneva without resource to intervene. The Italian seizure of Fiume and the later bombardment of Corfu, the Polish occupation of Vilna—these and a score of similar incidents testified to anarchy in Europe and impotence at Geneva.

Finally, the occupation of the Ruhr seemed to give the ultimate lie to all claims advanced on behalf of the League. It was the last circumstance in the long catalogue of deeds of violence which had marked the progressive disintegration of Europe following the making of the Treaty of Versailles. And once more Geneva was obliged to sit silent and idle, while there long continued a struggle which sapped the very foundations of European peace and order.

In all these bitter and dreary years the League was actually saved and prepared for future usefulness by a single circumstance. While the great powers consistently ignored it, the smaller nations, from the very outset, recognized that, for themselves, the League of Nations offered a resource and an opportunity hitherto lacking. In the Assembly they discovered a forum where they could be heard in defence of their own rights and a conclave in which the collective strength of many small states could at last exercise influence upon the policies of the great.

During all past time, the rôle of the small states in Europe had been at once insignificant and dangerous. Even in the periods when there had existed a Concert of Europe, the great states which composed it had never concerned themselves with the rights of small countries. On the contrary, these rights had always been sacrificed ruthlessly to the needs and the appetites of the great powers. Nor had there been any platform from which the small states could appeal individually or any meeting place where their scattered but collectively not inconsiderable influence could be exerted.

The League of Nations was thus for every small country a manifest promise. All, therefore, enlisted at once. To Geneva came not merely the smaller countries which had been created or expanded by the war, but the neutrals as well. The three Scandinavian countries, Holland, and Switzerland, together with the South American Republics, promptly seized upon the League as an instrumentality to improve their international situation and to provide at least a measure of protection against enduring dangers.

Again, while the great powers consistently and deliberately sent to Geneva small men whose political influence at home was slight and whose importance abroad was therefore insignificant, the little states were from the beginning represented by statesmen of first-rate ability and European reputation. Benes, Van Karnebeck, Branting, Hymans, Titulescu, Politis were among the names which frequently figured in important debates. A similar ability and distinction were also revealed in the men who represented the Latin-American republics.

As a consequence, during the years of its obscurity and impotence, the Geneva Society of Nations had actually been developing. A tradition of collaboration had been created. The men who returned year after year had acquired the habit of coöperation. What was even more important, there had been evolved a certain sense of European solidarity. For all the smaller states, future security was discoverable, not in nationalistic activities at home, but in international coöperation in Geneva. Accordingly, their representatives worked together in and for the League, not as Czechs, Swedes, Dutchmen, or Swiss, but as Europeans.

In another direction, too, the League had also made progress. Under the efficient direction of Sir Eric Drummond, a former under secretary in the British Foreign Office and the first Secretary General, there had been created a machine which was presently to disclose genuine skill in dealing with a variety of international problems. The salvaging of the finances of Austria and of Hungary, the rescue of the hordes of exiles from Asia Minor, flung destitute upon Greek shores, were later achievements counted to the credit of Geneva.

The solution of the problem of Upper Silesia, which was thrust into the hands of the League, following the deadlock between France and Britain in the summer of 1921, was at the moment less fortunate. British criticism and German resentment were equally violent. Nevertheless, later and soberer judgment recognized that, in the premises, the decision reached was fair and just. Thanks to the League, too, there was devised a system by which any immediate and fatal dislocation of the intricate and closely intermingled parts of this great industrial area was avoided. Thus, if political separation was established, a measure of economic unity was preserved for a period of years.

In a very real sense, therefore, when Edouard Herriot and Ramsay MacDonald set out for Geneva agreed to rescue the League by their presence and by their programme, they actually discovered a Society of Nations which had already acquired a vitality of its own. And they also found themselves confronted by European statesmen whose ability was manifest and whose influence within the League was not only potent, but constituted a factor which had to be reckoned with constantly. The isolation of the early years had been a blessing in disguise, for it had allowed a period for organization and preparation. Thus, in 1924, when at last the great powers condescended to recognize the existence of the League of Nations, it was, itself, a going concern.

As the very outset of the Fifth Assembly, Ramsay MacDonald delivered an address which supplied the basis for all the later discussions and actions of this memorable session. In an eloquent and even passionate speech he called upon all the European peoples not merely to accept compulsory arbitration, but also to scrap their separate treaties and disband their powerful armies. The basis of future security in Europe, he proclaimed, must be mutual confidence and not military force.

These declarations, equally consistent with MacDonald's principles as a Pacifist and with his position as the Prime Minister of an insular country, protected from invasion by the surrounding seas, awakened neither applause nor support among his hearers. Although all delegates at once affirmed the readiness of their respective countries to accept compulsory arbitration, none was prepared to stake the safety of his nation upon the assumed good faith of all others.

While Herriot for France and Benes for Czecho-Slovakia voiced the opposing views of countries one of which had recently been invaded and the other had just emerged from three centuries of servitude to foreign domination, it was left to Theunis, Prime Minister of Belgium, to reply for the Continent.

"Give us an assurance of safety," he declared, "and we Belgians will gladly dismiss our soldiers, but can you expect us to risk our security on words alone, *again and so soon?*"

From the long conferences which followed there presently emerged the famous Protocol which was mainly the work of Dr. Benes, the distinguished Foreign Minister of Czecho-Slovakia, who had become the most considerable figure in recent Geneva history. This programme for the organization of world peace was based upon the formula, "Arbitration, Security, and Disarmament."

Accepting MacDonald's proposal for compulsory arbitration, the Protocol envisaged the transformation of the League into a universal alliance which insured the security and integrity of all member nations by the agreement of all to join in the defence of any nation wantonly attacked. Once this contract had been accepted by all, the League was to undertake the task of limiting and reducing armies.

In effect, this Protocol did no more than amplify and reaffirm the principle originally expressed in Article X of the Covenant of the League of Nations. But the pledge of every nation to defend the victim of aggression was made explicit. At the same time, all the separate alliances were automatically merged in the greater compact. To the League was assigned the right to determine the fact of an aggression and the duty to call upon member nations for aid. These nations were free to determine the character and extent of their contribution, but the moral obligation to assist was unequivocal.

The experience of Ramsay MacDonald at Geneva was thus amazingly and amusingly like that of Woodrow Wilson at Paris. Both the American President and the British Prime Minister carried to an international conference a proposal to insure world peace which was consonant with the thought and tradition of the country of the author. Each in turn, too, was instantly brought face to face with a totally different conception which proceeded from the national experiences and traditions of Continental peoples.

Moreover, while Ramsay MacDonald, like Woodrow Wilson, reluctantly accepted a compromise, which alone could enlist the agreement of the Continental peoples, the British Parliament rejected the Protocol, as the Senate of the United States refused to ratify the Treaty of Versailles. In both cases, too, this rejection did immediate injury to the League of Nations.

The debates over the Protocol, both at Geneva and elsewhere, served to emphasize once more the eternal conflict between the views of insular and Continental peoples with respect of security. Those people who live safely behind frontiers covered by seas insist that the existence of armies explains the fact of wars. They argue that in the abandonment of large standing armies is to be found the true promise of peace. Believing this sincerely, they accept the fact that Continental peoples seek security in armies to be proof of militarism.

But, in precisely the same fashion, the Continental peoples, living behind open frontiers across which invasions have come frequently, see in their armies the same protection insular peoples derive from their ocean barriers. Moreover, Anglo-Saxon arguments for disarmament seem no more than proof of egoism and hypocrisy. Secure behind their seas the British and American peoples are unconcerned about the safety of Continental peoples. Unwilling to accept any responsibilities for the security of those whom they bid to disarm, they are satisfied to urge them to run risks which may prove fatal.

Viable compromise between these two points of view is impossible because they are mutually exclusive. Face to face with the disclosure of the strength and sincerity of the Continental conception, MacDonald accepted the Protocol as Wilson had adopted the Covenant and treaties of guarantee. But although the British people roundly scored the selfishness of the American people, as disclosed in the rejection of the Treaty of Versailles, their course with respect of the Protocol was not only identical, but was equally determined by their national tradition.

To the common sense and practical view of the Englishman the Protocol required of him that he agree to employ his fleet and his army to maintain all the territorial decisions resulting from the recent war. By its implications he would be morally bound to defend Polish sovereignty in the Corridor and Rumanian title in Bessarabia. In theory, at least, he would be called upon to engage his fleet to protect any South American country whose rights had been invaded by the United States.

In fact, the Protocol actually lodged in Geneva the right to determine in advance the action of the British Government. The League and not Parliament would rule on what constituted an aggression. When it had decided, Parliament might, to be sure, control the British participation, it could still limit the extent of British contribution, but the verdict which involved war would be reached not on the banks of the Thames but on the shores of Lake Geneva.

Conscious of their unanimous desire for peace, the British people were not prepared to defend the integrity of Poland or Rumania. At that precise moment they were not even in a mood to assent to any contract binding them to defend the integrity of France, although France had been a recent ally and Boulogne and Calais alike commanded the British shores and the sea approach to London. Above all they were utterly unwilling to surrender any portion of their control over their own decisions to any international body.

Thus, a few months later, Austen Chamberlain went to Geneva and announced British rejection of the Protocol. But this British decision had two inevitable consequences. In the first place, it insured the survival of all the separate alliances which had been made since the World War. In the second place, it put a practical end to all projects for disarmament in Europe. If the British and American peoples still continued to argue for disarmament as the real insurance of security and peace, the Continental peoples just as resolutely insisted upon security as the condition antecedent to disarmament.

The ultimate failure of the Protocol was a heavy blow to the League, because it was, itself, a creation of the Geneva society and it expressed the views of the nations and the statesmen who had been associated in the earlier period of League history. On the other hand, the coming of Herriot and MacDonald established a precedent which was followed thereafter. In fact, Geneva had now become, to a degree at least, the political centre of Europe. General agreement that Germany should be invited to join, also, insured the early presence of that great nation, whose absence had so long deprived the League of any real claim to speak for Europe.

One other consequence of the events of the Fifth Assembly deserves note. For the first time French statesmen perceived the patent truth that the League offered an incomparable field for French activity. Certain of the support of her allies, Poland, Czecho-Slovakia, and Belgium, united with Rumania and Jugo-Slavia in a common policy of maintenance of the *status quo* established by the Paris treaties, bound by every interest of her own to desire European peace and to oppose any attempt to disturb it, France was assured of an ascendancy within the League which was hardly to be challenged.

Few revenges of time have been swifter or more complete than that disclosed in the circumstance that, five years after the Paris Conference, the country of Georges Clemenceau had become the most influential member of the League of Nations of Woodrow Wilson. As a consequence, it was Aristide Briand, speaking not merely for France but for Europe as represented at Geneva, who welcomed Gustav Stresemann to the League of Nations two years later.

In this Assembly, too, there was revealed a growing European resentment of the attitude of the United States. Thus Ramsay MacDonald politely but emphatically voiced European refusal to attend any new disarmament conference in Washington, while the League reasserted its right to exercise control over such international discussions. Eagerness for American adherence was patently declining, and all thought of further waiting upon a reversal of American decision was abolished.

On the contrary, the Assembly listened with undisguised sympathy to a Japanese proposal which would have permitted the League to take cognizance of the domestic legislation of nations, when national laws disturbed international amity. This was a clear reference to the immigration laws of the United States in their relation to Asiatic peoples. Less important, but not without significance, was an Italian suggestion for some form of international control of the raw materials essential to national industries.

The later failure of the Protocol deprived these subsidiary proposals of value, but the Japanese and Italian suggestions, like the Protocol itself, were indicative of the spirit of internationalism which had developed at Geneva. This spirit, too, was equally unacceptable to the British and American peoples.

Closely upon MacDonald's return to London followed the fall of the Labour Ministry. The immediate cause was distrust and apprehension aroused by Russian negotiations. In the domestic crisis, MacDonald was guilty of defects in temper and judgment alike. Under the great strain of foreign and domestic responsibilities, his health had plainly broken down. The publication of a letter alleged to emanate from Moscow and openly seeking to promote British disorder accentuated the crisis. The "stunt" press seized upon it and for the moment all the old anti-Soviet passions were revived. Liberal defection instantly precipitated disaster.

Defeated in the House of Commons, MacDonald resigned, and in the election which followed the Tory party scored a sweeping victory. But although Labour lost forty seats, its voting strength was increased by more than a million. The Liberal party, by contrast, went to supreme disaster. Its membership in the House of Commons was cut in half; its disintegration was hastened. Thereafter, in the following years, it opened to right and to left, its members turning either to the Tories or to Labour, while Lloyd George was left a political Casabianca. The Labour position as the permanent opposition was, therefore, established.

Since Labour was at all times a minority party, its

loss of power was always assured. And in the larger sense it had fulfilled the mission which had been confided to it a few months before. Aside from the successful budget of Philip Snowden, Chancellor of the Exchequer, its domestic record had been undistinguished, but, thanks to MacDonald, British foreign policy had won new influence and British position in Europe had been restored.

Moreover, the supreme service of Ramsay MacDonald lay in the fact that he had not merely created a new atmosphere in Europe, but he had also revived Continental confidence in British good faith. The great failure of Lloyd George had not lain in the purposes which he sought to serve, but in the methods which he had employed. In the years following Versailles, he was not infrequently right. His fatal difficulty lay in the fact that his very skill and cleverness destroyed confidence, and confidence was, in the nature of things, the antecedent condition of achievement.

Stanley Baldwin, who succeeded MacDonald, wisely refrained from recalling Curzon to the Foreign Office, and, in fact, Curzon was already a dying man. Instead, he chose Sir Austen Chamberlain. The less distinguished son of a famous father, Chamberlain in later times was guilty of many mistakes and at times revealed undeniable blundering. His great merit lay in the fact that his honesty was unmistakable. He inspired confidence in Paris and Berlin alike.

Moreover, Baldwin and Chamberlain wisely adopted

both the policies and the methods of the Labour Prime Minister. Thus, the credit for the larger part of the later success of British policy and diplomacy belonged rightfully to Ramsay MacDonald. He and not Chamberlain was the true architect of Locarno. Without his contribution European anarchy might have been much more dangerously protracted.

CHAPTER TWENTY-TWO

LOCARNO

STILL another crisis followed the adoption of the Dawes Plan by the German Reichstag and failure to resolve it led to a new election. The results of this electoral test of the fall of 1924 are of real interest, because they disclose the domestic political situation which existed throughout the Locarno negotiations and, in fact, illustrate the fundamental incoherence which has cursed German public life ever since the Revolution of November 9, 1918.

On the face of the returns, the advantage lay with the moderate elements. Thus, the Social Democrats at the Left recaptured seats from the Communists. The Nationalists at the Right similarly regained places lost to the Super-Nationalists in the spring election, when the memories of the Ruhr dominated popular emotions and played into the hands of the extremists. Yet, despite the impressive successes of the Social Democrats, the steady drift toward the Monarchist camp was not interrupted.

Recognizing this unmistakable trend, Stresemann now undertook to make a combination which should for the first time in the history of the Republic bring the Nationalists into office. To this end he evolved a

Cabinet, headed by Dr. Hans Luther, Finance Minister in the recent Marx government, and a fine type of the best of the old Prussian civil servants. Stresemann, himself, continued at the Foreign Office, and several Nationalists also took portfolios.

Nominally, the Luther Ministry was nonpartisan. The Nationalists and the Bourgeois parties agreed in principle that for the present the Republic must endure. For the Nationalists, this concession was easy, because in point of fact the Monarchists were hopelessly divided between the partisans of the Prussian and Bavarian dynasties, as the French Monarchists had been split between Bonapartists and Orleanists after 1870.

Actually, however, the compromise was more apparent than real. Although the Nationalists were now eager for power and hungry for the fleshpots of public office, they were unable to restrain their hostility to the Republic. When Luther and Stresemann opened the discussions which finally led to Locarno, Nationalist opposition was immediate, and at the moment the Locarno Conference was gathering, the Nationalist ministers quit the Cabinet. Thenceforth, Luther and Stresemann were compelled to seek support for their foreign policy from the Social Democrats.

At bottom the bewildering chaos in the German political situation grows out of conditions which are without parallel in the United States. Thus, instead of two major parties, there are at least five considerable groups. Moreover, although these groups are of unequal strength, a majority in the Reichstag or in the country is possible only on the basis of combination between several parties.

These five groups are, too, divided, not merely horizontally, but vertically. Thus, while the Social Democrats and the Nationalists are squarely at odds both on the question of the form of government and the character of domestic legislation, the Catholic Centre and the Democrats are at one time Republican and Conservative. Finally, the People's party, while in principle Monarchist and as the representative of Big Business naturally reactionary, has accepted the Republic as the single possible form of government in all present time.

The problem for any chancellor who must command a majority in the Reichstag is, therefore, nothing less than a stupendous repetition of the once familiar puzzle of "pigs in the clover." Every Ministry since the Revolution has lived from hand to mouth. Each Cabinet has been compelled to bargain for support, now from the Republicans and now from the Monarchists, and in practice it has had to turn to the former when pursuing conciliatory policies abroad and to the latter when opposing radical legislation at home.

There is, too, one final source of infinite paralysis. While it still remains probable that there is an actual Republican majority within the Reich, were the issue of the form of government to be raised directly, the balance between the Republicans and Monarchists is so equal that it amounts to a deadlock. Thus, real majority government, in the American sense, is not only prevented by the incompatibility existing between the various political groups, but also because of the absence of an actual majority in the nation itself.

The difficulties are further aggravated by the existence of a considerable Communist party, equally hostile to the survival of the Republic and to the restoration of the monarchy, and always prepared to vote against any government or policy. Actually, these Communists hold the balance of power between the Republicans and the Monarchists. This fact was clearly revealed in the Presidential election of 1925, when the Nationalist candidate polled 15,000,000 votes, the Republican 14,000,000, and the Socialist 2,000,000.

The intricate and complicate political conditions in Germany make it excessively difficult for the foreigner and particularly the American to follow the course of events or understand the meaning of the various developments. But the real action of the play in all recent time has been discoverable in the effort of the People's party to create a majority based upon the combination of the Nationalists and all the Bourgeois parties, that is, of all the groups save the Social Democrats and Communists.

This manœuvre expresses the judgment of the People's party, representing finance and business, that the monarchy can only be restored by civil war. It is also based upon the equally sound conclusion that only a Republican Germany can hope to obtain the early evacuation of German soil by Allied armies of occupation. Moreover, while civil war would certainly produce chaos and prevent German economic recovery, it would also automatically interrupt the flow of foreign loans to Germany, and these have been an essential detail in German recovery.

The domestic programme of the People's party, which is Stresemann's, aims at transforming the German Republic into a thoroughly conservative and even reactionary state. It proposes to accept the Republic as permanent, but to make it less and less democratic. For the Nationalists, this programme is unappealing, because they have not yet accepted the Republic definitively. Nor are they unaware of the fact that mere habit may in the end insure the survival of the German Republic as it did that of the Third French Republic half a century ago. Their policy is always comprehended in the effort to perpetuate incoherence and thus to establish the conviction that Republican institutions are impossible in Germany. In this undertaking they are enthusiastically seconded by the Communists, whose aim is to reproduce the system of Moscow upon the ruins of both Potsdam and Weimar.

In the first days of 1925, Luther and Stresemann undertook to formulate a new foreign policy. Hitherto, German opinion had been sharply divided between two views, described graphically as the Eastern and Western Orientation. The former, generally accepted by the Nationalists, was comprehended in a programme of continued resistance to the Treaty of Versailles, consistent refusal to join the League of Nations and thus to cooperate with the victors of the war, and eventual combination with a renascent Russia to regain by the sword what had been lost in the World War. This policy was revealed in the Treaty of Rapallo, which wrecked the Genoa Conference in 1922. Historically, too, the policy reverts to Bismarck and even to Frederick the Great.

The programme of the Western Orientation, which was now adopted by Stresemann and has remained the basis of all his later foreign policy, was founded upon the belief that German recovery was impossible save in cooperation with Allied countries. The experience of the London Conference had convinced Stresemann and Luther that there had been a profound change in Allied opinion. The arrival of MacDonald and the fall of Poincaré had confirmed this belief.

While the Dawes Plan had already insured German escape from the most pressing of her dangers, her domestic situation was still dependent upon foreign loans for complete restoration. Moreover, although in the London Conference Herriot had agreed upon French evacuation of the Ruhr, the occupation of the Rhineland could continue legally until 1935. Unless France were freed from the nightmare of fear for her own security which had endured since 1870, Stresemann saw that Germany, now substantially disarmed, would be fatally exposed to any later French action provoked by a recurrence of French anxiety.

At the same time, long and patient German investigation of the Russian situation convinced the Foreign Secretary that Russia would not be available as an ally or even valuable as a market for a long period of years. And in the nature of things Germany could not wait. Like every other German, Stresemann was resolved not to accept as final certain of the decisions of Versailles, but he concluded that the restoration of Germany politically and economically was to be attained only by a policy of conciliation and that the period of passive resistance was at an end.

Actually, Germany had reached the parting of the ways. Moral considerations were also mingled with material. The German people were utterly weary of the isolation which they had endured since the beginning of the war. They still resented the treatment from which they had suffered. In German eyes Allied judgment still appeared unfair and unfounded. Nevertheless, German bitterness was balanced by the desire to resume the place among civilized peoples and the position in international affairs which had been German prior to 1914. Fear and hope were strangely mingled, distrust and dawning confidence equally discoverable in Berlin in the winter of 1924–25. But everywhere, save in Eastelbian circles, the desire to end the long nightmare on any honourable terms was unmistakable.

Against Gustav Stresemann, who now becomes the central figure in the German political drama, his critics both at home and abroad have charged that he is an opportunist and a realist. Confirmation of this indictment is to be found in his previous history. Always one of the ablest of German parliamentarians, his record during the war was so intransigent that, at the close of the conflict, the Democratic party refused him admission. As a result, he turned to the organization of the People's party, which presently became in his hands the most influential of all the many German political groups.

If Dr. Stresemann must be identified, not only as an opportunist, but also as a realist, it is still beyond debate that this opportunism and realism were fortunate for his country and for Europe in the critical years of 1924 and 1925. Simple justice, too, requires recognition of the courage displayed in the advocacy of a foreign policy which, in a slightly different form, had cost Erzberger and Rathenau their lives.

In all outward circumstance Stresemann is a German of the Germans. Indeed, physically, he is of that Prussian type dear to all international cartoonists. Yet, together with so much that is essentially Teutonic go a political genius and a parliamentary skill which recall Lloyd George. Nor is there lacking a certain *fantaisie* reminiscent of Briand. Challenged in the congenial atmosphere of a *bierabend*, to explain his foreign policy, Stresemann replied, "I want to be the German who makes peace with France." The response illuminates the man. Luther, who worked with Stresemann, is the only other considerable public man developed by post-war Germany. Admirably fitted to work together,

Luther and Stresemann performed their really colossal labours in an atmosphere of mutual jealousy, which was always amusing but rarely hampering.

In his decision, Stresemann was doubtless influenced by Lord D'Abernon, British Ambassador to Berlin from 1920 to 1926. Widely known in the Near East as Sir Edgar Vincent, D'Abernon is not merely an important, if more or less mysterious, figure in all the negotiations leading up to Locarno, but is also the single diplomat of post-war Europe who achieved considerable distinction. Hated by the French, who denounced him as pro-German, distrusted in many British quarters for similar reasons, D'Abernon's ability, finesse, and charm were conceded by all.

Stresemann's action was also hastened by the foreknowledge that the new Tory Cabinet in Britain was resolved to reject the Protocol, accepted conditionally by MacDonald, and this decision was bound to raise again the dangerous question of French security. Moreover, it was a matter of common report that Austen Chamberlain favoured a direct British guarantee of French security, such as had been contained in the Versailles pacts. This British guarantee was in the nature of things certain to have an anti-German appearance and to emphasize German isolation and Allied distrust.

Its hand thus forced, on February 9, 1925, the Luther Cabinet issued to the various Allied governments the note which was the point of departure of all the negotiations which led eventually to Locarno. The central circumstance in this communication was the proposal for a mutual agreement between France and Germany both to arbitrate further disputes and to recognize the western *status quo* created by the Treaty of Versailles. This undertaking was to be guaranteed by the British, who were to pledge their military and naval support to either Germany or France in case of unprovoked aggression. This proposal was to cover Belgian security in the same manner.

In London the German note instantly awakened an applause which at least suggested British inspiration. It at one time supplied a basis for that rejection of the Protocol which was announced in Geneva in March, and an avenue of escape from that exclusive guarantee of French security which had the character of a permanent alliance and was contrary to all British tradition. From the outset, therefore, British support of the Stresemann proposal was assured.

In Paris, on the contrary, criticism was mingled with approval. The French people were by no means blind to the double advantage of a voluntary German recognition of French title to Alsace-Lorraine and of a British guarantee of French security. Opposition, which at once became general, was based upon the fact that, while Stresemann's proposal covered the western situation satisfactorily, it made no reference to the eastern. And both Poland and Czecho-Slovakia were French allies. Moreover, the repercussions in Prague and Warsaw were immediate and impressive. The expulsion of thousands of Germans from Upper Silesia concomitantly aroused German fury and attracted European attention.

The issue of the eastern frontiers of Germany thus raised dominated all the discussions before the Locarno Conference; it was the main subject of negotiation at that meeting; it led to the fiasco in Geneva in the following March. Moreover, it remains, even after Locarno, the most acute and disturbing af all the problems surviving from the Versailles settlement.

On the German side, no party and no group within a party was prepared to accept the loss of Danzig, the Corridor, and the Silesian industrial district as permanent. Assailed because of the proposal to abandon German claim to Alsace-Lorraine, Stresemann would have been helpless in the presence of the aroused Nationalists had he even considered an eastern concession, which, of course, was totally outside his programme.

On the other hand, the suspicion that Herriot, under British urging, was flirting with the German suggestion, which involved the abandonment of Poland, produced his fall. In any event, he could hardly have survived many weeks, since his failure was now complete, but the Polish issue hastened his departure. Painlevé, who succeeded him and similarly represented the *Cartel des Gauches*, called Briand to the Quai d'Orsay. Thus, that veteran French statesman was now in a position to resume the negotiations interrupted by the catastrophe of Cannes, three years before.

Meantime, the outcome of still another election in

Germany not only intensified French fears but disturbed European confidence in the permanency of the German Republic. Ebert, the first President of the German Republic, whose services to his country had been distinguished, died suddenly in March. In the preliminary election to choose a successor, Marx, the Republican candidate, had led the poll. But, in the final test, the Nationalists nominated former Field Marshal von Hindenburg, and the old soldier won by a million plurality, although the Socialist vote made him a minority president.

For the moment, this sudden reappearance of the general who had been for all Allied peoples the symbol of the Hohenzollern régime in Germany destroyed faith in the reality of Republican institutions in the Reich and stimulated suspicion that Stresemann's programme was a fresh proof of the fundamental bad faith of the German. Stresemann, whose opposition to the Hindenburg candidacy had been determined, was thus placed in an excessively awkward situation.

In point of fact, however, all the contemporary fears excited by the arrival of Hindenburg were promptly abolished. The old soldier of the Kaiser not only swore allegiance to the Republic, but thereafter faithfully observed his oath. The mere fact of his acceptance of the Republic ultimately weakened the opposition, and in the succeeding years it was the Nationalists and not the Republicans who most frequently condemned the victor of Tannenburg.

While all Allied peoples were disturbed by the Hindenburg election, a similar German distrust was aroused by the failure of the Allied troops to quit the Cologne zone in accordance with the Treaty of Versailles. London and Paris explained this failure on the ground of German evasion of the disarmament clauses of the Treaty of Versailles. Although these evasions were established, the actual reason was the promise given by MacDonald to Herriot. To balance the French Premier's promise to leave the Ruhr in August, the British Prime Minister had agreed that British troops should stay at Cologne, covering the communications of the French forces in the Ruhr, until evacuation took place.

The German Nationalists seized upon this issue, as upon that of the Polish expulsions; German apprehension was excited; Allied good faith was called into question, and Stresemann was compelled to face attacks at home and abroad at the same moment. Moreover, the defection of the Nationalists from the coalition on which the Luther-Stresemann Cabinet depended for its majority was now becoming a matter of weeks. Stresemann, too, had counted upon the moral effect in France of a security pact offered by a Cabinet in which the Nationalists were represented, and their action was a fresh disappointment.

Hampered and harassed by domestic political difficulties, Stresemann and Briand continued discussions throughout the summer and in these Chamberlain played an important rôle. Always, however, France refused absolutely to abandon Poland or Czecho-Slovakia. But the Czech circumstance was never of great importance, since the Bohemian state had acquired no German territory.

Concomitantly, negotiations were carried on between Geneva and Berlin looking to the admission of Germany to the League of Nations. It was the French, too, who pressed the question and insisted upon German adherence to the League as a condition of the suggested settlement. Thus, six years after Versailles, Europe was treated to the amazing spectacle of a German proposal to guarantee French security and a French demand that Germany enter the League of Nations. At the moment, too, while the French distrusted the German offer, the Germans suspected the French demand.

In the negotiations between Berlin and Geneva, Germany claimed exemption from any obligation to use force to assist in any League operation against any nation guilty of wanton aggression. The German request was predicated upon the disarmament clauses of the Versailles settlement. But, in fact, the demand was made in response to Russian protest, based upon the Rapallo agreement, and Stresemann's course was determined by the Nationalists who still clung to the Eastern Orientation. In the end, however, the League denied Germany's request and insisted upon unconditional German entrance.

As a consequence of all these alarums and excursions,

which testified to the tension of the hour in Europe, it was not until the first week of October that representatives of Germany, France, Great Britain, Poland, Belgium, Czecho-Slovakia, and Italy met at the little Swiss town of Locarno, on the shores of Lake Maggiore and a few steps from the Italian frontier. In the modest *mairie* of this village there were signed two weeks later the famous Locarno Pacts.

Of the five treaties, four were no more than agreements between Germany and her neighbours to submit all future issues to arbitration. The fifth document was the Security Pact, which continued German and French pledges to accept the territorial *status quo* created in the west by the Treaty of Versailles, and the German promise to observe the conditions with respect of the demilitarized zone contained in the same compact. Great Britain and Italy also joined in guaranteeing this Security Pact.

The declaration of purpose and principle, which accompanied the several treaties and represented the formal expression of "the spirit of Locarno," was signed by Luther, Stresemann, Vandervelde, Briand, Chamberlain, Mussolini, Skrzynski, and Benes. The treaties, which were to be deposited at Geneva, were to become effective only when Germany had entered the League of Nations.

The Polish problem, which had produced such long delays and discussions, was thus covered by a compromise. Through the arbitration treaties, Germany renounced the right to recover her lost provinces by force. But she refrained from any such recognition of the *status quo* as was contained in her Security Pact with France. The French, on their side, reasserted their right to support Poland and Czecho-Slovakia, in case of unprovoked attack upon either, but determination of the fact of aggression was left to the League of Nations.

Examination of the broader implications of the Locarno Pacts belongs to another chapter, but no formal and routine description of the documents themselves can do justice to the larger significance of the conference at which they were framed. Meeting for the first time on the soil of a state which had been a neutral of the war, removed from all the atmosphere of lingering passions and continuing prejudices, the statesmen of Locarno for the first time worked together under conditions of peace.

If the German delegation to the London Conference had been received with utmost civility, and Marx and Stresemann had found in Ramsay MacDonald a colleague uninfluenced by war memories, it was, nevertheless, true that constraint and formality marked the occasion. "They treated us decently but never permitted us to forget that we were Huns," was the later and illuminating comment of a German official who made the London journey.

Locarno was in truth the first time when the representatives of the German Republic met the delegates of nations which had been hostile during the war, not merely upon the basis of technical equality, but upon terms of genuine cordiality. It was the initial occasion when the statesmen of the several nations worked together with the sense, not of ending by compromise some specific dispute, but of laying the foundations for a system of general pacification.

Nor was this temper restricted to the statesmen. Locarno was just as significant as providing the first opportunity for the resumption of contact between the representatives of the German and Allied press. A world which the war had abolished was suddenly restored. Friends who had parted in July, 1914, met again in October, 1925. By this renewed association, mutual comprehension of the national problems of all countries was made possible. The newspapers became once more an agency for international understanding and not merely a medium for national propaganda.

Excursions on the lake established relations between the journalists, themselves, and also between the statesmen and the pressmen of all countries. "I am glad to see that you are in the same boat with me at last," Briand smilingly remarked to a group of German journalists on one such adventure. The French Foreign Minister received the German correspondents, the German Chancellor talked to the French. The British Foreign Secretary admitted the correspondents of all nations.

At the same time, Briand and Stresemann and Briand

and Luther lunched in remote mountain inns and discussed not merely the international problems but also the political difficulties which each confronted at home. And the mutual confidence thus created stood the severe strain of the later Geneva fiasco of March.

The actual signing of the compacts was accompanied by an emotional explosion which attracted attention all over the world. There were tears and cheers, embraces and a few kisses. Above all, there was an unmistakable feeling on the part of all that one period in European history had come to an end and another had been begun. Under blue Italian skies, warmed by the Southern sun, surrounded by the sensational scenery of the Alpine lakes, the Northern peoples unconsciously laid aside something of their reserve, and even Austen Chamberlain revealed himself to unsuspecting Latins as a sentimental Englishman.

The spirit of Locarno, which lingered in the memory of all who shared in its inception, was manifestly bound to suffer in transplanting. Those who parted beside the shores of Lake Maggiore in the brilliant October sunlight were destined to meet at Geneva in the midst of a March blizzard. Romantic expectations and sentimental extravagances could not long endure in a Europe which still remained dominated by the consequences of the greatest war in human history.

Yet, allowing for all the exaggerations of the moment, Locarno did mark the end of the moral isolation of Germany. It did witness the final extinction of the spirit of Versailles. This larger meaning was perceived by all who were present at the Conference itself. And for that reason it recalled to them the thrilling moment in spring, when, at last, the ice breaks up and goes downstream, once more opening the great rivers of the North to navigation.

CHAPTER TWENTY-THREE

GENEVA AND THOIRY

WE HAVE now come to the closing act in the post-war drama, and it is measurably an anticlimax. The actual decision of the three great peoples, the British, French, and German, to end the period of conflict and chaos which had followed the making of the Treaty of Versailles, was expressed in the ratification of the Dawes Plan and the Locarno Pacts.

Yet, in this final phase, certain circumstances challenge interest. In the opening chapters of this book emphasis was laid upon the fact of democratic control of foreign policy. Attention was also drawn to the contrast between the fashion in which the kings had made peace in 1814 and the peoples in 1919. In a very real sense, too, the study of the years between Versailles and Locarno is psychological, not historical or political. It is the examination of the transition of the peoples of all countries from a state of mind produced by war to a state of mind in which they were at last able to see things as they existed, freed from the distortions of passion and of propaganda.

Peace could not be made in 1919, because the peoples were still unable to perceive the realities or accept the conditions upon which settlement was alone possible. But between 1919 and 1925 all European democracies did discover the truths, known in advance to the diplomats and sovereigns who made the settlements of 1814 and 1815. And, in the final year, which witnesses the completion of the programme of European readjustment, it is necessary to pay tribute to the skill and intelligence with which the peoples of Great Britain, France, and Germany employed the men and the machinery available, to achieve their own sound and sensible ends.

Nothing can better illustrate this fact than the situation which existed in the three countries in September, when German entrance into the League of Nations gave formal validation to the Pacts of Locarno. At that precise moment a Tory Cabinet in Britain was faithfully and frankly following the foreign policy of the Labour Government which had preceded it. In Germany, Socialist votes enabled a capitalist Cabinet to complete the policy of Locarno. In France, Poincaré was conducting domestic affairs, but Briand remained in control of foreign policies.

The people wanted peace abroad, but they just as clearly desired order at home. In 1924, the British and the French peoples turned out Tory and Nationalist Ministries because they had failed to end international anarchy. In 1925 and 1926, Baldwin and Poincaré returned to power. But neither the British nor the French reaction had the smallest repercussion upon foreign policy. In the same time the single certainty in German politics was that, whether Socialists or Nationalists entered the Cabinet, Stresemann would continue in Wilhelmstrasse.

Thus, while 1926 is marked not by one but by many political crises and by several Cabinet upheavals both in France and in Germany, all these resulted from domestic conditions. For the first time since the outbreak of the war, all three countries could concentrate their attention upon their domestic affairs. In France, it was the fall of the franc which made and unmade Cabinets. In Great Britain, the coal strike occupied attention. In Germany, the energies of the nation were at last absorbed in economic and financial restoration.

On the surface the change was little apparent. The battle between French and German Nationalists over the Polish Question was waged with all the fury of previous years. Both the French and the German people clearly indicated that there were limits beyond which neither would go in sacrificing national interests or national rights. Collisions were frequent and opposing positions were warmly defended. Nothing remotely suggested the arrival of the millennium.

Yet the statesmen who met in Geneva in March and again in September were at last assured of popular support for any reasonable compromise in the interests of adjustment. All were conscious of the dominating desire of their peoples to finish. The policy which for Marx, Herriot, and MacDonald in London in 1924 had been a dangerous experiment was without similar risk for

Stresemann, Briand, and Chamberlain in Geneva in 1926.

Moreover, in this same time, another change was noteworthy. For the first time since the war, Germans appeared in Paris and Frenchmen in Berlin. Intellectual association was resumed. French scholars lectured in the German capital, German in the French. Dramatic and musical interchange was renewed. If the beginnings were hazardous, there were few failures. The arbitrary barriers which had been established by firing lines and continued by post-war disputes disappeared. None of these things happened with dramatic suddenness. Yet anyone who left Europe in 1923 and returned in 1926 would have been astounded by the extent of the change.

French journalists explored the recesses of the German mind and reported that, if nationalism survived, Republican faith was not lacking. Although French and German nationalism continued to thunder across the Rhine boundaries, liberalism both in France and Germany began to find the first promise of collaboration. Even more interesting was the gradual resumption of business coöperation. Before German entrance into the League, French and German potash interests made a combination. Immediately after Thoiry, the steel industries completed a far more important cartel, which restored the pre-war partnership between Lorraine iron and Ruhr coal on the basis of business, not bayonets. In a word, while in this final year international relations did not become idyllic, they certainly became normal.

On French insistence, the Germans had agreed at Locarno to ask for admission to the League of Nations. The application was favourably received at Geneva, and a special meeting of the Assembly was called for March. On all sides there was equal eagerness to validate the Locarno Pacts by compliance with this final condition. For the French, German entrance meant a fresh acceptance of the *status quo* in Europe. For the Germans, it meant formal recognition as one of the great nations of the world.

Nevertheless, new complications precipitated another international quarrel. This dispute broke, too, at the moment when the Luther Cabinet had fallen in Berlin and the Painlevé Ministry in Paris. In Germany, the Cabinet crisis was finally resolved by the return of a Luther-Stresemann Government, supported now by the Bourgeois and Socialist groups, with the clear mandate to complete Locarno. In France, Briand succeeded Painlevé, but his situation was precarious and he fell momentarily in March, on the eve of the Geneva Conference, and, finally, in midsummer, at the height of the financial panic.

The latest of the European collisions rose from the fact that, at Locarno, Count Skrzynski had received some form of assurance that Poland, in return for assenting to the agreements reached there, would obtain a permanent seat on the Council of the League. The

German press and public opinion had already clearly indicated that the effort to recover the lost provinces of the East would now be carried to Geneva. The Council was thus bound to become the battleground of the new campaign. For the Poles, therefore, membership in the Council was of utmost value. It also carried with it quasi-recognition as a great power.

In an unguarded moment, Austen Chamberlain had encouraged this Polish aspiration. All the Locarno powers which were members of the League had, in fact, agreed upon a programme which was to expand the size of the Council by adding three new permanent seats. Brazil and Spain, which had long been promised this honour, were to profit with Poland. In addition, Germany was to obtain the seat promised at Locarno.

Opposition to this programme came from two directions. In Berlin, there was an instant explosion of wrath at the proposal to seat Poland beside Germany, and thus, from the outset, deprive German admission to the Council of most of its moral value. Driven by domestic protest, Stresemann publicly announced that Germany would enter the League only provided her accession to the Council was unaccompanied. He insisted that this was the contract of Locarno. The French, on their side, pressed the Polish claim and criticized an alleged German effort to impose conditions upon the League in advance of adherence.

Even more serious was the protest within the League. The member nations, which had not been parties to the

Locarno Conference, bitterly resented the fashion in which seats within the League had been traded in without reference to Geneva. Resentment of British rejection of the Protocol was general. Moreover, the long-standing dispute between the large and small powers over the Council itself was reopened. Even in advance of the March meeting, Sweden, speaking in fact for the small powers and acting as a champion of the League, announced her intention to veto any proposal to elect any new member of the Council save Germany.

At Geneva, the battle was joined instantly. Luther, Stresemann, and an enormous delegation of German journalists came to the Swiss city to assist in the restoration of Germany to European international society. But the Polish issue had not been settled, and a deadlock at once resulted. Meantime, the Cabinet crisis in Paris recalled Briand. Thus for days the admission of Germany was halted the delegates to the Assembly waited idly. The press of Paris, Berlin, and London quarrelled violently. The situation was at once critical and absurd.

In the end, a compromise was arranged between Germany and France and between the Locarno powers and the League. Czecho-Slovakia consented to resign its seat in the Council and Poland was to be elected to the vacant place in advance of German admission. No new seat was thus created; Poland did not obtain a permanent place, but only one of the seats filled annually. To this proposal Germany assented and Sweden yielded.

But Brazil, angry at the failure to obtain the permanent seat promised to it, stolidly refused to permit German admission.

Thus, in the end, the March session was an utter fiasco. The Germans returned home disgusted, to be greeted by the sneers and jeers of the Nationalists. The prestige of the League suffered manifestly. British criticism of the French for their Polish policy was general. All the Locarno system had to be laid aside for the time being. Never was a failure more complete, and the whole world shared in the disappointment. Only one circumstance justified continued confidence: the relations between Stresemann, Briand, and Chamberlain were never strained. These statesmen had succeeded in compromising their differences. It was the action of Brazil, not the issue between France and Germany, which had wrecked the meeting.

Moreover, despite all the quarrellings of German and French Nationalists from Paris and from Berlin, at Geneva not a little of the practice of Locarno had been repeated. Nothing in the relations between the Germans and the representatives of other nations recalled the spirit of the attitude of Versailles. While formal completion of the Locarno programme was postponed, the larger labour of European reintegration continued.

"Let us all go home to work in the spirit of Locarno and for the reconciliation of our countries," was the final appeal made by Briand directly to the German journalists, as they were departing, and the memory of these and other similar words spoken by British and French representatives deprived the Geneva experience of all bitterness for the Germans who had actually shared it.

As a result, at the regular meeting of the Assembly in September, the failure of the spring was redeemed. All the disputed issues were adjusted, Germany entered the League and the Council. Three semi-permanent seats were created, one of which fell to Poland and, in the election, Stresemann cast the German vote for Poland. Resentment in the League continued, protest was voiced both by Holland and Sweden, but the small powers bowed to the large. Only Brazil and Spain refused to accept the decision, and both retired from Geneva.

On September 10th, amidst great solemnity and with impressive simplicity, Luther, Stresemann, and Gaus entered the Hall of the Reformation. The German Foreign Minister delivered a dignified, restrained, and admirably phrased address. For the League and for France Briand replied. The situation was theatrical. Every member of the audience which crowded the dingy and dimly lighted hall felt the tenseness of the moment, when Aristide Briand, taking the platform, responded without notes or preparation to the carefully prepared address Stresemann had just read to his hearers.

Nor did Briand disappoint his audience. Never was his greatness as an orator better demonstrated. When he addressed the Germans directly, asserting that for both France and Germany the centuries of war had supplied glory and graves enough and that the time had arrived for new methods and a new spirit, something of the emotion of Locarno was repeated. Not since 1870 had any French statesman thus addressed a German publicly. Indeed, in all the centuries of Franco-German history, the circumstance was without precedent.

Beyond the parochial limits of Geneva, too, this day's proceedings had enormous and enduring repercussions. Yet the change which had taken place in the seven years which separate Versailles from Locarno was not accurately expressed by the emotional outburst of this moment. Nor was it correctly represented by the brilliant prospectus issued from Thoiry a few days later, when Briand and Stresemann lunched together and discussed the future. Exaggeration in both cases led to later reaction and disappointment. The French people could not so easily forget their devastated districts. The eloquence of Briand could not immediately banish the German memories of Versailles and the Ruhr.

Only those travel-stained pilgrims of the press, who had made the well-nigh interminable hegira, which had begun at Paris in 1919, could fairly measure the transformation. Listening to the words of Briand and Stresemann they could remember the opening episode, when Brockdorff-Rantzau had sat defiantly in the presence of the Big Three at Versailles. They could recall the successive stages—the threats of Paris, the ultimatums of Spa and of London, the panic and passion of Genoa, the early doubts and the later dawning of hope in

London in 1924. For them these memories were the background for Locarno and for Thoiry. Noting the flag of the German Republic flying from the Hôtel Metropole in Geneva, they could visualize the German delegation confined within the palisades which surrounded the Trianon at Versailles in April, 1919.

Others might see in the events of Locarno the promise of perpetual peace in Europe, discover in the conversations of Thoiry the forecast of Franco-German alliance, accept the League of Nations as the ultimate guarantee of the safety of the lamb under mandate to the lion. But these veterans of the score of conferences which mark the milestones between Paris and the final session at Geneva looked backward not forward. For them the measure of the promise for the future was not contained in the glowing prophecies of those whose imagination and faith were stirred by the immediate circumstances of the moment, but in their own exact knowledge of the distance already travelled in seven incredible years.

CHAPTER TWENTY-FOUR

THE EUROPEAN SETTLEMENT

THE entrance of Germany into the League of Nations formally established a new system of law in Europe. The Treaty of Versailles, as revised by the several conventions of London, Locarno, and Geneva, became the basis of future relations between Germany, on the one hand, and France, Belgium, Poland, and Czecho-Slovakia on the other. For Great Britain and Italy, as powers guaranteeing the Security Pact, this system also assumed unmistakable importance.

In examining this Versailles-Locarno compact, in its reference to European peace both present and future, it is essential first to inquire whether it is in accord with the balance of forces which exist at the moment in Europe. The Treaty of Versailles, as it was originally drafted, did not fail because it was morally bad, but because it was politically unsound. The partition treaties of the Eighteenth Century, which destroyed Polish liberty, were from the ethical point of view far worse than those made at the Paris Conference. They survived and remained in force with a slight interruption for nearly a century and a half, because, while they did violence to every consideration of justice they were, nevertheless, consonant with the political verities of

Europe in all these years. In fact, they endured, because Polish capacity for resistance was always inferior to the coercive power of the partitioning powers.

In 1919, by contrast, the strength of the victorious coalition was inadequate to impose the treaty which it made. Not only were the interests of the Allies conflicting, but the partnership itself was based upon temporary not permanent community of interest. Thus, German resistance, which was always inevitable in the premises, compelled the Allies to abandon the attempt to impose the Versailles Treaty and to arrive at an adjustment with the defeated by negotiation.

The fact that the present Versailles-Locarno compact was framed by negotiation and accepted voluntarily by all signatories removes any immediate problem of enforcement. It is, moreover, simple to demonstrate that this settlement is in accord with contemporary European conditions. Europe is, in reality, condemned by exhaustion to a period of enforced domestic reconstruction. All belligerent nations have equal need to concentrate their attention and their resources upon repairing the damages of the recent conflict.

The single requirement in any agreement to end the struggle was that it should bestow upon all nations an equal opportunity to restore their national edifices shaken by foreign war and, in the case of Germany, demolished by defeat and domestic revolution. And for all the Versailles-Locarno agreements contain this irreducible minimum. For ten, perhaps for twenty years, the state of facts resulting from the present adjustment is at least tolerable for every recent belligerent. For each a new conflict would impose hardships and involve dangers which are disproportionate to any conceivable advantage.

Beyond this period of one or two decades, at the close of the time within which exhaustion imposes peace, does the Versailles-Locarno settlement provide ground for the hope of permanent tranquillity? Is the system based upon an adjustment of forces and conditioned upon cirumstances which are likely to remain unchanged? Will a contract made between nations at the moment equally exhausted satisfy the demands of all when they have recuperated? The whole problem of peace or war in Europe in the future may conceivably rest here. But since the question relates to the future, discussion must be largely speculative, and dogmatic conclusions can have no place.

It is, nevertheless, true that the two great powers immediately concerned, France and Germany, have accepted the Versailles-Locarno settlement for totally different reasons. It is equally obvious that they give it absolutely dissimilar interpretations. In the phrase of M. Jacques Seydoux, for years one of the brilliant minds of the Quai d'Orsay, the present settlement is for France an end and for Germany a means.

At the close of the Ruhr war, the German nation found itself utterly exhausted. It was disarmed. Its industrial areas were in French hands. Its financial system was completely wrecked. Recovery was alone possible with foreign aid. But this help was to be obtained only on certain conditions. These conditions included the acceptance of the territorial decisions of Versailles and the payment of reparations, which were later fixed by the Dawes Plan.

No possible recovery for Germany was discoverable save as Germany met these terms. German assent, however, opened the way to a system of negotiated conventions which restored the Ruhr to German control and gave Germany protection against future sanctions. In a word, in return for certain promises, Germany was assured conditions under which she could not only live and work, but also hope within a period of years to recover most if not all the strength which had been hers in 1914.

Germany, in the end, accepted this contract. And its chief condition was contained in the Locarno Pacts which bound her not to undertake by force to revise the boundaries created at Paris. This was a definite pledge not to take up arms against France, Poland, Belgium, or Czecho-Slovakia. In the case of France, the Security Pact also included formal recognition of the *status quo* on the Rhine, and Germany not only proposed this compact herself, but even invited a British guarantee for this *status quo*.

In the German mind, however, these Locarno Pacts did not and do not represent any surrender of the purpose to recover the territories in the East taken by the

Versailles Treaty. They were not an end in the sense of a termination of German hopes. They were simply the sole means by which Germany could escape from the utter ruin which threatened her at the close of the Ruhr struggle. Thus every German is still resolved to recover Danzig, the Corridor, and Upper Silesia.

But neither in 1925 nor in any time which could then be measured by years was there any prospect of recovery of the old frontiers by arms. Surrounded by neighbours fully armed, helpless herself, Germany simply agreed not to undertake what was, in fact, beyond her power to achieve. The contract which she signed was in accord with the physical verities of the hour.

At the same time, however, the German people and the German government put the world on notice of their purpose to regain their lost provinces and also to seek Austrian union with the Reich by other means. And the basis of all German policy for the immediate future is Article XIX of the Covenant of the League of Nations. This provides that the Assembly of the League "may from time to time advise the reconsideration by Members of the League of treaties which have become inapplicable and the consideration of international conditions whose continuance might endanger the peace of the world."

German purpose is not based upon any forced interpretation of this provision. The article was drafted to cover precisely such questions. German action at Geneva in the next few years, therefore, will be comprehended in the attempt to obtain peaceful revision of her eastern frontiers and union with Austria by the application of this Article. And it is true that, technically, it is equally applicable to Alsace-Lorraine, although there is no present purpose to raise this issue. Nor is it less clear that the Germans also purpose to raise the question of German minorities, to press the disarmament issue and, finally, to demand the restoration of a German colony.

Thus, in M. Seydoux's phrase, the German people have accepted Locarno as the means by which to recover domestic equilibrium and political and financial strength. But they have not accepted it as a permanent solution of territorial problems. On the contrary, while renouncing the right to pursue their purpose by military force, they have concomitantly adopted a policy of seeking the same results by moral agitation. As Clausewitz declared, war was only an extension of policy; Stresemann has undertaken to give a similar translation to peace.

France, by contrast, has accepted Locarno as an end in the sense that the French people regard the whole territorial system created by the Versailles Treaty as a definitive settlement. For them peace can be preserved in Europe only as the territorial decisions of Versailles are accepted as permanent.

This view is based upon a logical and traditional interpretation of European history. It is, in fact, founded upon the principle of the balance of power. In all past time the rise of any European power to disproportionate strength and size has invariably resulted in its becoming a menace to the liberty of all other peoples. In this circumstance is to be found the underlying cause of all the great wars of modern times.

Were Germany to succeed in suppressing the Polish Corridor, regaining Upper Silesia, bringing Austria into the Reich, it would at once become a state of 75,000,000 inhabitants. Economically, Poland and Czecho-Slovakia would be isolated from the outside world. Their outlets would be in German hands. Czecho-Slovakia would be almost encircled by German territory. The presence of a considerable and discontented German minority within Czech frontiers would offer a ground for German intervention. Finally, German arrival at the Magyar frontiers would put the Reich in direct contact with all the Balkanized areas to the south.

In the French view this would be to restore that Mitteleuropa, which was the chief war aim of the Hohenzollern régime. German political and economic supremacy in central and southeastern Europe would be established. Military hegemony could hardly fail to follow. Thus for France the freedom of Europe can be preserved only as the territorial system of Versailles is maintained. And the preservation of Poland and Czecho-Slovakia as they now exist and the prohibition of Austrian union with the Reich are the bases of French foreign policy.

In the immediate case of Poland, too, the French see,

what is the fact, that, in the present state of the Polish mind, no new partition could take place except after war. Against it every Pole would fight to the death. Were Poland to be crushed, France would lose an invaluable ally. Were France to permit this to happen, then the Republic would repeat the blunder of Napoleon III. His refusal to support Austria in 1866 left France isolated in 1870 and Sedan was the inevitable epilogue to Sadowa.

All discussion of Franco-German reconciliation, such as that which filled the world at the moment of the famous luncheon at Thoiry, must therefore be predicated upon the clear perception that there is a profound and still-unbridged gap between the policies of the two countries. Locarno means something quite different in Paris and in Berlin. If it holds out hope of ultimate reconciliation, it also discloses the basis for present and future conflict.

Franco-German reconciliation is not prevented by recent or ancient memories, bitter as these are. Both peoples are far too practical to refuse profitable transaction for such reasons. Moreover, since France and Germany are industrially not competitive but complementary, the material circumstances which frequently promote political quarrels are lacking. Indeed, the combination of Ruhr coal and Lorraine iron is so natural as to be well-nigh inevitable. And, in fact, this combination has already been restored through the new steel cartel.

In both countries there is clear evidence of a real

desire for *rapprochement.* A renewal of war would mean ruin for each. Germany, to be sure, is bound eventually to be stronger than France, yet French hostility, based upon resentment over Alsace-Lorraine, made France the centre of a coalition which overthrew Germany in 1918. Moreover, this side of war, French opposition can block all German purposes at Geneva.

At the present time, France would welcome a permanent settlement with Germany, based upon German acceptance of the territorial situation in Europe, which exists and was created at Paris in 1919. Germany, on her side, would quite as gladly accept a settlement with France based upon French willingness to accept an irrevocable German guarantee of the *status quo* on the Rhine. It is on the Vistula and the Danube, and not on the Rhine, that French and German policies clash.

But it must be frankly conceded that real Franco-German reconciliation is hardly possible while this fundamental difference in interpretation of Locarno continues. Unmistakably, the atmosphere has changed between 1923 and 1926. But it would be futile to blink the fact that the hereditary enemies still remain, divided by a question which for one involves the problem of security and for the other the prospect of racial and national unity.

And it is essential to perceive, also, that, at bottom, French support of Poland and Czecho-Slovakia is based upon the maintenance of French security. While the British guarantee is valuable, no Frenchman forgets that it was Russian invasion in East Prussia which made victory possible at the Marne. While, too, immediate British military aid would be comprehended in an expeditionary army of 150,000 regulars; the two Slav states would together mobilize 1,500,000 conscripts in case of war.

German right to carry the territorial question to Geneva is beyond question, but the chance of obtaining any favourable action in any present time is slight. With France will stand her allies, Poland and Czecho-Slovakia. Rumania and Jugo-Slavia, in fact all the states created or expanded by the war, will be equally opposed to a programme which envisages the revision of frontiers. Nor is it unlikely that certain of the neutrals of the war will incline to the same view.

By contrast, Germany will be assured at once of the support of Hungary, Bulgaria, and Lithuania, all of whom demand revision and seek to regain lost provinces. Austria also may take the same side. But this is only to restore the alignment of the war. It is to pit the Continental victors against the vanquished again. It is not to unite Europe but to divide it.

In this situation, the course taken by the two great powers which have guaranteed the Security Pact, Italy and Great Britain, must be of great importance. Italian policy, however, remains obscure. Italy seeks a modification of the *status quo* in the Mediterranean and at the expense of France in Tunis. French and Italian relations are marked by extreme tension. Thus, Italian support for Germany might be conjectured.

German purposes, however, hardly square with Italian in Europe. The presence of a considerable German-speaking population in the Upper Adige has already provoked bitter words between Rome and Berlin. German wish to absorb Austria would bring Germany to the Brenner Pass, revive Italian apprehensions for Trieste, and immediately threaten ruin to all Italian ambition to play a considerable rôle in the Balkans. Thus, while Mussolini may support Germany in the Polish issue, he is just as likely to stand with France on the question of *Anschluss*.

British policy, as contrasted with Italian, is net. All British interest is comprehended in the desire to preserve peace on the Continent. It is a policy of peace at any price. The British have never accepted the Wilsonian solution of the Polish Corridor. They do not believe the Poles can hold the Corridor permanently. Therefore, they reason that it would be wiser and safer to give it back to the Germans.

Moreover, the British see clearly that the Polish Question is the immediate obstacle to Franco-German reconciliation. But if France and Germany fail to come to terms, war may one day result. In that case, Britain, as the guarantor of the Security Pact, would be involved. Consequently, the British not only do not support the French policy in the east of Europe, but steadily seek to persuade the French to abandon both Poland and Czecho-Slovakia and thus retire from all Central European disputes.

Under the immediate influence of recent Bolshevist activities, however, British sentiment in Polish matters has shown a certain modification. Nevertheless, the change is based rather upon Russian than German considerations. Thus, British support of German demands at Geneva, at least with respect to the eastern frontier, is assured.

Within limits, therefore, the situation which existed before Locarno continues. In the case of the new Treaty, as in that of the old, France and Germany are squarely opposed. And, in addition, now, as then, British policy takes a German rather than a French line. And, at the present time, as in all the Versailles struggle, while British support will encourage German purpose, French power remains sufficient to block German success.

There remains, too, the immediate problem of the armies of occupation in the Rhineland. For all Germans these constitute an intolerable circumstance. Locarno and the Security Pact, together with the entrance into the League of Nations, were accepted as a promise that the Allied troops would go, not in 1935 but in 1927. It was recognized that to hasten the departure financial inducements for the French were necessary. This was the basis of the Thoiry conversation.

But at bottom Thoiry involved the flotation of German industrial and railway securities to the amount of several billions. Only the American market could conceivably absorb these. But always the American insistence upon French ratification of the debt agreement seemed to block the way, although Washington was never officially consulted. Thus the collapse of the Thoiry programme brought disillusionment and disappointment to Paris and Berlin alike.

At the moment, evacuation is halted. The arrival of a Nationalist Cabinet in February, 1927, produced apprehension in France. Since the war, no steps have been taken to fortify the Alsace-Lorraine frontier, and France is open to invasion. Nevertheless, at bottom there is equal appreciation in Paris and Berlin that the occupation cannot continue indefinitely, without creating new frictions and fresh grudges. If, at the moment (March, 1927), negotiations have been halted, they are almost certain to be resumed. And the precedents of 1818 and 1873 serve as foundations for the belief that, long before 1935, the occupation will be terminated and both the Rhineland and the Saar returned to German control.

Last of all there is the Russian factor. While Russia remains outside the European circle, adjustments are provisional, policies subject to complete revision, forecasts pure speculation. Moreover, not only is the European situation, with Russia absent, abnormal, but there does not exist any knowledge upon which to base calculation as to when or how Russia will return.

It is equally possible that a renascent Russia may be

an ally of Germany against the West and of the West against Germany. The traditional rivalry between Slav and Teuton may easily reappear and Russia resume her historic rôle as the protector of the Slav fragments of the centre and south of Europe. Thus, eventually, Moscow and not Paris or Rome may undertake the task of blocking German expansion to the south.

For Germany, the Russian circumstance is all-important. Russia must be for her an ally and then a common policy based upon a renewal of the Polish Partition will unite the two nations. Or, by contrast, the old collision of interests will restore the situation of 1914. And it was fear of the great Slav neighbour which sent the Germans unprotestingly to the firing line in the opening days of the World War. Nor is it less patent that many Germans hold to the conviction that it was the abandonment of the policy of understanding with Russia, followed by both Frederick the Great and Bismarck, which prepared German defeat in the World War.

To-day, although all Germans refuse to accept the Paris solution of the eastern frontier and popular support for the purpose to seek a revision in Geneva is unanimous, it is in the Russian circumstance that the German people see the real hope of the recovery of Danzig, the Corridor, and Upper Silesia. For them Poland is an unreal creation of Paris, destined to endure only so long as Russia remains paralyzed by domestic anarchy. It is not the expectation of prompt revision which explains the policy of protest at Geneva. On the contrary, the German calculation is to keep the issue alive against that time when Russian recovery will bring a solution favourable to Germany. In such time, too, all Germans perceive that France will be powerless to protect the Polish ally.

As a consequence, while Stresemann accepted the Western Orientation and Locarno was made in the face of Russian protest, it was preceded by still another Russo-German pact, extending the agreements of Rapallo, and German policy steadily adheres to the purpose to keep the door open in the East. Moreover, in the present situation in Europe, and in the face of the unmistakable influence of France within the League of Nations, while Russia continues impotent, German power is narrowly restricted and German hopes have small chance of realization.

Thus, in the larger sense, it must be recognized that Locarno was an end and not a beginning. It terminated a war; it did not settle any of the larger issues which divide nations. Europe, after Locarno as before, is crowded with controversies. To-day, as yesterday, France and Germany are separated by conflicting policies which not only have their roots in the deepest traditions of two old peoples, but also have immediate and continuing relevance to contemporary conditions. Finally, while the riddle of Russia is unread, all policies and all purposes are subject to instant and complete transformation, and while on the surface all physical circumstances have been changed, at bottom the change is inconsiderable and Europe remains Europe.

In this situation must one accept the familiar American view that Europe is already headed for a new war and that the present calm is a truce of preparation imposed by exhaustion? Hardly. To do this would be to ignore certain unmistakable factors. Above all, it would be to exclude the all-important circumstance that for the first time in European history not only has a war ended without victory in any material sense, but the struggle has brought all the great peoples to the very edge of utter and enduring ruin.

Between 1914 and 1925 every European people was forced to confront, not merely the danger of devastating defeat in war, but also that of complete and utter disintegration in their domestic, social, and political systems. From 1918 to 1924, the shadow of Bolshevism rested over the whole Continent. Men and women did not then, as now, consider that a new war would mean the extinction of European civilization; they were compelled to face the possibility that the World War, itself, had resulted in this catastrophe.

Actually, after Locarno, Europe at last arrives at a period and lives in an atmosphere in which the lessons of the long decade of strife can be analyzed objectively. Despair, passion, resentment born of wrongs which were immediate and intolerable, have disappeared. Before Locarno, Europe sought, not to preserve peace, but to possess it. The emotion which attended the signing of the pacts did not arise from the belief that perpetual peace had been established, but that actual peace had been attained.

Moreover, the whole system of pacts, which constitute the settlement of Locarno, even the separate alliances which unite certain states and divide others, have been related directly to the League of Nations. This is more than an accident, and it is just as clearly the evidence of a new factor in the European equation. The League of Nations is not a solution, it is an experiment. Nevertheless, it is manifest to anyone who knows the various European democracies of the hour that there is a real and growing demand on the part of all peoples that the experiment be made.

At the moment, the situation in Europe is clear. Negotiation and voluntary agreement have established a system of peace which is in present time tolerable. Exhaustion has imposed conditions which for all nations equally preclude new conflict in all present time. Necessity and public opinion alike direct governments to make use of the League of Nations. From 1924 onward, peoples have given not one but many impressive evidences of their support for policies which envisage conciliation and of their rejection of the men and the methods which lead to conflict.

Viewed from a distance, it is easy to see Europe unchanged; to believe that the peoples, like the Bourbons before them, have learned nothing and forgotten nothing. Seen at close range, however, it is impossible not to feel that, while the physical circumstances have changed astonishingly little, the psychological mutations have been almost incalculable. The transformation may be temporary, the new atmosphere may be transient, but to-day it is the real fact in the European situation. It is the imponderable, and it is expressed in the "*drang nach Genf.*"

CHAPTER TWENTY-FIVE

THE LEAGUE OF NATIONS

SINCE not merely the Locarno Pacts, but all of the various treaties of alliance and security which constitute the framework of the new European system, have been directly related to the League of Nations, the Geneva organization has in recent years become increasingly a vital circumstance in European affairs. And, in fact, since Herriot and MacDonald decided, in 1924, to make the League the basis of French and British foreign policy, Geneva has more and more been the political centre of Europe.

In spite of the European development of the League, however, in America it has steadily remained difficult to examine it with any degree of objectivity, because of the survival of political prejudices and personal grudges. While the League has thus continuously evolved, opinion in the United States has on the whole remained unmodified and unvaryingly hostile. Moreover, while, in Europe, Geneva is the battleground between Liberal and Nationalist camps, in America, the considerable support which the League undoubtedly commands, lies outside both party organizations. Not even in liberal circles are League sympathies pronounced or general

Again, discussion of the League in the United States is rendered well-nigh impossible by the existence of two sets of equally erroneous convictions. On the one hand, those who support the League claim for it limitless and almost unimaginable achievements. By contrast, the opponents deny it every useful attribute. To the former it is Utopia, in full and efficient operation. To the latter it is failure, already established beyond debate.

It follows, therefore, that any discussion of the League, as it exists, must be prefaced by the double explanation of what it is not and of what it actually is. For, as is inevitable, the truth lies midway between both contentions. Moreover, the initial reality about the League is that, despite general and popular conception, it is not an institution which has within itself authority or power to preserve peace or to prevent war. Indeed, not only does it lack force, but all the recent evolution of the League has been away from the idea of force.

This evolution was not, however, the result of any absence of effort to clothe the Geneva institution with the authority and bestow upon it the power to prevent war by the exertion of force. Article X of the Covenant was expressly designed to provide the new Society of Nations with command of the necessary military, naval, and economic weapons to prevent aggression or to protect a state wantonly attacked.

The rejection of the Treaty of Versailles by the United States Senate destroyed the vitality of this article.

The American action, too, was definitely based upon the assertion that the American people were unwilling, in the interests of general peace, to assume responsibility for the forcible maintenance of peace in Europe. The idea of a continuing obligation to send troops to Europe to defend the frontiers or liberties of European peoples, at the decision of the League, was contrary to American tradition and was unacceptable to the American people.

American rejection removed one of the great nations whose strength might have been available. Later quarrels between the British and French nations had a similar consequence. Yet the idea of force was not abandoned. On the contrary, it reappeared in the Protocol of 1924. In this proposal, the principle was reaffirmed much more concretely. By the terms of this contract, member nations not only subscribed to the formula of "arbitration, security, and disarmament," but accepted the obligation to defend each other against unprovoked aggression. Here was a very definite military and naval alliance to preserve peace by force.

Once more, however, the project was blocked by an Anglo-Saxon country. Great Britain, which had already rejected the Cecil memorandum, looking in the same direction, now definitely refused approval to a programme which would have imposed a moral obligation to send British troops and ships to war without regard to immediate British material interests, simply upon the decision of the League of Nations.

In both cases the Anglo-Saxon nations acted for the

same reason. In the eyes of the British and American peoples, the risks were in excess of the advantages. Neither country was willing to permit its sovereignty to be impaired to the extent of permitting the decision of war or peace to be made for it, not in Parliament in London nor Congress in Washington, but in the League at Geneva. Neither was convinced that the costs incident to a war precipitated to restrain an aggressor might not be out of proportion to the benefits resulting from the Protocol itself.

These two failures, however, left the League destitute of all physical power to enforce its decisions. Its duty to pronounce judgment in cases of aggression not only remained, but was emphasized by the various other treaties which were made. But, great as might be the moral value of the decision, it was the limit of its power. And this situation has continued. All criticism of the League for its inability to prevent war or preserve peace is, therefore, utterly unjust, because the failure arises uniquely from the refusal of the two Anglo-Saxon countries to consent to delegation of power.

Parallel with the effort to arm the League was another effort, which was first expressed in the treaties of Guarantee made at the Paris Peace Conference. By these treaties, Clemenceau, who did not believe the League would ever acquire power adequate to guarantee security, sought the British and American pledge to defend France against any later German attack. This French demand aroused protest from all friends of the League, because they believed that it was designed to establish a system of separate alliances in place of the central League authority of the Covenant. Woodrow Wilson, however, agreed, because for the moment, since the League was yet to be organized, it could obviously accomplish nothing.

When the Guarantee treaties fell with the American rejection of the Treaty of Versailles, French statesmanship turned elsewhere to search for security. Thus, there were framed treaties of alliance between France, Belgium, Poland, and Czecho-Slovakia. All these alliances were defensive, all were modelled upon the original Guarantee treaties. Not only were all registered at Geneva, but it was left to the League to establish the fact of aggression.

This is the basis of the system of alliances which exists in Europe to-day. These alliances result from the fact that the United States and Great Britain refused to enter a general alliance to insure mutual protection for all countries. In addition to the French treaties, similar compacts bind Rumania, Jugo-Slavia, and Czecho-Slovakia in the Little Entente and Poland and Rumania. These are founded upon the perfectly patent truth that, while in theory and in principle it is the duty of all nations belonging to the League of Nations to unite in common defence, in fact, only those nations whose material interests are directly involved will take up arms. The immemorial question, "Am I my brother's keeper?" is thus answered by the statement, "Only where fraternal interests are identical and defence of my brother is defence of myself."

British opinion, however, was hardly less hostile to the system of separate alliances than it had been to the collective partnership of the Protocol. Not only did the British object to these alliances in principle, but in practice they saw that, in the existing situation in Europe, French influence would be enormously fortified by them. Thus France became actually the controlling member of a coalition of all the countries similarly interested in the preservation of the territorial *status quo*.

When the question arose over the guarantee of French security, the British consistently refused to undertake a separate alliance with France while France remained associated with her several Continental allies. Faced, however, with the necessity of establishing some system of security in the West, where British interests were directly affected, the Tory Cabinet finally adopted the system of the Security Pact. By this, Great Britain guaranteed, not one nation against another, but a *status quo* satisfactory to British interests against the two nations which might disturb it, namely, Germany and France. Once more, as in all other cases, it was left to the League to establish the fact of aggression. In this pact Italy also participated on the same terms.

Three systems to insure peace have thus been experimented with in Europe since the war. First, that of the Covenant and the Protocol, which was a general compact and would have given the League real power to preserve peace; second, the separate alliances, which left to the exposed and therefore interested nations the right to act on League judgments. Finally, the Security Pact formula.

In Europe to-day, therefore, judicial power to decide the fact of aggression resides in the League. But police power rests entirely with the nations which have material and therefore selfish reasons for action. And the purpose to exercise this power is disclosed in the several treaties of alliance and in the Security Pact.

It would, of course, be absurd to overlook the moral power which belongs to the League. Within limits, no nation would care to invite the judgment of Geneva that it had been guilty of unprovoked attack and of a wilful disturbance of the peace of the world. What is to be recognized is not that the moral power is unimportant but that it is the actual limit of League power. And, in this sense, while the League can license defensive war, it cannot prevent offensive.

There is a second and peculiarly American illusion as to the League. Not unnaturally, but quite without reason, many Americans see an analogy between the meeting of European states in Geneva and of American at Washington. They conceive the League to be a nascent United States of Europe, if not of the Universe. It becomes for them a "federation of mankind" and from the Geneva galleries they look down with sorrow and shame upon the vacant chairs, which, to their minds, should be occupied by American delegates.

But, in point of fact, while the future arrival of a United States of Europe is possible and Geneva may well be its capital, the post-war evolution of Europe is not in the direction of political union. The British rejection of the Protocol was a significant evidence that the British people were not willing to permit their sovereignty to be impaired in the interests of international union. On the Continent, moreover, the results of the war have been enormously dissolving, and not only has the number of states been increased but also the division between peoples has been greatly emphasized.

Any patient and careful study of contemporary Europe will certainly demonstrate the fallacy of the attempt to establish analogy between the present relations of Continental countries and those which had developed between the Thirteen Colonies at the close of the American Revolution. It may be true, as many argue, that Europe must federate or perish, but it is not less true that, at the moment, this process is not even beginning. The idea of the League gains ground, but association within the League is predicated upon unimpaired sovereignty. This is a patent paradox, but is just as obviously the present truth.

The League of Nations cannot prevent war by force. On a continent in which the centrifugal influences of nationalism march visibly, it is not becoming the framework of any United States of Europe discoverable today. Must one then accept the judgment of American critics of the Geneva institution? On the contrary, while the evolution of the League is steadily away from American conceptions, its growth and development continue.

And, in fact, it must be perceived not merely that the machinery of the League has been invoked in the application of all the intricate system of agreements and alliances, which are the bases of European peace, but also that the idea of the League has become the first principle in all Liberal and Democratic political groups in Europe. Concomitantly, too, Geneva has become a centre of political relations to a degree unparalleled in modern history.

Nor is it less obvious that all this extension lies outside the immediate reality of the institution itself. The League which is visible to the eye is a useful and even invaluable organization, which with increasing efficiency performs the necessary international chores of civilization. But the idea of the League is at once something far more considerable and less concrete.

To appreciate the relation of the League of Nations to present-day Europe, it is essential to establish the difference between the American and European history of the idea, itself. In the United States a great wave of enthusiasm for the proposal of a league of nations came and went. It was an emotional and evangelical explosion. It was evanescent because it was unrelated to any immediate and controlling necessities. American conditions did not compel the American people or their public men to face the question of war and peace as one of future life or death for their country. After the World War, as before, the United States was impregnable, its prosperity and safety were unimpaired.

Thus, the League represented an adventure in idealism. This idea developed with the war. It supplied a moral justification for what was otherwise, in itself, international murder. But, while the promise of a new and better world, consequent upon the adoption of the League, was inspiring, the American world, even without a league, was not only possible but very far from unattractive. Thus, in the United States, sentiment for the League was never the expression of a dominating and controlling necessity.

By contrast, the development of the League idea in Europe had little of the American circumstance. The proposal aroused slight enthusiasm at the outset. On the contrary, in its first stages it excited general and cynical criticism. American arguments for it seemed at once naïve and incomprehensible, and Europe laughed with Clemenceau. Undoubtedly, the League idea found supporters, but for the European world, it seemed an Americanism which was wholly untranslatable. Throughout the period of the Peace Conference the European attitude toward the League was that it was the toy of a wealthy child, who must be humoured.

After Paris, the first distinct move toward the League came from the small powers. But it was not in any sense a moral or idealistic move. It had its origin in the perception by the practically minded political leaders of the smaller countries that certain very definite and material advantages could be drawn from the institution. And, in this preliminary stage, the League ceased to be a moral reform; it was no longer the project of idealists, it became a political experiment.

It was not until after the occupation of the Ruhr that the British, French, or German peoples began to look to Geneva. Ten years of war and post-war anarchy had, however, produced a very definite conviction in the minds of masses of European people that the alternative of the future was between some form of international compromise and collective European collapse. The bankruptcy of nationalism, which had been steadily and inevitably hostile to the League, almost insensibly sent the Liberal and Democratic opposition, now developing, to Geneva.

Again, as in the case of the smaller powers, this drift of the Left in the great powers toward the League was very largely determined by physical circumstances. It was not faith in the principles of the League, but plain perception that the League offered the single alternative to the programme of nationalism, which had failed, that led to ultimate adoption of the idea of the League by the *Cartel des Gauches* in France, by Liberal and Labour parties in Great Britain, and presently by the Socialist and Bourgeois parties in Germany.

Thus, while the idea of the League was only transiently a basis of political conflict between the two great political parties in the United States, it became and it remains one of the main points of divergence between the two European camps which represent, broadly speaking, the two ideas of nationalism and liberalism. Moreover, the success of liberalism in Great Britain and in France in the elections of December, 1923, and May, 1924, resulted in the adoption of the League as the basis of foreign policy in both countries. A year later, the Republican Left in Germany sustained a Cabinet which had accepted Locarno and the League in a similar fashion.

As a result, although it is perfectly true that the League has enlisted a considerable idealistic support in Europe, this is not, as in the United States, the real basis of League strength. On the contrary, the League has become a practical political question in the largest possible sense. And the question arises from the greatest problem which faces Europe or can face it in our own time. Moreover, despite temporary reactions, it is not merely patent that liberalism is gaining ground in Europe, but also that nationalism finds itself, even in periods of temporary success, unable to reverse the movement toward Geneva. This is not true in Italy, where the conditions are unlike those elsewhere among great peoples, but it is true in France, Great Britain, and Germany. Moreover, in Europe, generally, the support of all the small states, without regard to domestic political divisions, is constant.

Liberalism in all countries and all parties in small countries have decided to adopt the idea of the League as the basis of foreign policy and to coöperate in the effort to make the League of Nations which does now exist at Geneva the expression of this idea. It is, however, clear, that in its present form the League does not even measurably fulfil the minimum requirements. It is, itself, at best an imperfect and rudimentary sketch of the institution required to express the idea. It is, in reality, only the beginning of an experiment. But, always, it must be remembered, the beginning of a political and not a moral experiment.

In this preliminary stage, therefore, Europe has had recourse to a fiction, which is to-day the largest fact about the League of Nations. At the bottom of the European conception of the League is the perception that a new conflict means probable extinction of European civilization. And international compromise is the single alternative. As a consequence, while the machinery of the League of Nations is totally unready to perform the necessary task, while, too, the present nationalistic state of mind in Europe rigidly rejects any such surrender of national sovereignty as would be involved in clothing the League with the necessary powers, Europe goes to Geneva and compromises, outside of the actual limits of the Society of Nations, itself.

When Chamberlain, Briand, and Stresemann met at Geneva in March, 1926, to validate the Locarno pacts by German entrance into the League, the differences which had arisen were compromised, not by the League, but by these statesmen directly. When Briand and

Stresemann met at Thoiry, they met as Foreign Ministers of their respective countries; the League was not directly involved. When they met at Geneva again at the close of the year and adjusted the question of German armaments, later definitively settled in the agreement of February 1, 1927, the decision was reached by the statesmen; the League was, in reality, only the pretext which made their conference possible.

Thus, in a sense, the League is nothing. But in another sense it is everything. For there has developed and is still growing in Europe the realization of the fact that international differences must be adjusted by compromise, and all peoples have more or less completely accepted the view that Geneva is the place where compromise is to be made. It is not the actual operation of League machinery which promotes these compromises, but it is the popular idea of the League which permits them to be made.

Similar adjustments might conceivably be made elsewhere, but popular assent to these afterward would be vastly more difficult to obtain. In a word, the idea of the League has outstripped the fact. The machinery is, as yet, totally inadequate to perform the task nominally incumbent upon it. It is even conceivable that no such capacity will ever be attained, but the results actually reached at Geneva are not largely affected thereby.

Nothing is more difficult than to explain to any American public this extraordinary paradox of the League of Nations at the present hour. The phenomenon is at once metaphysical and intensely European. It reverts to the Truce of God of the mediæval world and it just as clearly discloses the influence of modern democratic evolution. It represents an incredible compromise between the centrifugal influences of nationalism, which the war undoubtedly stimulated, and the centripetal necessities, which the prospect of any new conflict creates. Every effort to translate it into the dangerous simplifications of American experience is unsatisfactory, because, while the outward resemblances are often striking, the inward spirit is as different as the history of the two continents.

Nevertheless, there can be no doubt of the fact that the League has become a continuing fact in European life. It has also become the basis of the fundamental difference between two schools of European political thought. The idea has been accepted by masses of the peoples in all western countries except Italy. Not only is the experiment to continue, but it will in the future be carried on, not by emotional idealism, but by practical political leadership, because it has become, not a question of moral reform, but a problem of practical political existence.

The League, is, moreover, not merely an idea but a place. It has become the point of contact not only of the statesmen but of the pressmen of Europe. Twice a year the foreign ministers of all countries assemble at Geneva. Nominally, they come to attend the Council or the Assembly. Actually, their presence makes possible innumerable conferences and discussions. No similar contact has been possible in modern European history. The immunities supplied by the League deprive the meetings of any character of incidents which might provoke domestic comment and criticism.

It is impossible to exaggerate the value of this phase of the League activity. It lies totally outside of the League institution. But again, it is the fiction of the League which makes possible a fact of enormous importance. And precisely the same contact takes place between the journalists of Europe. Those who make policies and those who make opinions meet. Moreover, the foreign ministers of all countries receive the correspondents of every nation. All the pending problems of the year can find authoritative explanation and illuminating elucidation. It is a cross section of Europe which one meets on the quays and bridges of Geneva each September. Few of the journalists ever attend the League sessions; the statesmen go only on ceremonial days. But, except for the League, none would be in Geneva.

Thus, it must be perceived how little of all that is most important in the achievement, not primarily of the League, but because of the League, relates to those phases which were the bases of the American political debate. As an institution the League of Nations has evolved slowly and, after all, slightly, but as an idea and a place its expansion has been well-nigh incredible.

No circumstance in recent League history is more puzzling to the American world than the relation of

Geneva to the question of limitation of armaments. None, too, better discloses the fundamental difference between the conceptions of the two continents. In the United States it seems axiomatic that the way to disarm is to disarm; that the problem is simple and arithmetical. Since results do not flow from disarmament discussions at Geneva, American opinion easily concludes that the League is a failure and the episode a new evidence of European hypocrisy.

Such views are not only possible but natural for a country seated between Canada and Mexico and behind the Atlantic and Pacific oceans. American military and naval strength is not based upon American policy. It only vaguely represents American estimate of concrete dangers. It is an insurance against a possible conflagration, but it is an insurance based on a rate which is established haphazard and by accident.

In Europe, on the contrary, armaments are the disclosure of fire risks very carefully estimated and scientifically adjusted. Limitation of armament involves the reduction of the fire risks themselves. The rate of insurance will only be reduced with the diminution of the danger. And, in fact, as the prospects of peace in Europe increase, the size of armaments diminishes automatically and proportionately. Therefore, all discussion of the limitation of armaments promptly resolves itself into the examination of those political circumstances on which armaments are based.

And, in the end, reduction of armaments in Europe

will not result from decisions reached at Geneva. At most, the League will only be the instrument which records the gradual evolution of European spirit away from fear and toward confidence and thus toward compromise instead of conflict. The League will not impose upon Europe or upon any European state a standard of military or naval strength.

Nowhere more clearly than in this direction is disclosed the fact that the League is primarily an idea and not an institution, a method and not a machine. It is measurably the expression of a European purpose, but it is the development of the purpose which will dictate the decisions of Geneva. In the United States the question of limitation of armaments is absolute and is confined to guns and ships. In Europe, it is an infinitely complex puzzle in balance. On our side of the water it is the primary circumstance in peace; on the other, it is utterly secondary.

It is not in the least true that disarmament makes small progress at Geneva because the European nations desire war, cling to militarism, and disguise old purposes behind new pretences. The reality is that the organization of peace in Europe is, in the very nature of things, complex almost beyond believing, and disarmament is no more than a barometer which records the progress toward adjustment. Promise of peace does not come from the reduction of armies. But the growth of the confidence in peace steadily sends the strength of military establishments downward.

All reduction of armaments in Europe must be predicated upon the extension of political adjustments. Nations will not surrender their own views of their needs in the direction of military guarantees against dangers which are real. But the reduction of the apprehension of danger will modify the national estimates of the amount of protection required. Thus the development of the League idea in Europe will enormously influence the future strength of armies. But no disarmament conference at Geneva will much hasten the spread of the idea and can never anticipate its consequences. Nothing will be settled by such a conference, but every modification of European dangers will be there recorded.

A disarmament conference at Geneva is not a meeting for a definite and specific purpose limited in time and space. No concrete results can be reached and final adjournment taken. On the contrary, such a conference must have something like the character of a continuing and even a permanent congress. No definitive solution of the problem of armaments will ever be reached. Agreement will only record the changes which have actually taken place in the European estimates of the perils and promise of contemporary conditions.

Underlying the rejection of President Coolidge's proposal for a new conference to fix naval ratios, made in February, 1927, was the Continental conviction that the political adjustments on which such a programme could be based had not been made. To the French, it seemed a characteristic American attempt to persuade

Europe to abandon the consideration of a foundation and start construction at the ground floor. It endeavoured to bring Europe to deal with its most complex and intricate problem as if it were a simple sum in arithmetic. Finally, it was made by the country which utterly refused to share in the effort to adjust the larger question and simply asked that Europe turn its attention to the only detail in which the United States was concerned or interested.

No examination of the League of Nations can be complete, however, without the frank recognition that it is now in full crisis. It was at first completely the concern of the small nations. Not until 1924 did the larger powers turn to Geneva. But even then it was only the Allied nations which came. The entrance of Germany and the obvious purpose of the Germans to carry to Geneva problems which divided Europe open a new page in League history.

At one time the German purpose must give additional importance to Geneva sessions and supply the first real test of the vitality of the spirit which lies back of the institution. Everything so far has been in a very real sense preliminary. There have been established an idea and a place. But none of the greater questions which divide Europe have been posed. Two processes have gone forward simultaneously, the war has been liquidated outside of the League and the League has developed in Geneva, or, more exactly, the idea of the League has taken form and found acceptance in Europe.

It is the problems of the future which now appear on the agenda. The question of whether compromise is possible or eventual conflict inescapable must be answered, not once, not definitively, but again and again, from year to year. No one can, of course, foretell the outcome. But it is clear that the single conceivable basis of hope for the future, which has emerged from the catastrophe of our own time, is the idea which is instinct in the popular conception of the meaning of the League of Nations. Geneva may fail, but the experiment of European peace is to be made there and nowhere else.

Democratic control of foreign policy has become absolute. The machinery of diplomacy which was adapted to the old order has broken down and in large measure been discarded. The forms remain, but year by year they lose vitality and value. But in all European democracies there has been discoverable in the past three years the growing purpose to make use of the idea underlying the League as the new basis of international relations.

The war and the post-war anarchy for the first time drove the democratic groups and parties of Europe to the consideration of foreign policy and international relations. Inevitably, their struggle had hitherto been concentrated at home and upon domestic problems. Power had come to their hands, but not only was experience lacking but the impelling force of necessity was not felt. The problem was not practical and immediate. Nearly a decade and a half of continued and intense misery and suffering have, however, intervened to emphasize the relation of foreign affairs to domestic existence.

In this situation it is, perhaps, more than an accident, that the Democratic parties and political groups in all European countries have with unmistakable unanimity adopted the League idea as the basis of their foreign action. If the process has been instinctive, it is not less logical. It may well reveal the effort of democracy to fashion an instrument to its own hands, consonant with contemporary conditions, and to make it serve the purposes diplomacy fulfilled in the era of kings. At all events, the facts remain, Democratic control of foreign policy continues, and all the European democracies have adopted the League of Nations. If nationalism resists, its fight unmistakably has the character of a rearguard action.

Only in the United States does the opposition to the League of Nations successfully hold its ground. But the explanation is simple. It was not idealism and the urge for moral reform which produced the revolution in opinion with respect to the League which has certainly taken place in Europe in the past eight years. On the contrary, the whole movement has proceeded only under the driving impulsion of immediate necessity

In the United States the idea of the League of Nations has always been associated with the dream of a better world. In Europe, it is being accepted slowly as the single alternative to the complete and utter destruction of the existing world. For the American people the

League has appeared a dangerous adventure into the unknown. For Europeans, it increasingly represents the single avenue of escape from the known.

Woodrow Wilson's purely American conception of an ideal solution for world problems has, therefore, with the passing of years, been translated into a system based upon the political realities of Europe. The sea change which it has suffered has made it largely unintelligible to American experience and unrelated to American needs. But, by contrast, the Wilsonian conception of an American mission to regenerate Europe has about vanished. Concomitantly, the Irreconcilable suspicion of a European conspiracy to destroy American independence is passing.

As a consequence, the perception of the possibilities and the necessities of coöperation with the League of Nations in questions which have common interest is developing on this side of the Atlantic. Within the limit of national tradition and interest, too, the process is bound to continue and the coöperation to be extended. American refusal to join the League may stand indefinitely, but American appearance at Geneva is likely to be increasingly frequent. And in practice the distinction is unimportant.

CHAPTER TWENTY-SIX

AMERICA AND EUROPE

WHILE Europe was making peace without America, there was also proceeding another operation which constitutes a definite part of the whole post-war settlement. During the course of the struggle, four of the opponents of Germany had made vast borrowings in the United States. Indeed, in April, 1917, when the American declaration of war was published to the world, the first and most urgent appeal of all the nations which thus became our associates was for financial aid.

During the balance of the war and in the immediate post-war period upward of $10,000,000,000 was loaned to Great Britain, France, Belgium, and Italy. During several years thereafter, the question of the liquidation of this huge debt remained in abeyance. At the moment the borrowers had given their notes of hand for the loans, and these notes bound them to pay 5 per cent. interest. The United States, in its turn, had obtained the funds by the sale of Liberty bonds within its own areas, and the cost of carrying this foreign lending was thus transferred to the shoulders of the American taxpayer.

It was only in 1922 that American opinion and policy finally began to take form in the matter of these debts. In that time sentimental feelings had rapidly cooled.

Sympathy with European suffering had been moderated by suspicion. Europe seemed resolved to prolong conflict and to pursue policies which to the remote American mind appeared calculated to prevent any real restoration of peace. The loans themselves thus constituted, in American opinion, foundation for new wars. Payment was judged to be a sure way to deprive Europe of the means of continuing the conflict.

This American insistence upon payment opened a new period in the relations between the two continents. The American refusal to honour the signature of Woodrow Wilson and to ratify the Treaty of Versailles had resulted in grave misfortunes for all the European belligerents, and in their eyes it had taken on the colour of an evasion of a moral obligation on the flimsiest of legal technicalities.

European resentment at the American withdrawal was now accentuated by the demand for repayment of moneys advanced during the struggle. As to the legality of the claims, there was no question. But while all the European peoples recognized the legal strength of the American case, all equally rejected the idea that the debts had moral warrant. American policy in the matter of debts, joined to American policy in respect to the Treaty of Versailles, therefore constituted for all European nations a grievance and henceforth all relations were poisoned by the consequences of the dispute over the debts.

On the American side, the government and the majority of the people adopted the view that the loans were commercial transactions. They were regarded as lying outside the area of war contributions to a common cause. There was an absolute refusal to consider any sentimental or moral elements. The Harding and Coolidge Administrations, alike, laid down the principle that the debtors must pay in full, save as integral payment was patently beyond capacity.

American public opinion felt itself further fortified by the fact that, while the European associates took large profits in territories both European and colonial, the United States had declined all share in the fruits of the common victory. France had recovered Alsace-Lorraine and acquired the Kamerun and Syria. Italy had annexed Trieste and the Trentino and seized Fiume. Great Britain had taken German East and Southwest Africa, with other mandates in Asia, including Palestine and the Iraq. America had obtained neither a foot of territory nor a dollar of indemnity.

Europe, by contrast, rejected the legal for what it conceived to be the moral interpretation of the facts. It reasoned that the World War was always a collective operation and America always concerned. It argued that in remaining neutral for three years, the United States had, in fact, left it for the other belligerents to fight its battle. Thus American failure to enter the struggle before April, 1917, imposed disproportionate losses upon the other opponents of Germany.

On this basis Europe measured its casualties and its

vast property losses with American. It asserted that it had paid a price in blood and treasure, which, in fact, represented the cost of American neutrality. If it had borrowed vast sums in the United States after America entered the war, this borrowing had been the inevitable consequence of carrying on the struggle for three years without American aid. At the very least, the loans represented a fair counterweight and cancellation by the United States would be no more than an act of justice.

This broad principle found general European acceptance. There were, naturally, variations in the several countries. The French based their view upon 1,400,000 casualties and the vast extent of devastation in their northern departments. They urged that France had paid her share in blood and ruin. To be asked to pay again and in gold was for all Frenchmen totally unjust and even immoral.

The British, while endorsing the basic principle, took a more practical view. In their eyes war debts and reparations were obstacles to the restoration of normal economic life in the world. America, like Britain, was a trading nation, it was interested in the reopening of markets and the restitution of the purchasing power of all countries. Such reintegration was impossible while the ordinary flow of international trade was hampered by the abnormal conditions resulting from vast payments alike of reparations and of interallied debts.

Cancellation for the French was thus an act of justice, for the British quite as much a duty of statesmanship.

This view underlay the Keynes thesis, the Balfour Note; it remains the foundation of all British conception. Thus the British, who were owed large sums by their allies and were entitled to approximately a quarter of German payments, proposed and continue to urge general cancellation and proportionate reduction of German payments.

Since the people of the United States rejected the French thesis as without moral basis and similarly rejected the British, because in practice it put the whole costs of the general process of cancellation upon America, the European debtors were faced with the fact of the American demand for payment. They were also quite as squarely confronted with the American purpose to refuse access to American financial markets to all countries refusing to fund their debts and to begin payment.

And at the moment American loans were still the foundation of all European reconstruction. The British could not put the pound sterling back to par, the Belgians could not stabilize their currency, the Italians could not order their finances without fresh American borrowings. France faced the inevitable consequences of a long extended period of inflation. Thus, the power of coercion lay with the United States government and when, in 1922, the United States disclosed the purpose to use its power, all four countries undertook negotiations which led in due course to the signature of treaties establishing the modalities of payment.

Judged simply on the basis of ordinary business transactions, the four settlements cannot be condemned as unreasonable or unfair. Thus, while the original capital sum had amounted to $10,000,000,000 and more than $2,000,000,000 interest had accumulated, the aggregate capital of the debts as fixed in the several agreements is but $7,000,000,000. For the Italians, too, the reduction on the sum actually borrowed amounted to nearly two thirds, while for the French and Belgians to approximately one half. In addition, to meet the existing crises in the domestic situations of all countries, earlier payments were fixed at exceedingly low sums.

Great Britain, Belgium, and Italy ratified the Baldwin-Mellon, Theunis-Mellon, and Volpi-Mellon settlements. France has so far rejected the Berenger-Mellon agreement. French opposition has been based upon the American refusal to grant a saving clause which would permit French reductions proportioned up, on German failures to pay reparations. But although this concession is contained in an Anglo-French debt settlement made on similar lines although on terms naturally less generous to the debtor, the French Chamber has also refused to ratify the British contract. On the other hand, the French government has undertaken, both in the British and American cases, to make payments in conformity with the provisions.

In the aggregate, European payment to the United States during two generations will average $315,000,000 annually, although it will fall below $250,000,000 in the opening years and rise to $400,000,000 in the closing.

Except in the case of Italy, too, there is no basis for any argument that the payments are beyond the capacity of the debtors. In addition, if German reparations payments continue at the totals fixed by the Dawes Plan, the European creditors of Germany will receive $625,000,000 annually, or approximately half the average payment to America.

Present opinion in the United States assumes the debt question to have been settled, save as the French ratification has been postponed. Yet it is not less clear that Europe regards the whole transaction as temporary. It does not accept the principle of payments of large sums between nations continued over two generations as rational or possible. It continues to look forward to an eventual international conference in which the principles of the Dawes Plan will be still further applied. And because of this expectation, the European creditors of Germany have so far refrained from fixing the period of years during which German reparations payments are to continue.

As is inevitable in all cases of difference between national opinions, the debt dispute has aroused passion on both sides of the Atlantic. Thus, at the moment when Europe was making peace at Geneva and Germans were able again to walk unmolested in Paris streets, Americans were insulted and stoned. If, too, the franc crisis added exceptional bitterness to French sentiment, it is not less clear that anti-American opinion has passed all national limits and is tending to become European.

Moreover, there is a fundamental weakness in the American case which lies outside its intrinsic merits. In an odd way, the American position in the matter of debts is coming to resemble that of the French in the matter of reparations. The effort of the French to collect reparations, to which they were legally and morally entitled, did violence to the self-interests of most other European peoples. Thus, while France was widely condemned for alleged offences against justice, she was actually assailed because she put French material interests above those of other peoples.

When France entered the Ruhr, the spectacle of military coercion exerted against unarmed and helpless populations aroused world-wide protest. But it is just as unmistakable that the United States, by exercising financial coercion to compel payments by peoples exhausted by vast sacrifices in blood and treasure, is similarly provoking world criticism. American prosperity and wealth stand out in sharp contrast to the poverty and suffering of most of the debtor nations. The use of money power has clear and unhappy resemblance to the employment of military. Moreover, as French rights were in conflict with the interests of other peoples, American rights are similarly contrary to the interests of all Europe.

Yesterday the world was filled with denunciations of French militarism. The press was crowded with criticisms of the French purpose to make military power the foundation of European hegemony. To-day the same denunciations are levelled at American "dollar" imperialism, and there is the similar charge that the United States is seeking to establish financial hegemony on the basis of money power.

Nor does the parallel stop here. Precisely as the French people were angered by world criticism and saw foreign denunciation based upon the self-interest of other nations, the American people have been roused to indignation by the European campaign for cancellation. Like the French, they regard the moral and sentimental arguments advanced as no more than clever but dishonest attempts to destroy American rights. They are at one time satisfied as to the legality and the morality of their debt policy and convinced that they are faced by an obvious manœuvre to abolish these rights by the most hypocritical of all conceivable tactics. Thus American temper is at the present moment quite analogous to French, before the Ruhr.

Since the conflict continues, prophecy as to its outcome is idle. In the matter of reparations, France had finally to consent to compromise her legal rights under pressure of world opinion and in the face of the collective and conflicting material interests of other peoples. The American situation is patently far stronger than the French. But, on the other hand, it must be perceived that world opinion is at least as strongly united against the United States and that moral arguments are just as generally employed to support material interests. While the dispute continues, too, American unpopularity is bound to endure and even to increase.

In the last analysis, however, the causes of the present misunderstanding between Europe and America lie much deeper. Material issues have produced irritating disputes and contemporary bad feeling. But beyond all these relatively insignificant circumstances lies the essential fact that the whole period between Sarajevo and Locarno has been interpreted in one fashion in Europe and in another in America.

For Europe, these years of strife and anarchy have brought the most stupendous explosion since the French Revolution. Empires have fallen, new states have risen. Changes within national frontiers have been almost as great as those without. Moreover, if the first consequence of the upheaval was to stimulate rival nationalisms, the latter developments have demonstrated inescapably the interdependence of European peoples.

In the storm and stress of the war and post-war years, the whole system under which European peoples lived either broke down utterly or functioned with complete inefficiency. International anarchy was accompanied by national misery. The peoples of all countries endured almost unexampled suffering and privation. And because of this universal agony, millions of men and women were compelled to recognize the limits of national power and to consider the necessities of international coöperation.

By contrast, in the United States, these same years were marked by the greatest prosperity known in human history. Every physical circumstance, foreign and domestic, contributed to reinforce the natural belief in the superiority of American ideas, political, economic, and moral. While Europe was driven by privation to seek change, America was led by prosperity to resist it. In the period during which European nationalism passed through bankruptcy, American nationalism flourished beyond comparison. Having escaped the common fate of all European nationalisms, American nationalism remains confident, self-sufficient, satisfied. It is conscious of no need to modify its will in the presence of that of other nations. Convinced of the essential rectitude of its own purposes and the absolute justice of its claims, it is neither patient under foreign criticism nor impressed by foreign example.

To-day Europe is escaping from the immediate physical consequences of its recent catastrophe. Reintegration of European life both national and international is proceeding swiftly. But European thought is still dominated by the lessons it has drawn from the universal calamity. Out of this time of suffering European liberalism has brought the profound conviction that international conciliation and coöperation are the sole means of escaping common ruin. A similar experience has produced the same results in France, Germany, and Great Britain.

In America, on the other hand, while dislike of European nationalism as encountered at the Paris Conference continues, there is not the smallest sympathy for European liberalism. Mussolini and not Ramsay MacDonald is the most popular European figure in the United States. Fascismo and not Labour wins the approval of the American democracy. While solidarity develops between Liberal and Democratic groups in all European countries, American political opinion is equally hostile to European nationalism and liberalism.

That European nationalism should resent and even hate the United States is not surprising, since, in recent years, we have acquired much of the power and prestige which formerly belonged to Europe. The growing distrust and dislike of European liberalism is, on the whole, more surprising. Yet it is the inevitable consequence of the fact, that, while the war unmistakably stimulated internationalism among all Liberal groups in Europe, it just as patently reinforced nationalistic tendencies in both American political parties. As a consequence, Liberal Europe discovers in America political thought precisely the same spirit of uncompromising nationalism which it holds responsible both for the war and the post-war anarchy. Divided, therefore, on all other issues, the Right and Left in Europe are able to agree upon the American question.

Retiring from Europe immediately following the Paris Conference, the United States has increasingly ignored European circumstances. The profound and progressive revolution which has taken place in European political thought has passed unnoted on this side of the Atlantic. The impressions of Europe acquired between 1917 and 1919 have not only not been modified, but have tended to become traditional and thus immutable. The suspicions roused at Versailles have hardened into enduring distrust. Political isolation has involved intellectual and moral separation.

As a consequence, while the gulf between America and the Old Europe was profound and not to be bridged, the distance between the United States and the New Europe, which is unquestionably taking form, is visibly widening from year to year. In fact, the American people have dismissed the idea that there can be a new Europe. Not only is there no American concern with what is happening beyond the Atlantic, but there is also neither general interest nor considerable curiosity.

It is the conviction that America is a world in itself and sufficient to itself, which actually forbids understanding between Europe and the United States. American indifference is an even more impressive obstacle to mutual comprehension than suspicion or distrust. It is not merely that European complexities are difficult to understand, it is even more that there is no general perception of any necessity to comprehend them. In the past ten years, America has become a very real and important circumstance in European opinion, but Europe has only transiently affected American opinion.

In this situation, American administrations are far more concerned with the dangers of American public opinion than with the discomforts of European sentiment. American foreign policy is based upon popular estimates of European conditions rather than upon any actual appraisal of existing conditions. All our proposals abroad are addressed to our electorate at home. Notes sent to foreign governments are invariably directed at the domestic voter. Secretaries of State are occupied mainly with the thought of the repercussions in the United States Senate; what the responses evoked in Europe may be are unimportant by comparison.

Thus, in recent years, it has never been quite possible to escape the disquieting suspicion that, while the American government continues to cherish the eagle as a domestic symbol, it is to the ostrich that it turns instinctively for an example in all questions of foreign policy.

THE END

INDEX